Writing Travel

Series Editor, Jeanne Moskal

WRITING TRAVEL
Series Editor, Jeanne Moskal

The series publishes manuscripts related to the new field of travel studies, including works of original travel writing; editions of out-of-print travel books or previously unpublished travel memoirs; English translations of important travel books in other languages; theoretical and historical treatments of ways in which travel and travel writing engage such questions as religion, nationalism/cosmopolitanism, and empire; gender and sexuality; race, ethnicity, and immigration; and the history of the book, print culture, and translation; biographies of significant travelers or groups of travelers (including but not limited to pilgrims, missionaries, anthropologists, tourists, explorers, immigrants); critical studies of the works of significant travelers or groups of travelers; and pedagogy of travel and travel literature and its place in curricula.

Other Books in the Series

Vienna Voices

A Traveler Listens to the City of Dreams

Jill Knight Weinberger

To Donna and George,
I hope you enjoy these
glimpses of "my" Vienna —
With thanks,
Jill Knight Weinberger

Parlor Press
West Lafayette, Indiana
www.parlorpress.com

Parlor Press LLC, West Lafayette, Indiana 47906

SAN: 254-8879

Library of Congress Cataloging-in-Publication Data

Weinberger, Jill Knight, 1953-

Vienna voices : a traveler listens to the city of dreams / Jill
   Knight Weinberger.

   p. cm. -- (Writing travel)

Includes bibliographical references and index.

ISBN 1-932559-88-4 (hardcover : alk. paper) -- ISBN 1-
   932559-89-2 (pbk. : alk. paper) -- ISBN 1-932559-90-6
   (adobe ebook) 1. Vienna (Austria)--Civilization--20th century. 2. Vienna (Austria)--Intellectual life--20th century. 3.
   Vienna (Austria)--Description and travel. I. Title. II. Series.

DB851.W5347 2006

943.6'13--dc22

                              2006012174

Cover design by David Blakesley.
Printed on acid-free paper.

Parlor Press, LLC is an independent publisher of scholarly
and trade titles in print and multimedia formats. This book is
available in paper, cloth and Adobe eBook formats from Parlor
Press on the World Wide Web at http://www.parlorpress.com or
through online and brick-and mortar bookstores. For submission
information or to find out about Parlor Press publications, write
to Parlor Press, 816 Robinson St., West Lafayette, Indiana,
47906, or e-mail editor@parlorpress.com.

In Memoriam

Marianne Kathryn Knight Farrell
1950 - 2004

For Mikey, whose voice, whose laughter,
Filled our hearts and graced our lives.
May she be at peace in her own city of dreams.

Series Editor's Preface

Our book series, "Writing Travel," seeks to publish the best works in the field of travel studies. This field has been given new urgency by debates about globalization and terrorism, by fresh dialogue between practitioners and scholars of travel writing, and by emerging insights from many disciplines (post-colonial studies, gender studies, literary studies, geography, religious studies, and anthropology) about the ways in which travel and travel writing engage such questions as religion, nationalism/cosmopolitanism, and empire; gender and sexuality; race, ethnicity, and immigration; and the history of the book, print culture, and translation. Our list will include original travel writing; editions of out-of-print travel books or previously unpublished travel memoirs; English translations of important travel books in other languages; biographies of significant travelers or groups of travelers (including but not limited to pilgrims, missionaries, anthropologists, tourists, explorers, immigrants); critical studies of the works of significant travelers or groups of travelers; and pedagogy of travel and travel literature and its place in curricula.

We are pleased to present Jill Knight Weinberger's *Vienna Voices: A Traveler Listens to the City of Dreams* as our inaugural volume. Weinberger's memoir engages one of the pervasive issues in travel writing—the travel writer's double vision that surveys a new venue of human suffering while delighting in the pleasures of a novel place and culture. Historically, much travel writing has evaded this difficult double vision, choosing either touristic delight or political discussion at the expense of the other. As James Buzard notes in *The Beaten Track: European Tourism, Literature, and the Ways to "Cul-*

ture" 1800–1918 (Oxford: Clarendon, 1993), the erasure of politics from popular tourism was one of the foundational moves of nineteenth-century British publisher John Murray, a founder of the travel-guide-book industry and the predecessor of Baedeker and other popular guides. Murray incorporated many memorable passages from Lord Byron's poetry into his guidebooks, but strategically omitted Byron's passages decrying political oppression or advocating causes such as Italian unification. Buzard concludes that Murray thus produced for his reader-travelers the frisson of Byronic passion without the worrisome pangs of conscience that direct political allusion would prompt. This divorce of delight from political awareness remains a staple of the present-day travel industry of much travel writing.

Weinberger writes a different kind of travel book. The daughter-in-law of Holocaust-era exiles from Vienna, she recounts her search for the specifics of her adopted family's dispossession and murder, including the bureaucratic paper trail documenting the "Aryanization" of Wilhelm Weinberger's hardware and household-goods stores and the stamp collection of a fledgling philatelist who never got to grow up. Countering the trend described by Buzard, Weinberger directly engages the contradictions created by the delights of the city— its coffee houses, architecture, and musical heritage—and the pervasive awareness that the Austrians voted overwhelmingly in favor of annexation to Nazi Germany. Characteristically, she gives funny advice about getting the attention of a busy Viennese waiter while noting that her fellow customers in the coffee house are children of those Austrian voters. With bravery, subtlety and humor, she anatomizes for her reader Viennese charm and Viennese guilt. Moreover, Weinberger opens up the possibilities of her own threshold position as outsider, as not-quite tourist in Vienna, as one who acquired the German language by study among its native speakers, and as a child of Yankee Protestants married into a Jewish family, to create a window into the outsider position of the Viennese Jews whose psyches and histories she seeks to understand.

This memoir is especially timely as an act of compassion and preservation in these days when the last survivors of the Holocaust are dying. It will appeal to armchair travelers and to students of travel literature, Austrian culture, and Judaic studies, as well as to anyone interested in the intricacies of remembering historical and family trauma.

—Jeanne Moskal
Series Editor, Writing Travel

Preface

I am tempted to begin by suggesting what *Vienna Voices: A Traveler Listens to the City of Dreams* is not. It is not a book about the Holocaust, or a history of the Jews of Vienna. It is not a family history, in the conventional sense, nor is it a travel guidebook. And yet, it contains elements of all these.

My aim in writing *Vienna Voices* was to present the city through my particular set of lenses, which has, I readily admit, been tinted by long acquaintance and by my slow absorption of fact, images, and experiences over the past twenty years. I have traveled to Vienna often during that time, both alone and with my husband, G. J., whose parents were born there and then forced to leave when Hitler came to power in 1938. The living memories of these loved ones are never far from consciousness whenever I travel to Vienna and whenever I look back on my time there.

I have toured the palaces and cathedrals of this handsome city, wandered its medieval streets and through its neighborhoods, dallied in its coffeehouses and pastry shops, followed its footpaths through legendary woods. But I have learned as much about this place through listening, through filtering the city's clamor, the Viennese speech, its whispers, songs, poetry, and theatre into some level of understanding. Perhaps this book, then, is best described as kaleidoscopic, in that it brings together fragments of Vienna, bits and pieces that add up to a kind of portrait of a place, one that suggests not a single, unified image, but rather one that is richly complex, layered, ambiguous. The Vienna of popular imagination, the elegant city of waltzes and choir boys and dancing white horses, does indeed exist, but no one really lives there except the most willfully sentimental of foreign visitors, and surely even they cannot sustain the illusion for more than a few days. A far more interesting Vienna, darker and less nostalgic, is the one with which I have become acquainted. It is a place of which I have grown fond, in spite of myself, in spite of what I think I know about its character. And that is the Vienna, so often called the city of dreams, I have attempted to render in this book.

ACKNOWLEDGMENTS

I am profoundly grateful to the many people, both in Vienna and closer to home, who supported my efforts throughout the research and writing processes. These include those who assisted me in obtaining Weinberger family, school, and business records: Luise Schuster of the Wiener Handelsakademie, Mag. Rita Tezzele of the Wirtschaftskammer Österreich, Mr. Lambert Schön of the War Archives Sections of the Österreichischer Staatsarchiv, Dr. Gerda Barth of the city of Vienna Plakatsammlung, and the staffs of the Waltergasse and Albertgasse Realschulen and the Kultusgemeindearchiv. In addition, I thank the able librarians of the University of Vienna, the Nationalbibliothek, the Theresianum, and Central Connecticut State University for their help in locating and retrieving old newspapers and periodicals. For giving generously of their time and expertise, I thank Hebe Jeffries, Regina Anzenberger, and Mag. Consul Gertrud Tuchhammer. Special thanks go to Josef Köber of the *Kronen-Zeitung* for allowing me to adapt an anecdote from his book, *Weanerisch;* Simone Furtlehner of the Hundertwasser Archives, who kindly facilitated permission to reprint the artist's statement that appears in Chapter Seven; and Susan Widmer of the Vanderbilt University Library for her help in dating Ernst Waldinger's "Ich bin ein Sohn der deutschen Sprache." Thanks, too, to several of Vienna's tour guides, whose knowledge of and passion for the city are always inspiring: Elisabeth-Joe Harriet,

Maria Husa, Brigitte Timmermann, Barbara Timmermann, and Eleonore Neubacher.

My time in Vienna—several extended stays over the past two years while organizing and writing and thinking about this book—was enriched by pleasant evenings spent with Peter Schwarz and Dorith Salvarani-Drill and their son, Emanuel, and with our cousins, Louis and Marion Mieses. To our Vienna landlords, Alfred and Barbara Punzet-Krammer, we owe a million thanks for providing us a home away from home on Darwingasse and for their kindly interest in our comfort and well-being. But among our Vienna debts, the greatest is owed to Eva and Pauli Wertheimer and their son, Patrick, who welcomed us, fed us, introduced us to their friends, and with whom we forged a renewed family bond.

Work on *Vienna Voices* would not have been possible without the support of Central Connecticut State University, which granted me a sabbatical leave during the 2003–04 academic year and additional professional leave. I thank also those administrators and faculty who awarded me two CSU-AAUP research grants (2002, 2003). My colleagues in the English Department generously covered my teaching, advising and committee assignments during my absence. Special thanks to Gilbert Gigliotti, Christine Doyle, Leyla Zidani-Eroglu, Mary Anne Nunn, Matt Ciscel, Steven Cohen, Jeff Partridge, and Cheryl Chatfield.

My friends Barbara Baker and Jane Hikel traveled all the way to Vienna to meet me for coffee, and I thank them for many lovely hours walking and talking and sampling the pastry. To Virginia Tubeck-Drozd, who did not travel to Vienna, heartfelt thanks for the sound and supportive commentary over coffee at our local Starbucks. I wish also to thank Katharine Sands of the Sarah Jane Freymann Literary Agency, who listened to my first thoughts on this project and suggested to me the title, *Vienna Voices*. My editor, Jeanne Moskal, and publisher, David Blakesley of Parlor Press, proved both wonderfully professional and collegial, as they charted a steady and enthusiastic course from proposal to book.

I hardly know how to thank all the family and friends who contributed documents, stories, memories, photographs, and good conversation to the making of *Vienna Voices:* Helly Kohn, Lisl Lederer, Gerty Schaier, Herta Schwarz, Didi Zwirn, Ernst and Irene Wiesner, and Gaye Wiesner. I can only hope this book, which touches on their lives as well as my own, honors them as it means to do.

Finally, two special men in my life made incalculable contributions to my work. Despite his ill health, and at a time of life when he should be excused from having to revisit the painful past, my father-in-law, Ludwig Weinberger, generously shared with me his memories and knowledge of Vienna, as well as his insights into the city of his birth. He gladly answered questions both intrusive and trivial, strove in every way to be helpful, and gave *Vienna Voices* his blessing. Sadly, he passed away in August, 2005, while the manuscript was being prepared for publication. My husband, G. J., assisted me in all practical aspects of the work, read every word—indeed, listened to every word—of the manuscript, collaborated on translations, served as interpreter, helped with the research, and traveled with me to Vienna when he surely would have preferred new destinations.

And, in the darkest of hours, he held out the warmest and steadiest of hands.

A note on translations: unless otherwise indicated, translations of primary documents and literature were made by G. J. Weinberger and me. G. J. was responsible for providing a rough, literal translation from German into English, which I then polished. A process of negotiation routinely ensued, as we consulted our dictionaries or sought outside advice, debated the subtleties of word choice and analyzed tone until we were both satisfied with sound and sense. I, however, take full responsibility for any infelicities or mistakes that readers may find.

J.K.W.

Contents

Vienna Voices

1 Vienna Faces

PORTRAIT OF THE WRITER AS A THIRTEEN-YEAR-OLD

Growing up in Connecticut, I had only the slightest knowledge about Vienna, and most of it deriving from an album of Strauss waltzes sent to my parents by the Columbia Record Club because my mother forgot to mail in the alternative request for Tony Bennett or Dean Martin. The record wound up in my room and I played it until tics developed in *The Emperor's Waltz* and *Tales from the Vienna Woods*. The music captivated me, as it does still, but I do think this was a little strange for a thirteen-year-old circa 1966, and so did my older sister and younger brother, who liked nothing better than to find me conducting the Vienna Philharmonic in my silent room, arms waving about, big clunky earphones plastered to my head. That is now family lore and I am stuck with it.

And for a long time I was stuck with the album cover image of Vienna—the gilded figure of Johann Strauss, Junior playing his violin superimposed on a wide angle shot of the city, all palaces and cathedral spires. After my marriage, then, I had everything to learn, starting with the notion that Vienna was no city of waltzes for the Weinberger family and no Strauss soundtrack accompanies their story.

KAFFEE KLATSCH

On a recent afternoon at our home in Connecticut, G. J. and I hosted a small party of old folks—old Viennese folks. All had

3

been refugees who by various means, including sheer luck, survived the journey in the late 1930s from their birthplace, Vienna, to whatever safe havens in the world they, as Jews, could find: Uruguay, the Dominican Republic, Curaçao. All eventually emigrated to the United States, settling in and around New York City.

It is a gathering dominated by the German language, specifically the funny and lovely-sounding Viennese dialect, and by one inescapable and inexhaustible subject: their identities as Jews, as Americans, as Viennese, as survivors. It is a gathering and a conversation familiar to me, perhaps incongruously, as the youngest person present, the non-Jew, the non-German speaker, the deeply-rooted New Englander. But when I married Guillermo J. Weinberger, I took my place at the table and listened. What I have heard over the past twenty-three years from this dwindling community of exiles are stories that have chilled my blood and left me shaken, that have enlarged my world and forced me to confront my ignorance. And they have contributed, no doubt, to my evolving *Weltanschauung,* my way of looking at the world.

G. J. has heard their stories all his life, and so today is a trifled bored, wants his dessert and coffee while the old folks are still nattering away over their stuffed chicken breasts and mesclun salad.

"I don't know what it is I'm eating, Jill, but it's very good," says Helly, pronouncing my name, as they all do, "Jeel." I know what she's saying: this is no "spread," no lavish array of cold meats and salads and bagels and rye and liptauer cheese that is usually brought forth on such occasions. Allowances, however, are made for the "American" daughter-in-law who is a sweet girl and who tries so hard to please.

On this day, the discussion turns to the term "Holocaust survivor." I bring up the subject. There is a woman who lives at my father-in-law Ludwig's retirement home, Summerwood, who introduces herself as a Holocaust survivor, as if no other introductory phrases were necessary. When she did it to me, it felt, somehow, like a rebuke. Had her Jewish radar informed

her I was no Jew and had she therefore felt compelled to remind me of the Holocaust, lest I forget? Ludwig's friend, Lisl,
also a resident at Summerwood, says that isn't it, that she says
it to everyone. When Lisl pressed her for details one day, it
turned out she had not been imprisoned in any of the camps,
but that she had been, simply, a refugee from Germany.

"But that doesn't mean she *isn't* entitled to call herself a
Holocaust survivor, right?" I ask. I'm puzzled by this periodic
discussion over who is and who is not a "survivor."

"You are all survivors," I argue. "Just because you weren't
in the camps doesn't mean you aren't victims of the Holocaust."

That sets off a minor ruckus. All my guests—Ludwig,
Helly, Lisl, and Gerty—insist upon the special status of concentration camp survivors.

"We are," Lisl says, "merely refugees."

FLÜCHTLINGE

Regina Anzenberger, who runs a photographic agency in
Vienna, invited me recently to take a look at an exhibit in
her small gallery—two dozen or so black and white shots of
Chechnya taken by one of her photographers just back from
that forlorn place. We seem only to hear of Chechen rebels,
not refugees, but here they are, lining the walls like grim
shadows.

I, an American-born woman, do not know what it is to be
a refugee. As a child growing up in rural Connecticut, I doubt
I ever heard the word, unless it was embedded in some school-
room lesson about the Statue of Liberty and Emma Lazarus's
poem. We had no refugees that I knew of in my small hometown, Granby. Immigrants, yes: the occasional Polish or
French-Canadian family would move to town, usually into
some rundown property they would attempt to brighten with
a few potted geraniums or a front yard vegetable garden. I
thought no more about this matter than that the school bus

route would be longer for having to stop for the new batch of kids, who sometimes seemed a little paler than the rest of us.

I look up the German word for refugee: *der Flüchtling.* I don't think I have ever heard it aloud from any of the old German speakers of my acquaintance. Ludwig always uses the English word, pronouncing refugee with a soft "shhhee" sound.

When I say—attempt to say—*Flüchtling,* I hear its relationship to a more familiar German noun, *Flug,* or "flight." *Flug* is a word I know well: the words for airplane (*Flugzeug*) and airport (*Flughafen*) and excursion (*Ausflug*) and all sorts of travel-related terms are built around it, and thus I encounter it frequently when G. J. and I travel to Austria and Germany. It has no dark connotation for me, rather the opposite—travels, journeys, holidays. But I learn from my *Oxford Duden German Dictionary* that a second way of translating the English "flight" is *die Flucht,* but the sense of this word is closer to "fleeing," as in, say, the Jews' flight from Egypt in Biblical times. Jewish history is a record of such flights: from Pharaohs, Catholic monarchs and their inquisitors, Cossacks, village mobs, Nazis.

Ludwig and his friends Lisl, Helly, and Gerty fled Vienna. They fled because they had to; because Hitler found in them highly marketable scapegoats around whom to consolidate his power; because life became unbearable in the city of their birth; because their Viennese, that is, Christian, neighbors vigorously, and often maliciously, demanded they go. Helly, in fact, was one of those forced from her apartment in Ottakring to scrub the street, while the good burghers watched, some silently, some not.

But they had to be nimble of mind as well as body in order to face the present reality and look into the grim future. And they were courageous enough to see no future and prescient enough to see only a short-lived opportunity to leave Vienna. In 1938 and 1939, before Wannsee, the Nazis were more interested in expelling the Jews than in exterminating them. Of the nearly 200,000 Jews living in Austria in 1938, most of them in Vienna, some 130,000 became *Flüchtlinge.* They left behind homes, families, lovers, businesses, art, books, aspirations, ambitions, a way of life, a city they loved. Of the remaining Jews who did not or could not flee, some 65,000 perished in labor or concentration camps, mainly Dachau, Mauthausen, Theresienstadt, and Auschwitz. In 1945, at war's end, Vienna's Jewish population was estimated at between 4,000 and 5,000.[1] How they survived I hardly have the courage to imagine.

VIENNESE CHARM

Everyone admits that much of the charm of Vienna is due to the Viennese people. They are remembered by the visitor even more than the great beauty of the city, but the Viennese possess and give out a great deal more than charm. They are full of courage, they know how to take defeat without a whimper, and they are, as a mass, extremely intelligent. Another characteristic that ultimately guarantees success, they are not afraid of work, and we are living in a workaday world. I find the best word in which to sum up the Viennese character is Gallantry.

The world needs just what Vienna has to give it—courage, beauty, charm—is not this true gallantry?

There is a lilting song, one of those Viennese melodies which, when once heard, are so hard to forget, and which sums up what Vienna means to those who know and love her:

"Wien, Wien, nur du allein,

Wirst stets die Stadt meiner Träume sein!"

(Vienna, Vienna, you alone are the city of my dreams!)

Alfred Granger, *The Spirit of Vienna* (1935)[2]

LUDWIG

I have never called him by his nickname, Viki, the way his family and old friends, and even the children of his old friends, do. He is, to me, Ludwig ("like Ludwig van Beethoven," he tells new acquaintances). That is what my late mother-in-law, Jula, invited me to call him, and to do otherwise still seems after all these years a liberty—no, an intimacy—to which I am not entitled.

Sometimes Ludwig will sign "Papito" on G. J.'s birthday card, a relic of the family's life in Uruguay in the 1940s and early 1950s, but never have I heard G. J. call his father that— or "Dad," or "Pop," or even "Father." He calls him "Viejo" or, in a joking kind of way, "Herr Vater," in the exaggerated formality that was once characteristic of upper middle-class Viennese families. That was, indeed, how Ludwig addressed his own father, Wilhelm Weinberger.

Ludwig's shoulders hunch over—he has osteoporosis, a dowager's hump, although he insists he does not—and his hands shake a little. Now 90, he suffers from congestive heart failure and thus must carefully engineer every exhausting move out of a chair or down a hallway. He is nearly always short of breath, often taxed by the effort simply to speak, his lips bluish and thin. Ludwig's face reflects a man exhausted by life itself. Too often these days I hear him say, "*Das ist kein Leben mehr*," this is no life anymore.

While it is difficult to see any youthful traces remaining, Ludwig's long thin face is marked by strong features: a high brow, a goodly but well-proportioned nose, heavy eyeglasses. He is dignified, patrician, even, with his cap of thick wavy gray hair, the only man I know who still uses Brylcream, or something like it.

"People think I am younger than I am," he likes to say. "It's the hair."

There is something unmistakably old world about Ludwig, something of the "Herr Professor," although the academic life he yearned for when he was a young man was not to be.

He remains attached to the old courtesies, standing up, or at least attempting to, when a woman enters a room. He won't let me pick up the tab for lunch, motions me into the elevator before him, and often notices when I'm wearing something new. Reserved and rather formal, kind and generous, he no longer possesses the nimbleness that enabled him to survive the catastrophe of the Nazis, only the tenacity.

"They didn't catch me," he says.

HERR VATER

A framed photo portrait of Wilhelm Weinberger sits on a table in our living room. He wears the self-satisfied expression of a prosperous burgher, the maker of the family fortune, the ambitious son of a respectable but undistinguished middle-class Czech Jewish family. He wears a dark, heavy-looking suit jacket, a white shirt and a tie fastened with a cravat pin. Ludwig is unsure of the date of the picture—probably the 1920s—for the smooth, unlined face, the short dark hair suggest a man in his thirties. His pince-nez lends a bit of *gravitas*—or perhaps pretension—to his portrait. (He looks a bit in this portrait like Karl Kraus, the legendary Viennese writer and satirist, who was also Jewish, also born in what is now the Czech Republic, and who also sported a pince-nez.) And while Wilhelm's face does not remind me of Ludwig's, I see his resemblance to G. J., his namesake, the somber brown eyes, the full lips, the moustache linking grandfather and grandson. They are linked in other ways as well.

Ludwig once told me, "I was more Fürth than Weinberger, I took after my mother." There was always tension between the status-conscious businessman and his dreamy, book-loving son. There was tension, too, between Alice Fürth, Ludwig's mother, and Wilhelm. The couple were legally separated and lived apart for most of their marriage.

Although obscured by the mat of the frame, Wilhelm's signature appears at the bottom of the photograph in a fancy script, very much like G. J.'s calligraphy-like cursive that he learned in his Uruguayan primary school. Stamped in purple ink on the back of the photo is the Weinberger firm calling card:

Specialhäuser für Korklinoleum
Ledertuch u. Wachstuch
Wien
X. Favoritenstrasse 73, Telef. 1295/VIII
V. Schönbrunnerstrasse 119, Telef. 1114/VIII
XX Wallensteinstrasse 5, Telef. 5030/VIII
Inhaber Wilhelm Weinberger.

Eventually, there would be more Weinberger shops in Vienna that sold linoleum, carpeting, draperies, and other household goods, enough shops to employ an extended network of sisters, brothers, brothers-in-law, nephews, and cousins. Wilhelm or Onkel Willy ("Villy"): patron, patriarch, and oh, how his portrait reflects the ease with which he wore the mantle of family power and hints at the iron determination with which he wielded it.

FRAU FRISCH, CLICK, CLICK

"Küss die Hand, Frau Frisch," said the Herr Ober, the maitre'd, taking her hand and bowing towards it.

How disappointing to learn that no actual kissing is involved anymore in Vienna's ritual greeting. But this remnant of courtly manners was one of the reasons G. J. and I loved receiving an invitation to meet Frau Frisch—Ludwig's cousin Gretl—at the Intercontinental Hotel, which overlooks the Stadtpark. A niece of Onkel Willy's, Margarete (Gretl) Fischer Frisch had retired from her job as the hotel's Group Sales manager but still commanded the respect of the staff whenever she appeared. And that is precisely what G. J. marveled at: "They practically click their heels when they see her!" Dining with Gretl at the Intercon was always an event.

Since Gretl died in 2001 at the age of 80, Vienna has not seemed quite the same. We miss her, and not only because she had a kind and generous spirit but because she was a woman to whom we could talk easily and frankly (her English was excellent), who unfailingly welcomed us despite long intervals between visits, who gave us a precious sense of family connection to Vienna.

Gretl was 62 when I first met her in 1983. She seemed not to age at all over the next 18 years. True, her hair color gradually gave way to pure white from tinted blonde, and she grew stouter. She was short and barrel-shaped, her spindly legs hardly seeming to support her expanding waist and ample bosom. But she dressed impeccably, favoring expensive looking knit dresses and sweater sets; never did I see her in a pair of slacks. I suspect she would not have set foot out of her apartment on the Neubaugasse for even a quick trip to the market unless more than decently attired and neatly coiffed. In winter she wore a fabulous silver mink coat. At times, I aspired to be her: *I* wanted to be an elegant old lady at home in an elegant old city, traveling about by taxi, meeting elegant old lady friends in the coffeehouses for *Jause,* afternoon cake and coffee. But this was my fantasy, far removed from the reality of her day-to-day life.

Sometimes we would meet Gretl at a coffeehouse or a *Konditorei,* a pastry shop. We dragged her to the famous ones, Demel and Gerstner and Heiner, for a long time not fully understanding how much she disliked these places. Once, when I was writing a travel article about the pastry shops, I asked her for her favorite reminiscences about them, peppering her with silly questions—"What was your favorite one growing up?" "Did you ever meet any young men in them?"—until she finally told me about her very first date: "He took me to Heiner, on Wollzeile."

"Do you remember what cake you ordered?" I asked.

"I was too shy to order a cake, but I remember I had a raspberry soda."

"Whatever happened to him?"

"I heard he died at Mauthausen. He went first to Dachau."

Into my article went the raspberry soda, but not Mauthausen, one of the worst of the concentration camps, site of the
infamous "staircase of death," where unspeakably cruel labors
were forced upon Jewish prisoners by their Austrian and German guards.

Gretl always took an interest in what we were up to in
Vienna—what museums or exhibits we had taken in, which
performances we planned to attend. And, of course, she told
us about life in Vienna. Eventually, we understood that she
lived merely in peaceful coexistence with the city, and was
most definitely not on terms of affection with it. And why
should she have been? It had wanted her gone or dead. She
had managed in 1938 to get a visa to go to England, where
she became fluent in English and after a stint as a housemaid,
trained as a nurse. She adored London and told her daughter
Eva that she hardly realized the war was raging overhead. She
wished never to return to Vienna. When she did, in the late
1940s, it was because her new husband, Erich Frisch, insisted.
But here, she refused to work as a nurse despite the shortage.
Eva told me her mother just could not bring herself to employ
her skills or expend her compassion on people who just a few
years before would have had her deported to a concentration
or a labor camp, most likely to die.

Gretl came to terms with Vienna, but never with the Viennese.

"The worst mistake I made in my life," she never failed to
tell us, "was returning to Vienna after the war."

"Nothing in Common"

I myself have some very good friends who are not
Jewish and whom I have known for many years,
even my parents knew their parents, but whenever
the conversation comes to a certain point e.g. speaking about the war etc. we have nothing in common
and, therefore, we are avoiding speaking about it,
even though I definitely know that they were not

"Nazis." On the other hand, my brother Leo had a life-long friend, who declared himself to be a "Nazi" when Hitler come to Austria. Nevertheless, he was hiding my brother in the apartment of his parents when the police was looking for him, he was the person who went with Leo to the ship which brought him to—at that time Palestine, carrying his small suitcase, he was the only one to say good by to my parents in a very touching way, and he was the first one to welcome me in Vienna when I returned; until now I don't know how he found out the date of my return or my address! I am still in very good contact with him and he is the only one with whom, and with his wife, I can speak quite openly.

Gretl Fischer Frisch, Letter, September, 1992

"Wie schön wäre Wien ohne Wiener"

How often I have heard Viennese friends and family sigh, "*Wie schön wäre Wien ohne Wiener*"—how lovely Vienna would be without the Viennese. For the longest time, I didn't know this was actually a song title, the refrain of a parody by the cabaret artist Georg Kreisler, who had set his scathing lyric to an old sentimental ballad about springtime in the city, with trees blooming in the Prater and the wine flowing in Sievering.

> How lovely Vienna would be without the Viennese,
> As beautiful as a sleeping woman.
> The City Park would be much greener,
> And the Danube would finally be blue.[3]

A people capable of satirizing themselves cannot be all bad. Just as they have cultivated their own mythos of a musical, pleasure-loving people with a bent toward the nostalgic, so have the Viennese enjoyed a long tradition of lampooning that very image.

G. J. reminds me, however, that Kreisler was Jewish and a refugee: "He's not satirizing himself."

No one was better, however, at exposing the reality behind the carefully cultivated illusion—or more brutal—than the writer Karl Kraus, for the record, a Jewish convert to Catholicism.

"I put my pen to the Austrian corpse," he wrote, "because I persist in believing there's life in it."[4]

Not-so-Famous Women of Vienna

Dr. J. Alexander Mahan described the "typical" Viennese woman in a chapter titled "Women in General" from his book, *Famous Women of Vienna,* published in 1930.

> They are not taller nor shorter than those of other cities; perhaps a little fatter, but not much. Their faces are Teutonic, but not so markedly so as those of their sisters in Berlin and many of the other cities to the north. Blue eyes and brown hair predominate; red-haired Viennese are very rare. Mouths as a rule are well formed, certainly not too small; noses are neither long, hooked nor flat; cheeks are well rounded; chins about right; and in youth the complexions are rosy and fresh as the petals of garden flowers. Busts are shapely, quite often plump, and, since the advent of modern skirts, we are sure their limbs are neat and trim, at least as an average.[5]

What kind of chin is "just right," Dr. J. Alexander Mahan? And may I tell you that Ludwig's late sister Nora was a redhead, a gorgeous one at that, I am told?

I have read lots of stupid things about Vienna, and this is one of them. Vienna in the 1920s and 1930s, when this book was written, was (as it always had been and largely remains) a melting pot, the former capital of a once vast empire that comprised a multitude of ethnic, religious, and linguistic groups: Hungarians and Czechs, Poles and Ukrainians, Slovenes and Slovaks, Italians and Jews, Bosnians and Croats, and on and on. Its earliest inhabitants included Teutons, yes, but also Romans and Celts and other migrating tribes. Perhaps the only generalization possible is that traces of all of these should have been, as they are today, evident to Dr. Mahan in Vienna's faces.

When I am in Vienna, I invariably find myself studying the faces of the city—a traveler's habit, a writer's habit. It is a walker's and a trolley rider's city, slow paced enough to feel I am in the midst of a moving portrait gallery. Some faces worry me, like that of the lady I watched from the trolley who soberly poked through her change purse and then did not get on board. She looked around—*What do I do now?* She inhabited that grey area between middle-aged and old; she wasn't shabby but not solidly middle class looking, either. Within about 30 seconds I had constructed an epic life's story of hardship and heartache. Some faces just break your heart, even if you only see them for a second or two.

Then there is the Bag Lady of the Schwedenplatz, a little disheveled, shuffling about between the flower kiosk and the *U-Bahn* entrance. But one summer morning, it was only 9 o'clock or so, I spotted her with a huge pink ice cream cone from the Italian *Eissalon* that must have just opened for the day. She was greedily sucking it in, and looking a bit worse than usual in a flimsy housedress and slippers, her hair uncombed and unwashed.

Why do I take particular notice of old ladies? Perhaps because I will be one in due course. Not all of them evoke my sympathy, though. I watch the old Viennese ladies who sit side by side in the heavy green chairs lining the Volksgarten, loden-clad against crisp summer mornings. They make a pleasant, picturesque scene as they chat or close their eyes against the sun, framed by roses and neatly groomed gravel paths, by fountains and flower beds. I watch them, too, in the pastry shops having their *Jause,* their strudels and *Tor-*

ten lavish with whipped cream. Often, their faces remind me of those other old ladies from Vienna who occasionally sit around my table in Connecticut. I like Vienna all the more for offering me such genteel scenes, but here is my dilemma: try as I might not to, I wonder if these gentle-looking old people cheered Hitler's victory lap into the Heldenplatz on March 15, 1938. Did they, or their husbands, hurl stones into Jewish shops on the night of November 9, 1938, the infamous Kristallnacht? Were they the ones who demanded Ludwig's friend Helly go into the street and watch, laughing, as she scrubbed the pavement? I regret these thoughts, for they spoil my mood, they spoil Vienna for me and supplant the graceful scene before me with images of terror. I try to shoo them away. I *try* to think, "Perhaps they were rescuers or resistance workers." And if they were not, shouldn't I take pity on their powerlessness to stop the expulsion and eventual destruction of their neighbors, their fellow Viennese? But I cannot ask them which version is true. I cannot bring myself to ask them anything, not even the time of day.

WALULISO

On visits to Vienna, G. J. and I often take an evening stroll along the pedestrianized streets of the *innere Stadt,* the "inner city," along Kärtnerstrasse, Graben, and Kohlmarkt, the core of Roman and medieval Vienna. We stop to listen to street musicians: a Russian fingering a balalaika, Bolivians making the breathy music of the Andes with their pipes, a Hungarian violinist playing Liszt. We look for the old lady in a rumpled smock and babuschka—is she Polish?—who plays, of all things, the saxophone. She's been around for years. We thread through the crowd of Japanese, Italian, and American tourists, young mothers pushing strollers, Palestinian newspaper sellers, periwigged and frock-coated concert ticket sellers, *Profis*—Vienna's young professionals—and outdoor café habitués: the cosmopolitan hodgepodge, as varied as the world itself. Well, not quite. There are noticeably few black faces.

Kärtnerstrasse is where we used to spot Waluliso in the 1980s and early 90s, an old fellow in a white toga, carrying a staff or a banner, his head wreathed in greens. He was one of the city's eccentrics, a *Wiener Original,* as they say. He patrolled the street, nodding and sometimes smiling, tolerating the tourists' giggles and finger pointing, stopping to talk to the curious.

Years later I came across his picture on the Internet and learned Waluliso is a contraction of the words for water, air, light, and sun: *Wasser, Luft, Licht, Sonne.* His message—his mission—was to raise awareness of environmental issues. He had waged a successful campaign in the 1970s to maintain the Danube Island as a recreational park, staving off commercial development of the site, collecting thousands of signatures to support the cause.[6]

Waluliso's real name, I was delighted to learn, was Ludwig Weinberger. No relation, I am sorry to say.

DER KAISER

Lots of Vienna faces stare back at me as I wander through the city's museums and galleries: the naked, soul-searing self-portraits of Egon Schiele, or those of Gustav Klimt's women, his muse Emilie Flöge (with the great frizzy hair) and the chic, doe-eyed, black-haired Adele Bloch-Bauer. But these twentieth-century faces, reflecting a dawning modern age with its angst and ardor, coexist with faces of the nineteenth. And of the latter, the images of Kaiser Franz Joseph I and his empress, the Kaiserin Elisabeth, are omnipresent. There is no escaping them. Their faces appear on posters and postcards, on teacups and knick-knacks, on book covers and knock-off portraits in hotel lobbies and restaurants, their images the linchpin of a mighty tourist marketing scheme based on nostalgia for the old empire. Until the end of its thousand-year epoch the Habsburg corporation was a fairly well-oiled machine that ensured at least an illusion of stability and which regulated in fine detail the lives of its millions of citizens. But in its closing decades, the empire had but one great and enduring symbol of power and stability, the Emperor himself. To the public, he was not so much absolute ruler as a patriarch who managed to keep his squabbling polyglot children together, if not in loving harmony then at least within the family. Franz Joseph ruled for 68 years, from 1848 to 1916, longer than either Britain's Elizabeth I or Victoria. My father-in-law, Ludwig, was born during his reign and was nearly two years old when he died. His father, Wilhelm, born in 1883, was a child of the old empire. Not long after Franz Joseph died, Austria-Hungary collapsed at the end of an apocalyptic war that would send tremors through the remainder of the century.

One of Ludwig's favorite books, Joseph Roth's *The Radetzky March* (1932), chronicles the end of the Habsburg epoch. The novel traces the fortunes of the Trotta family, whose rise and fall over three generations are inextricably linked to their emperor. The protagonist, a young Infantry Lieutenant, Carl Joseph von Trotta, is haunted by two figures: his late grandfather, the "Hero of Solferino," who long ago saved the young emperor's life in battle, and the Emperor himself, whose power would devolve slowly into the merely symbolic:

> There was Franz Joseph in a sparkling-white general's uniform, the wide blood-red sash veering across his chest and the Order of the Golden Fleece at his throat. The big black field marshal's helmet with its lavish peacock-green aigrette lay next to the Emperor on a small, wobbly-looking table. The painting seemed to be hanging very far away, farther than the wall. Carl Joseph remembered that during his first few days in the regiment that portrait had offered him a certain proud comfort. He had felt that the Kaiser might step out of the narrow black frame at any moment. But gradually the Supreme Commander in Chief developed the indif-

ferent, habitual, and unheeded countenance
shown on his stamps and coins. His picture
hung on the wall of the club, a strange kind
of sacrifice that a god makes to himself. His
eyes—earlier they had recalled a summer
vacation sky—were now a hard china blue.
And it was still the same Kaiser! This painting also hung at home, in the district captain's study. It hung in the vast assembly hall
at military school. It hung in the colonel's
office at the barracks. And Emperor Franz
Joseph was scattered a hundred thousand
times throughout his vast empire, omnipresent among his subjects as God is omnipresent in the world.[7]

Franz Joseph's face is still scattered not only throughout
the former empire, but the world, even in Connecticut. When
I reach into my own cupboard each morning, I pull out a Bohemian porcelain coffee mug stamped with the iconic portrait
of the Emperor Roth describes. My father-in-law is amused
by this souvenir—silly girl, he no doubt thinks. G. J. was less
amused when I bought it and a companion cup bearing the
image of Empress Elisabeth. But over the years he and I have
enjoyed having breakfast with our now fading Habsburgs.

The collapse of the world of Franz Joseph so powerfully
depicted by Roth has done nothing to diminish the popularity of his image, especially the one of the Emperor in old age, a
white-haired and whiskery grandfather, his "china blue" eyes
not so much hard as simply glazed by old age. There are even,
I am told, a few old monarchists left in Vienna. I have seen
their tributes—candles and wreaths—left beside the Emper-
or's tomb in the Kapuzinergruft, the crypt of the Capuchin
brothers where generations of Habsburg have been laid to rest.
Ludwig's late boyhood friend, Pudi, was frequently teased on
account of his enduring affection for the Old Man. For all
that was rotten in the empire, certain conservative and com-

fortable and middle class values—tradition, propriety, orderliness—remain attached to his name. It is perhaps the ultimate Viennese triumph of image over substance, of illusion over reality.

Sissi

The Empress Elisabeth, known as Sissi, is something of a Viennese industry in her own right, and her image sells everything from candy to costume jewelry. She is, rather weirdly, contemporary Vienna's supermodel, the subject of a long-running musical, and often compared to the late Princess of Wales, Diana. The twin of the Winterhalter portrait of Franz Joseph described in *The Radetzky March* is one of the 18-year old Elisabeth standing in three-quarter profile in a billowing white gown, her mass of dark curly hair trailing down her back and adorned with star-shaped ornaments. Her expression, to me, is shy—or is it merely coy? No strong personality emerges from her face, only a vacant sort of loveliness. She was a beauty, but a mostly miserable one who was negotiated into a marriage with her cousin Franz Joseph at age 15, saddled with a truly frightful mother-in-law, the formidable Archduchess Sophie, and overwhelmed by the rigid court protocol. Her unhappy marriage, constant travels, obsessive vanity, her son Rudolf's suicide at Mayerling, and her assassination by an Italian anarchist in 1898 are the hallmarks of her legend, these and her beauty. Awed by this earthly goddess, cheering her every public appearance, Sissi's subjects were never bestowed so much as a smile, for behind this loveliest of façades lay a carefully guarded secret: a mouthful of rotten, unsightly teeth.

Lady Mary Wortley Montagu Meets the Empress of Austria, Elisabeth Christina of Brunswick-Wolfenbüttel

Vienna, Sept. 14, 1716

To the Countess of Mar.

I was perfectly charmed with the empress: I cannot, however, tell you that her features are regular; her eyes are not large, but have a lively look, full of sweetness; her complexion the finest I ever saw; her nose and forehead well made, but her mouth has ten thousand charms that touch the soul. When she smiles, it is with a beauty and sweetness that forces adoration. She has a vast quantity of fine fair hair; but then her person!—one must speak of it poetically to do it rigid justice; all that the poets have said of the mien of Juno, the air of Venus, come not up to the truth. The Graces move with her; the famous statue of the Medicis was not formed with more delicate proportions; nothing can be added to the beauty of her neck and hands. Till I saw them I did not believe there were any in nature so perfect, and I was almost sorry that my rank here did not permit me to kiss them. But they are kissed sufficiently; for every body that waits on her pays that homage at their entrance, and when they take leave [. . .][8]

EVA

Ten-year-old Eva Frisch had a crush on her cousin from America, an 18-year-old the family called Bobi. He gave her some chewing gum and that was that; her heart was his. She likes him still, but now in a cousinly sort of way. We like her, too, and her husband, Pauli, and son, Patrick.

The first time I met Eva Frisch Wertheimer was at a family dinner in her mother Gretl's apartment on Neubaugasse. She was European chic, elegant like her mother but up-to-the-minute stylish. She knew how to wear makeup—still something of an arcane art to me—and although not a classic beauty, was an arresting presence with her green eyes and sleekly coiffed hair. I thought she was gorgeous. Next to her, I felt frumpy and unsophisticated and certainly uninteresting, entirely the provincial American. It was a struggle to find some common ground, so finally I asked her about her work for a Jewish relief agency which aided immigrants in their transition through Vienna from Eastern Europe and the former Soviet Union.

"So, you are a social worker," I said.

"What I do has nothing to do with parties," she said tartly.

I stumbled to explain what I meant by "social worker," but she seemed not to listen. I implored G. J. with a "help me out here" look. He shrugged, thinking it didn't matter, but it did.

While we never saw quite as much of Eva and her family as we did of her mother, over the years we built a relationship that slowly moved from merely cordial to truly familial. And now that Gretl is gone, we rely on Eva to keep us connected to Vienna. It is a role she has, in a sense, inherited as the only Weinberger relation left in the city.

"I always remember," she told me one day as she sipped her *kleiner Brauner,* "that if any of the family came to Vienna, they came to my grandmother. Also, you know, I found some letters recently from Israel, very polite, nice, warm letters to her. You *had* to come to her, you had to give her the honor, and something like this I feel now."

"I think people felt the same way about your mother," I said.

"My mother tried to be the same, yes."

"And now it's you we all come to see."

"*Ja,* but, you know, I can't be that good!" she laughed. "You know in our family how it is, not everyone is talking to each other. What shall I tell you? You know it. But everyone was talking with my mother and also with my grandmother. She was connected to everyone, and my mother, too. But between themselves people didn't always talk. I don't have to tell you. So it is."

So it is with all families.

My cousin Eva—I claim her as kin, if only through marriage—is still gorgeous, and I still feel frumpy beside her, although she never fails to admire my smaller frame. Like her dear mother, Eva has grown plump, but it has only enhanced her beauty: she is *saftig*, bosomy, womanly.

We are still learning about each other's lives. On a recent trip, Eva asked me about my job at the university, adding, "You are a mathematics professor, right?"

Wrong. And the question astonished me and caused G. J. nearly to choke. Why on earth did she think *that*? What *she* remembered from our first meeting at her mother's was that I had played a game with young Patrick, giving him some numbers to add up so he could show off his arithmetic skills.

"Well, we all knew you were a professor, so we assumed you taught math," she said.

"THE MARTYRDOM OF THE TEN THOUSAND CHRISTIANS"

In the Kunsthistorisches Museum on the Ringstrasse, that grand and stolid repository of the former empire's art treasures, there are, of course, thousands of faces to look at. One in particular haunts me, and it's not even a Viennese face. I came across a Dürer painting, "The Martyrdom of the Ten Thousand Christians," that I am compelled to revisit whenever I'm in Vienna. It depicts a scene of mass murder, a supposedly historical event of Christians set upon by a Persian potentate and his army. The slaughter is graphic and hideous: men being speared, tossed off cliffs, decapitated, crucified. One of my art books tells me that the work was commissioned by a German Elector, Frederick the Wise, in 1507, but that Dürer might have gotten bored with the project and thus produced a rather uninspired work, for which, he apparently complained, he had not been paid enough.[9]

What interests and disturbs me about the painting is not the blood and guts but that Dürer placed himself in the midst of all the carnage. Clad in black, accompanied by a male companion, he holds a small banner bearing his name and the date, 1508. What on earth is he doing there? Is he a Dante wandering through Hell with his Virgil, as one critic suggests?

Is the banner meant to symbolize a warrant of safe passage through this treacherous landscape? Or is he, as the museum commentary asserts, chillingly I think, simply an "uninvolved observer"?

And this painting troubles me, for it reminds me a little of my own journey through Vienna. Unlike Ludwig's and so many others', mine has been a safe passage through a magnificent and welcoming place which so many have called a *Traumstadt,* a City of Dreams, but which has been for so many others a City of Nightmares. My journey through the Vienna of the past—aided by history books and literature, artworks and the stories of my family and friends—has been at times painful. I can no longer be, if I ever was, an "uninvolved observer." To know Vienna, I am learning, is to face up to its enigma. It has been both Hell and Heaven, a place of plague and massacre, of enlightenment and culture. Is it possible to pass through Hell unscathed or through Heaven untouched? It is the enigma, perhaps forever unsolvable, that Ludwig's dying generation of refugees—and to some extent G. J.'s—must live with. But so too must those lovely old ladies who meet by the roses in the Volksgarten. And so, of course, must I.

2 German Is the Language of Liebe (Love!)

Even though my mother thinks I speak German, I do not. My passing grade on a German reading comprehension exam required for my doctorate was evidence enough for her, however, despite my protests to the contrary. So, dear reader, please believe me when I confess that after more than 20 years' exposure to the language, a couple of college courses under my belt, and a notation on my academic transcript that certifies I fulfilled my language requirement, I still neither speak, read, nor write German with anything close to fluency. At best, mine is a simple survival-mode grasp of the language, a traveler's storehouse of words and phrases that allow me to eat, drink, find my way around, and exchange stock pleasantries with strangers: *Grüss Gott! Wie geht's?* I reconnoiter best in German when conversing with speakers I know; that is, with family and friends whose German has become as familiar to me as their faces. My father-in-law often tells his friends, "Her German is good, she understands a lot." He gives me more credit than I deserve, the old dear. He forgets that intimacy is created through repetition—we say the same things over and over to those we see daily. Of course I understand him: our conversations *auf deutsch* follow a predictable pattern and are defined by my limitations in German and his now narrow scope of activities.

I came too late to the study of German to do more than dabble in it, for there has been no time for either total immersion or a systematic study of grammar and syntax in the midst of a whole other career as an English professor. I have learned German, therefore, mainly in snatches: a noun here, a verb there, a phrase, an idiom as necessity dictates or serendipity allows. Serendipity—a lovely word. *Wie sagt man daß auf deutsch?* (Now there's one of the most useful questions I know: "How do you say that in German?") Here it is in my *Oxford Duden German Dictionary: glücklicher Zufall*. The same number of syllables and a similar rhythm as serendipity, but requiring two separate words; it has an umlaut, which I love the sound of (*eeeeuuuu* and pucker); and a "z" which is really a "tz" sound. *Glück* I already know: it means both luck and happiness. *Zufall* I do not know, so back to the dictionary. Chance. Lucky chance, happy chance. Perhaps a bit of *glücklicher Zufall* will permit me to use my new word sometime soon and won't I feel a little thrill? But I predict Ludwig will say, "What? I don't understand you."

"Ich bin nicht dein Schames"

Jula Mieses Weinberger was a sympathetic mother-in-law. On my maiden voyage to Vienna in 1983, she taught me my first complete German sentence as we sat in a restaurant on the Naglergasse. "You tell your husband," she said, pointing to G. J., *"Ich bin nicht dein Schames."* She enunciated it slowly: *eeessh beeeen neesshht dyne sshhaaam-eessssss.* I repeated it a couple of times, and found it pleasantly sibilant and nicely ripe with vowels, a real pleasure to pronounce.

"She doesn't know what a *Schames* is," said G. J., so this turned out to be a little more than a language lesson. *Schames* isn't even a German word, but Yiddish, referring to the beadle, the custodian, of the synagogue. Linguistically as well as geographically, I suddenly felt worlds away from the rural Connecticut town I had come from.

Jula was keen for me to have a retort in the mother tongue—my husband's mother tongue—to unreasonable demands; in other words, "I'm not your servant, go get it yourself." Turns out, I had far less occasion to use it than Jula did, but I practiced it from time to time so I wouldn't forget. Just in case.

MOTHER TONGUE

I am struck by a line from Eva Hoffman's essay, "The New Nomads": "To lose an internal language is to subside into an inarticulate darkness in which we become alien to ourselves."[10] Although it did not, this *might* have happened to G. J., who as a child in the early 1950s overheard a woman aboard a Manhattan bus chastising Jula for speaking German to him. "Speak English to the little boy," the stranger admonished her. She heeded no such advice and the family continued to speak German after leaving Uruguay and resettling in New York, English gradually displacing Spanish as their second language. Many refugees, however, abandoned German altogether, or refused to teach it to their children, who then did not share a mother tongue with their parents. Many of G. J.'s peers, the sons and daughters of the wartime immigrant generation, did not grow up bilingual, a knowledge of German thought to be a handicap, a constant reminder of the world—the old world of Vienna or Berlin or Munich—from which their parents had fled.

And that generation has not easily shaken free of such notions. At Summerwood, where Ludwig lives among elderly Jews from a variety of backgrounds, German is rarely spoken, although there are several native speakers in residence. I asked our friend Lisl, who also lives there, if she thought this to be a kind of "political correctness." No, she said. It was worse than that. One of her neighbors told her, "Those German speakers just think they're better than everyone else."

"I Am a Son of the German Language"

Though I may not hum the psalms of old,
I walk along my fathers' trail of tears;
I feel as one with every creature here,
No matter what the mask its face enfolds.

Death rages forth from them—and death is
mute;
Screams and raw oaths of vengeance shrill
forth.
I'm only a son of the German tongue
But no German—all the better for me.

I'm only a son of the German tongue;
Whatever sorrow my people suffered
Is clarified by my words and proves

My Jewish blood and that the human soul
Is the stronger—: from many darkest hours
I've found my way home to the poem's
light.

> Ernst Waldinger, "Ich bin ein Sohn der
> deutschen Sprache" (1943)[11]

Code Talkers

As a newlywed, I found conversations with my in-laws, Jula and Ludwig, both exhilarating and daunting. Hard as they and G. J. tried to stick to English, they would invariably lapse into a bewildering combination of English and German, a kind of linguistic stew strewn, like so much parsley, with bits of Spanish, a legacy of their years in Uruguay. A simple dinner table request like, "Pass me a piece of bread, please" might be rendered—and often was—"Pass me *ein Stück pan, bitte.*"

My friend and colleague, Matt Ciscel, himself a speaker of English, German, and Romanian, tells me there is a term for this blending of languages: code switching or, more pre-cisely when it occurs within sentences, code mixing. Com-mon to most, if not all, bilingual persons, code switching, Matt says, is an essentially creative act, a piecing together of languages that both enriches personal expression and solidi-fies the speaker's cultural or social identity. Matt knows a lot about this, and not just because, as a professor of linguistics, it is one of his academic specialties. As a son-in-law of a Roma-nian- and Russian-speaking family from Moldova, he shares my wonderment at the phenomenon. Learning Romanian hasn't solved all his family communication problems, though. "My in-laws discuss family matters in Romanian, but argue in Russian," he once told me. Among fully bilingual speakers, one language tends to predominate in certain situations, serv-ing what Matt refers to as "higher functions" like argumenta-tion. The other language serves "lower functions," those in-volving intimacy or solidarity.

When Ludwig and his old Viennese friends gather, they speak German. When I enter the room, the discourse switch-es to English. This is not entirely out of courtesy: I am still enough of a stranger to change the nature of the gathering from private to public. When the code switching begins, which it invariably does, I feel less an intruder and more a member of this tiny club, yet, still, only an auxiliary member, often silent but always listening.

P.S. FROM WOLFIE

In his letters to his mother and sister, Nanerl, Mozart loved to play with words, often presenting code mixing messages like the following, rendered in Latin, French, German, and Italian:

> Vienna, August 12, 1773
>
> hodie nous avons begegnet per strada Do-minum Edlbach welcher uns di voi compli-

ments ausgerichtet hat, et qui sich tibi et ta
mere Empfehlen läst. Adio.
(Today we met Herr Edlbach in the street
who brought us greetings from you and
who wants to be remembered to you and
Mama. Adio.)[12]

WIENERISCH

Only a few weeks (or was it days?) after enrolling in a beginning German course at my university, I learned a couple of
bits of crucial information. One, G. J. was no help in guiding
me through the intricacies of German grammar; turns out,
he didn't know any: "I don't know *why* you use *den* instead of
dem in that sentence, you just *do.*" And two, there was even to
my inexperienced ears a difference between how my teacher,
Herr Professor Lothar Kahn, and my husband spoke German.
The clear, crisp enunciation of Herr Kahn's rich baritone
Hochdeutsch bore only a passing resemblance to the sounds I
heard across the dinner table. G. J., somewhat to my horror,
slurred his words and changed the proper endings.

"*Geh' ma,*" he would say, impatient to get going as I fid-
dled with my purse.

"What do you mean, '*Gay-ma*'?"

"*Geh' ma*—let's go,"

"Shouldn't you say '*Gehen wir*'"?

"No, it's '*Geh' ma.*'"

Where did that "m" sound come from? Twenty years later,
I know only that it is the wrong question. To G. J., "*Gehen
wir*" is the equivalent of "Do let us go" (add a British accent
to underscore the point), and who, for heaven's sake, talks like
that?

Certainly not the Viennese, who have their own lingo
called *Wienerisch,* a term derived from Wien ("Veen"), which
is what the city is called in German. G. J. insists, though, that
with some exceptions—like *geh'ma*—how he speaks reflects
merely a Viennese accent, and Ludwig tells me, "We spoke

proper German at home," and tsk-tsks any implication otherwise. Both assert that the authentic *Wienerisch* dialect belongs
to the working-class neighborhoods of Vienna, to Ottakring
and Hernals and Simmering, where "w"s are routinely shifted
to "m"s and other permutations of the so-called "standard"
German can be readily heard: consonants dropped, vowels
shifted, and word endings contracted. (Just as in any other
colloquial form of language—including English.)

I leave the finer distinctions between what is dialect and
what is sub-dialect to the linguists to sort out. What does
seem clear, though, is that the Viennese share with south-
ern Germans and Austrians generally (except those in the far
western end of the country, along the border with Switzerland and Liechtenstein) a similar form of standard German
sometimes referred to as Austro-Bavarian. So people in Munich and Vienna understand each other well enough linguistically, but put a Berliner in Wien or a Wiener in Berlin and
the stuff of comedy arises out of differences in pronunciation
and vocabulary. Just think of a New England Yankee in the
heart of Dixie, or a Texas cowboy on the streets of Manhattan, and you get the idea—people confounded by a common
language.

BUTTER ON HER HEAD

The Viennese are right up there with the Irish in their gift
of gab and their adoration of the mother tongue, celebrating the rich variants of the standard language. On a display
table in the Morawa bookstore on Wollzeile, Vienna's version
of Borders, I find an ample number of titles about the city's
Mundart—meaning dialect, but fashioned out of the words for
"mouth" and "style": *Sprechen Sie Wienerisch?* (*Do You Speak
Wienerisch?*), *Wienerisch—das andere Deutsch* (*Wienerisch:
The Other German*), *Wos Wea Wo Waun Wia En Wean* (*What,
Who Where, When, How in Vienna*), to name a few.

At home in Connecticut I browse through G. J.'s copies
of *Wie sagt man in Österreich?* (*How Do You Say It in Aus-*

tria?) and *Cassell's Colloquial German: A Handbook of Idiomatic Usage,* which is useful because it is in English but not a particular help in the study of Wienerisch. Our favorite, though, is Josef Köber's *Weanerisch,* which includes a glossary as well as a collection of jokes in dialect. With its generous number of words and phrases related to drinking, sex, and bathroom functions, it is a book that amply illustrates the writer Ruth Kluger's comment that the language of Vienna shares "an insolent humor and an aggressive, colorful verbiage" with the English she learned on the streets of New York City.[13] Insults abound: I learned eleven different ways of expressing *Dummkopf,* which probably needs no translation for English speakers, and almost twice as many for those who have consumed a few too many *Wiener Schnitzel.* The *Wiener Schnitzel,* by the way, the breaded veal cutlet that is one of Vienna's signature dishes, is aptly defined here as a *Breslteppich,* a breadcrumb carpet.

I trotted out this book recently over lunch with some of Ludwig's old Vienna friends. Lisl, Helly, and Gerty recognized hardly a single word or phrase, and seemed more bemused than amused by usages reflecting a city and a culture they hadn't lived in for over 50 years, a place profoundly different from the Vienna that gave them their mother tongue. I should not have been surprised for as I grow older, I find that my students bring to the classroom—and to their writing—words and references that baffle and bewilder me. And quite often I am not amused either.

Whenever I am in Vienna, though, I listen for local idioms, but finding them is usually a matter of serendipity (*glücklicher Zufall!*), since it requires G. J. to hear them and then turn them over to me for my collection. Here is a good one: we were on the #18 trolley when a woman sitting in front of us, talking on her cell phone—her *Handy*—asked, incredulously and clearly, "*Hast an Vogel?*" G. J. whispered to me, "She's asking her caller, 'Are you nuts?'" How can I explain this? If I were to say that the "proper" German is "*Hast du einen Vogel?*" it would be irrelevant to its meaning because she's using an idiom which has nothing to do with having a bird (*Vogel*). But I like this phrase—I can probably put it to good use.

Ludwig told G. J. and me one day that his home health aide had been extra solicitous of him that morning, that whatever misunderstanding had occurred between them the day before had clearly been resolved, apparently in his favor.

"*Sie hat Butter am Kopf,*" he said, in an "Ah ha! See? I was right!" kind of spirit.

She has butter on her head? It means she has a bad conscience or is feeling guilty. There's a good example of *Wienerisch,* I thought, and stored it away. But I happened to spot in the Köber book a phrase that was translated as "*Butter am Kopf.*" The next time Ludwig has reason himself to feel guilty over some transgression, I'll tell him, "*Dreck am Steckn håm.*" Dirt clinging to his walking stick makes about as much metaphoric sense as having butter on his head. Maybe a little more.

IT'S SO . . . GUTTURAL

I love the sound of German. But to so many Americans, especially baby boomers like me, notions about German have been shaped—distorted—by portrayals of Nazis in the movies, by buffoonish Captain Klinks and Sergeant Schultzes, by *Saturday Night Live*'s Hans and Franz, and by the Terminator English of the most famous Austrian alive today, Arnold Schwarzenegger. Indeed, well-educated and well-traveled friends of ours not long ago took, at our prompting, a detour from their holiday in northern Italy to drive over the Brenner Pass into Austria to spend a couple of days in Innsbruck. By their own account, they became so disoriented, even frightened, by the sound of German, by the complete foreignness of it, by their inability to recognize any cognates, that they turned tail and headed right back into Italy, their stay lasting barely 24 hours. They confessed to us upon their return their irrationality in the matter. But one of them told us he simply could not disconnect the language, both the sight and sound of it, from the terrifying newsreel images of World War II, of Hitler, of the liberation of the concentration camps he had seen as a child in darkened theatres in Ohio.

Our friends' visceral response is forgivable, perhaps even understandable; but more perplexing and irritating is the commentary of other of our friends and acquaintances, who thoughtlessly say to G. J. about his mother tongue that it is unpleasing to the ear, harsh sounding. "It's so guttural," we hear. To me, German sounds neither guttural nor threatening. I perceive its melody, if not always its meaning. Whenever I hear it, especially at home in Connecticut, I discreetly eavesdrop, not to gather intelligence but to listen for a moment or two to a welcome sound. Even Mark Twain, when not lampooning the complexities of German grammar, betrayed his love for the sound of it: "There are German songs which can make a stranger to the language cry. That shows that the *sound* of the words is correct—it interprets the meanings with truth and with exactness; and so the ear is informed, and through the ear, the heart."[14]

Special

My friend Barbara Baker fondly remembers her undergraduate German courses, and not only because she was in love with a boy in her class and because of the Friday afternoon beer-and-conversation-sessions her instructor held at a local pub. She, too, loves the sound of German. When she visited me in Vienna recently, we rode on the trolley one morning and traded favorite words and phrases. She likes: *besonders, bedeutet, Träumerei, die ganze Welt, heilige Nacht, frisches,* and *Stammtisch.* I like: *Mutti, fünf, Gabelfrühstück, mein Deutsch ist nicht sehr gut, ausgezeichnet,* and *gnädige Frau.*

Mark Twain, der Wiener

It is difficult for an American to write about the German language without quoting Mark Twain, who made some hilari-

ous—to non-German speakers, that is—observations about
it. Here is one of my favorites: on the subject of those impossibly long compound nouns German speakers invent at every
turn, he wrote,

> These things are not words, they are alpha-
> betical processions. And they are not rare;
> one can open a German newspaper any time
> and see them marching majestically across
> the page—and if he has any imagination he
> can see the banners and hear the music, too.
> They impart a martial thrill to the meekest
> subject.[15]

One of Twain's most famous nonfiction pieces is an 1879
essay titled "The Awful German Language" that appeared at
the end of *Tramps Abroad*. One might understandably think
that Twain's object was merely to have a good laugh at the expense of the language of Goethe and Schiller, to deflate some
of its perceived pomposity. Well, yes. But "awful," I think,
must be read as a pun, for the author was filled, as am I, with
wonder at and admiration for this dynamic, creative, complex, and vexing language.

America's most famous nineteenth-century author took
up residence in Vienna for nearly two years, from September
1897 to May 1899, while his daughter, Clara, studied piano
with one of the great master teachers, Professor Theodor Le-
schetizky. It is fair to say that Vienna left its mark, so to speak,
on Twain and he on it. For one thing, he made great newspaper copy and the press reported his comings and goings
assiduously throughout his stay, although not always in the
most favorable light. He managed to step on any number of
toes during his visit, perhaps the most sensitive of all having to
do with the German language. Two months after his arrival,
he was invited to address the prestigious Concordia society, an
association of journalists and writers. In a ten-minute speech,
delivered in German to the surprise and delight of his audi-

ence, he lampooned the German language, as he had done in print before, proposing on this occasion some "reforms":

> I would very much also like to reform the separable verb a bit. I don't want to let anyone do what Schiller did: he stuffed the whole history of the Thirty Years' War between the two parts of a separable verb. That aroused even Germany itself and Schiller was—thank God!—refused permission to write the history of the Hundred Years' War.[16]

A quick lesson in German: the separable verb to which Twain refers is the bane—one of many—of every student of the language. As the term indicates, some verbs have prefixes which grammar dictates become detached and deployed elsewhere within a sentence.

The point about Twain's speech, though, has nothing to do with German grammar and everything to do with his audience, which included that night such luminaries of Vienna's high culture as composer and conductor Gustav Mahler, the Burgtheater actor Alexander Girardi, the writers Hermann Bahr, Richard Beer-Hofmann, and Theodor Herzl. Recounting the episode in his *Our Famous Guest: Mark Twain in Vienna,* Carl Dolmetsch writes that Twain

> seems not to have been fully aware that those he was addressing were, after all, artisans of their language, as he was of English, and just as he made of his mother tongue a fine-tuned instrument, so did many of these Viennese writers in their use of German, the language they instinctively cherished. His insensitivity on this occasion betrays a boorish streak he shared with too many of his compatriots then and now. [17]

"Half-Truths and One-and-a-Half Truths"

"My language is the common prostitute that I turn into a virgin,"[18] wrote Karl Kraus, one of Vienna's greatest satirists, a man whose character and body of literature defy easy categorization or analysis. Not well known to American readers, Kraus (1874–1936) was a profoundly important author and critic—a critic of just about everything, it seems: literature and journalism, art and architecture, feminism and psychoanalysis, politics and government, Vienna and the rest of the world. It would be easy simply to refer to him as the intellectual contrarian or coffeehouse curmudgeon of the nineteenth-century *fin-de-siècle,* a sort of Viennese H. L. Mencken. In fact, his was one of the most vital voices in the European culture of his time, his journal *Die Fackel* (*The Torch*) in equal parts admired and reviled, but always avidly read.

On perhaps no other subject was he as passionate as that of language, "linguistic corruption," forming, Jonathan McVity writes, Kraus's "lifelong nemesis."[19] Long before George Orwell exposed crimes against English in his landmark essay, "Politics and the English Language," Kraus had pointed to and protested assaults on German, warning that truth, accuracy, and ethics are inextricable from the language in which they are expressed, that what you write or what you say *is* what you think and who you are. "Through his worship of language," writes William M. Johnston, "Kraus exalted Viennese aestheticism: for him words were the supreme, nay the only reality."[20]

Although he is best known for his journal, Kraus also wrote poetry and drama, as well as aphorisms, a literary form notoriously difficult to translate because of its wordplay and brevity. ("You cannot dictate an aphorism into a machine," Kraus wrote. "It would take too long.")[21] Witty and savage, Kraus's aphorisms may wreak havoc with readers' sensibilities, provoking anger and laughter, inspiring thought and startling them into self-recognition, wounding and confounding. As his biographer Edward Timms writes, "A complex aphorism may pursue this collision of ideas through a sequence of dialectical stages without ever reaching a fixed conclusion."[22]

Hence, the word (or world?) according to Kraus, translated by Harry Zohn:

> "You'd be surprised how hard it can often be to translate an action into an idea."
>
> "I have drawn from the well of language many a thought which I do not have and which I could not put into words."
>
> "The closer the look one takes at a word, the greater the distance from which it looks back."
>
> "A linguistic word translated into another language is like someone going across the border without his skin and donning the local garb on the other side."
>
> "The most incomprehensible talk comes from people who have no other use for language than to make themselves understood."
>
> "An aphorism never coincides with the truth: it is either a half-truth or one-and-a-half truths."[23]

THAT RAT PACK FEELING

The city of Mozart, Beethoven, Schubert, Brahms, Mahler, Schönberg, and several Strausses was offering among its entertainments recently a Rat Pack tribute show. What middle-aged American in temporary residence could possibly resist? (For the record, G. J. could have and would have.) The very idea was deliciously incongruous to begin with, but what sealed the deal for me was the program title: *"Rat-Pack Songs wienerisch."*

In the grand and gilded Wiener Konzerthaus, a venue that would only days later host such distinguished artists as

Monserrat Caballé and Vladimir Ashkenazy, a local "*Song &*
Danceman," Michael Seida, brought to a seriously dressed up
audience "*das Ratpack-feeling von Las Vegas.*" Tall (what long
legs!), elegant in his tux and slicked back hair, Seida provided
an evening of "*Songs und Stories der 'Grossen 3': Sammy Davis
Jr., Frank Sinatra, Dean Martin!*"

Backed by Richard Oesterreicher and his Big Band, with
"*special guest*" Cole Hunter, a local singer known as *the Voice
von Heanois* (Hernals), Seida indeed conjured up a bit of 60s
Vegas entertainment. He was on stage a guy with all the right
moves, a hipster, a cool cat, a ringadingdinger of the old
school, brandishing a cigarette (smoking is certainly no crime
in Vienna), and talking about the heyday and the hijinks of
the *Grossen 3*.

His Dino was spot on, better than his Frank or Sammy,
although as a dancer, his "Mr. Bojangles" was a highlight of
the show, a lump-in-the-throat sort of tribute to Davis. But
his voice best captured Dino's insouciance, and the Wienerisch lyrics for some of Martin's greatest hits were hilarious
to the audience and incomprehensible to me. Sammy Cahn
and Jimmy Van Heusen's "Ain't that a Kick in the Head,"
recorded by Martin in 1960, turned into "Waun di' die Liab
Amoi Pockt," which G. J. translates into standard German
as "Wann dich die Liebe einmal packt" and into English as
"Once Love Grabs You." The Lee Hazelwood song, "Hous-
ton," which I hadn't heard in years, turned into a parody
called "Grinzing," which is the name of the famous wine village on the outskirts of Vienna. Listen: "Hew-*stun*, Hew-*stun*,
Hew-*stun*" . . ."Grin-*tzing*, Grin-*tzing*, Grin-*tzing*."

Seida's program was cheeky but reverent. He told a sweet
story of traveling to Paris as a kid to see Sinatra perform.
Frank was introduced, the audience gave him a standing O,
but the kid continued to clap well after the rest of the audience had taken their seats, drawing the singer's attention and
acknowledgment. It was the only time he "met" Sinatra, Seida
said, although his show biz credentials are enhanced a bit by

program pictures of him posing with Liza Minelli and Dino's old comedy partner, Jerry Lewis.

The Sinatra selections included awful pop covers ("Bad Bad Leroy Brown" and "Sunshine of My Life"), classic Frank ("Where or When," "The Lady is a Tramp"), and blockbusters ("New York, New York," "That's Life"). Seida sang some in English, some in Wienerisch, and some in a code-mixing combination of both.

Through it all, Viennese *Song und Danceman* Michael Seida stood tall and did it all *sein Weg*.

An Empire Divided by Language

In 1897 a bill was introduced in the Austrian Parliament, that stately, neoclassic structure on the Ringstrasse, requiring government officials in Bohemia to speak Czech as well as German. What ensued over this seemingly sensible, rational piece of legislation is complicated and convoluted, involving Tammany-style politicking; a duel between the Prime Minister (Count Badeni) and a nationalist scoundrel (Karl Hermann Wolf) who earned the admiration of—and later a pension from—Adolf Hitler; one of the longest parliamentary filibusters on record; a police action to quell the rioting politicians; and the invocation of a constitutional clause which restored dictatorial powers to the Emperor. This was neither the first nor would it be the last time the issue of language threatened to divide an already linguistically and ethnically divided empire.

One of the spectators viewing the Parliamentary mayhem from the Visitors' Gallery was Mark Twain, who published an account, "Stirring Times in Austria," in *Harper's Magazine.* Twain marveled at the lack of decorum and although clearly horrified by the debasement of democratic process, seemed to relish the insults shouted at the various players in this high drama:

Schönerer uplifts his fog-horn of a voice and shakes the roof with an insult discharged at the Majority.

Dr. Lueger. "The Honorless Party would
  better keep still here!"
Gregorig (the echo, swelling out his shirt-
  front). "Yes, keep quiet, pimp!"
Schönerer (to Lueger). "Political mounte-
  bank!"
Prochazka (to Schönerer). "Drunken
  clown!"

During the final hour of the sitting many happy phrases were distributed through the proceedings. Among them were these—and they are strikingly good ones:

Blatherskite!
Blackguard!
Scoundrel!
Brothel-daddy!

This last was the contribution of Dr. Gess-man, and gave great satisfaction. And deservedly. It seems to me that it was one of the most sparkling things that was said during the whole evening.[24]

AT THE CAFÉ GRIENSTEIDL

We were sitting at a sidewalk table at the Griensteidl when a man walked by wearing a T-shirt that read, *"Ois hot sei end."* Translation from *Wienerisch* into standard German: *"Alles hat sein Ende."* Translation into English: "All things must come to an end."

3 By Bim

There is a rich local parlance by which Vienna's lovely old red and white *Strassenbahnen*, or streetcars, are known. Old folks, including Ludwig, still call it the *Elektrische*, which stems from the system's conversion from steam (and horse!) powered to electrical back in the first decade of the twentieth century. Our twenty-year old Viennese cousin Patrick and his friends, however, call it the *Öffi*, which is blessedly short for *Öffentlicher Personennahverkehr*, most simply translated as "local public transportation."

However, the term I like best is *Bim* (beem). How easy and sweet and playful it sounds: "'I ride the *Bim*,'" and, as an inveterate passenger, I think it correct to say I am a *Bim*-er. Patrick's mother, Eva, says the term is onomatopoetic, drawn from the BEEMBEEMBEEM of its not so-sweet-and-playful warning bell that its drivers are not at all averse to ringing. I like, too, that the *Bim* celebrates itself. Many of the cars offer a touch of whimsy in the messages they bear on their exteriors, in white on red: *Bim unterwegs*, "Bim under way," which is also a pun, G. J. tells me, on *Bin unterwegs*—"I'm on the way." Some bear the nice summertime suggestion: *Bald im Garten bei Bim*, for which I can only provide a wordy, interpretive translation: "You can soon be in one of the city's gardens by taking the Bim." German *can* be economical.

Bim by the Numbers

Recently I found a copy of *Wien von A–Z,* a compendium of information and anecdotes published in 1953. It even includes a chart of Vienna's streetcar and bus lines. Fifty years ago, there were 61 *Bim* and 18 bus routes. The *Strassenbahn* alone had 3,107 cars with 197,587 seats. System-wide, the trolley tracks stretched some 656 kilometers or just shy of 400 miles. The bus lines traversed an additional 143 kilometers, or about 86 miles.[25]

My copy of *Enjoy: Wilkommen in Wien* magazine, thrust at me by a lovely young thing as I was heading towards the baggage claim at Vienna International Airport, states that in 2003 the entire city public transportation system comprised some 919 kilometers (551 miles). There are "117 underground, tramway and bus lines with more than 4,300 stops."[26]

My *Verkehrslinienplan Wien 2003,* indispensable for planning my outings *bei Bim,* states there exist precisely 32 *Bim* routes, 86 bus lines, and 5 subway lines, numbered 1, 2, 3, 4, and 6.[27]

According to these statistics, the evolutionary thrust of Vienna's public transportation system is clearly indicated: the *Bim* is headed towards extinction.

"It's a Vonderfoll System"

However else he may feel about Vienna, when the subject of its streetcars comes up, Ludwig never fails to note, "It's a vonderfoll system." He can tell me, still, which lines he took to school and to get around town, although some of these routes or route numbers no longer exist. And, he admits, once he acquired his beloved Fiat, the *Elektrische* held no further thrill.

It thrills me, though. I have a country-raised and suburban-living American's awe for such convenient city infrastructure: hop on, hop off, almost anytime and almost anyplace. True, not every one of the city's 23 *Bezirke* or districts is accessible solely by street car, but the extensive network makes it possible to penetrate many neighborhoods outside the *innere Stadt,* and to do so at a stately, decorous pace, distinctly unlike that demanded by the city's *U-Bahn,* or subway. The buses are nice, and they are far more comfortable and rattle less than the trolleys, but . . . the *Bim* is truly the *grande dame* of Vienna transportation, as much a part of the city's collection of iconic images as Kaiser Franz Joseph, the Sacher Torte, or the white frocked debutantes waltzing at the Opera Ball.

I certainly owe my grasp of Vienna's geography to long and leisurely forays *bei Bim,* but that isn't claiming much, really. Although the city occupies some 160 square miles and comprises a remarkably diverse set of landscapes—marshy river land and Alpine foothills, skyscrapers and vineyards—it is not an overwhelming task to find one's way around; hence, I, too, consider the transportation infrastructure quite vonderfoll for such a big city.

"Vienna's a big city?" Patrick asked in response to some comment I once made about its size and its many charms. To him, Vienna is "Hometown, Austria," a small place, a sometimes frustratingly provincial European capital compared to Paris and London. Nothing proves his point more than a walk with his mother, Eva, through the *innere Stadt,* what she calls "the city." (No *Bim,* incidentally, penetrates the historical city center, only buses and subways and *Fiakers,* horse-drawn carriages.) I tease Eva about knowing everyone in Vienna, because inevitably she stops to greet someone, or many someones, along our way. "Oh, he owns the shop over there," she'll say, waving to a man sipping a coffee at a sidewalk café, or, "Patrick has been friends with her since Kindergarten," after having stopped to kiss a pretty girl on both cheeks. She was walking me to the Schwedenplatz one rainy afternoon so I could catch the #21 back to my apartment when a man in a black fedora whizzed by, but not without exchanging pleasantries with Eva on the fly. "Yes, that is the Chief Rabbi of Austria, not just Vienna, mind you, but all of Austria. A good man. Always busy. He's an old schoolmate of mine," she said.

Splendid Village

I had heard someone say that Vienna combined the splendour of a capital with the familiarity of a village. In the Inner City, where crooked lanes opened on gold and marble outburts of Baroque, it was true; and in the Kärntnerstrasse or the Graben, after I had bumped into three brand-new acquaintances within a quarter of an hour, it seemed truer still, and parts of the town suggested an even narrower focus. There were squares as small and complete and as carefully furnished as rooms. Façades of broken pediment and tiered shutter enclosed hushed rectangles of cobble; the drip of icicles eroded gaps in the frozen scallops of the fountains; the statues of archdukes or composers presided with pensive nonchalance; and all at once, as I loitered there, the silence would fly in pieces when the initial clang from a tower routed a hundred pigeons crowding a Palladian cornice and scattered avalanches of snow and filled the geometric sky with wings.

Patrick Leigh Fermor, *A Time for Gifts* [28]

The Ring

I never feel I have quite arrived in Vienna until I have taken the full circuit of the Ringstrasse on the #1 or #2 trolleys, which exist solely for that purpose: round and round and round they go, traveling the two mile route in opposite directions from 5:30 a. m. to midnight. Strictly speaking, the Ring does not comprise a full circle but only three-quarters of one; the remainder of the route follows the Franz-Josephs-Quai that

runs along the Danube Canal, which, like the Ringstrasse itself, was another nineteenth-century public works project.

One of the most famous urban thoroughfares in Europe,
the Ring is a handsome piece of civil engineering, although its
design generated plenty of contemporary criticism. But down
came the old defensive fortifications walling in the medieval
city, and up went a series of grand—perhaps grandiose *is* the
right word—public buildings interspersed with parks and
monuments and privately held real estate. It was the defining
stamp Franz Joseph I placed on the appearance of his imperial capital, and his brief 1857 decree set in motion Vienna's
transformation into a modern city:

> It is my will that the expansion of the inner
> city of Vienna be undertaken as soon as
> possible [. . .] For this purpose I permit the
> removal of the walls of fortification of the
> inner city as well as the moats around them
> [. . .] Around the inner city there shall be es-
> tablished a beltway of at least forty fathoms
> in width, comprising a road with pedestrian
> and horse lanes on both sides [. . .] This belt-
> way should include an appropriately unified
> design of buildings alternating with open
> spaces intended as gardens. [29]

Franz Joseph got what he willed, even if took about 30
years. Up went the State Opera House, the Court Theatre,
the Parliament, the City Hall, and so on, each represent-
ing an interpretation of a past architectural epoch (Gothic,
Renaissance, Classical), but collectively forming a unique
style now called Ringstrasse Historicism. "These buildings,"
writes historian William M. Johnston,

> resemble the symphonies of Mahler, with
> their profusion of melodies—no composer
> before Mahler ever used so many different
> melodies—or the dream analyses of Freud,

who discerned in dreams layer upon layer of
accreted memories and associations. For the
Viennese, the past is assimilated and accom-
modated rather than pruned or directed.
Like Proust, the Viennese lives in a perpet-
ual recherche du temps perdu and proclaims
whatever he encounters in the present to be a
revival of some aspect of that past.[30]

When the first of the great buildings, the Staatsoper, was
completed, a local wag dubbed it "The Königgrätz of
Architecture." The 1866 battle of Königgrätz was very nearly
to the Austrians what Waterloo was to Napoleon. The architects, August Siccard von Siccardsburg and Eduard van der
Nüll, were lambasted in a little ditty, loosely translated as:

> Siccardsburg and van der Nüll,
> Neither one has any style,
> Gothic, Greek, or Renaissance,
> Of all these bits they build a pile. [31]

Both men died in 1868, the year prior to the opera house's inaugural performance of Mozart's *Don Giovanni*. Van der Nüll
hanged himself, although whether directly in response to a
criticism about his design from the Kaiser remains unknown.
One of the great legends about the Kaiser, however, suggests
he felt so horrible about the architect's death that thereafter,
whenever asked his opinion of anything in public, he con-
fined himself to a formulaic, "*Das war sehr schön; es hat mir
sehr gefreut*": "That was very nice; I liked it very much."

"Second Viennese Elegy"

Yes, I see you now, how you, decked out in spring's jew-
    els, brilliant,
stretch yourself for miles around, conscious of splendid
    beauty.

You are truly unique! Who can count the towering
    buildings
that form the Ring, at once noble and magnificent?
Here, a jewel in stone, the newest cathedral; the delicate
 pinnacles of its double towers reach up to the sky;
There, with its wide façade and grave arcades, the
    mighty town hall—
and, crowned with four-horse chariots, Attic marble
    beam.
High up in the ether the domes of both museums
    dream,
while Habsburg's venerable home charmingly regains its
    youth.
And thus it continues round, broken only, and lovingly,
by the softly sparkling green of open garden preserves.
Truly, a sight enchanting to behold, for every onlooker,
whatever land he comes from, in joy admires what is
    here.
The Hesperian gladly forgets even his classical home—
and on this warmer splendor is shattered Nordic pride.

    Ferdinand von Saar, "Zweite Wiener Elegie" (1893)[32]

Love a Parade

In 1999, G. J. and I embarked on the most intrepid journey of our lives: we took a group of our university students
on a ten-day tour of Vienna and Prague. We arrived on a
Saturday morning in late June, got the young folks checked
into our hotel, then set off on the nearest *Bim* for a trip to
the Ring, where we would begin our walking tour. We found
the Ring closed to traffic because there was a parade in progress—the Rainbow Parade. Our students' first real glimpse
of the Ringstrasse, of Vienna, was not of stately buildings,
the charming rose gardens, or horse-drawn carriages driven
by portly fellows in bowler hats, but of a huge, raucous street
party celebrating gay life. Floats dedicated to lesbian domina-

trices and crossdressers rolled right by us and right under the nose of the Pallas Athena, goddess of wisdom, who graces the fountain in front of the Parliament.

"I didn't think Vienna would be anything like this," whispered Amy.

Three years later, G. J. and I were again in Vienna during June, this time without students. On a Saturday afternoon, we exited the Natural History Museum on the Ring, only to find that something called the Free Parade was under way. It wasn't, somehow, as lively or interesting as the Rainbow Parade—lots of protest speeches distorted by bullhorns into inarticulate noise, mostly, I gathered, about globalization and police brutality. But following hard behind the convoy of floats was a battalion of bright orange municipal garbage trucks, immediately sweeping up every scrap of paper and cigarette butt that the protesters had flung onto the Ring.

That, dear Amy, is very like Vienna.

ALONG TABORSTRASSE

Lately, when G. J. and I have stayed in Vienna for more than a few days, we have rented an apartment on Darwingasse in the second *Bezirk,* just a block away from the intersection of two trolley lines, the "N" and the #21, both of which could carry us to the hub at Schwedenplatz, at the edge of the *innere Stadt.* We became quite spoiled, for if we happened to miss one trolley, we had merely to step around the corner to the other stop. The ridiculous thing, though, was that should we be forced to wait for more than five minutes, we grew impatient.

I am particularly fond of the "N" and the #21 because you don't hear much English spoken except between G. J. and me and sometimes by tourists heading for the Prater on the #21. Actually, it's possible at any given time not to hear much German, either. Leopoldstadt has traditionally been Vienna's most ethnically and linguistically diverse district. In the nineteenth century it was the neighborhood to which the Empire's eastern Jews gravitated, so many that it was referred to as the Matzoh Island. Living here today are Turks, Middle Eastern Arabic speakers, sub-Saharan Africans, Hasidim, Asians, Russians, and Balkan peoples, among many others. The neighborhood boasts Turkish groceries and travel agencies, a Jewish high school and kosher butchers, a mosque, and a hair salon catering to African women. Along Taborstrasse, the Kebab König holds court in his tidy booth alongside the old Carmelite church, while a couple of blocks further on, the Jambo African restaurant is packed with young black men.

My own refuge is on a side street off Taborstrasse bearing the unlovely name Schmelzgasse: a small traditional Konditorei, the neighborhood cousin of two famous cafes of the *innere Stadt,* the Landtmann and the Mozart. I didn't know it existed until Eva tipped me off: she used to have coffee here while waiting to pick up Patrick from school. Here, I can sit and read the papers, sip a *Melange,* a frothy coffee and milk, and contemplate the display case of delectable cakes, tarts, and pastries. But even the baked goods remind me of the melting pot of Vienna: the marzipan confections originated in the Middle East, the streusel-topped cakes and homely fruit buns from Bohemia and Moravia. And the quintessentially Viennese apple strudel? The Hungarians claim to have invented it.

Herr Schaffner

Vienna's trolleys used to have a conductor, a *Schaffner,* on board who dispensed and punched the tickets as passengers entered the car. He or she (women were employed as conductors starting in 1914) would also call out each stop. Eventually ticket machines and automated recordings made the position obsolete, but it took a remarkably long time to phase them out. Indeed, Vienna's very last *Strassenbahnschaffner* did not retire until 1996. Herr Peter Winterhalter had been a conductor for 25 years, the last few on the #46. His final ride from Ottakring to the Ringstrasse and back took place on December 20, 1996; shortly after 7 p.m. on that day he called out the end station, "Joachimthalerplatz" one last time, an "historic moment," one newspaper account called it.[33]

I never met Herr Winterhalter, to my regret, nor rode the #46 on his watch. For the 22 years that I have been visiting Vienna, I have heard only one voice announcing on a pre-recorded tape each trolley stop, and periodically reminding passengers to give up their seats for the elderly and handicapped, and for pregnant women and parents with small children. Whenever I return to Vienna and board the *Bim* and hear this voice for the first time again, I somehow feel greeted by an old friend, marveling at the disembodied sound emanating from within the trolley car—every trolley car—like an omnipresence. And after an extended stay in the city, I carry it home in my dreams.

In addition to being male, it is also a middle-aged voice, with a characteristic Austrian German intonation—nasal, even a little cartoonish. It is also flat toned, but given the public announcement nature of the text, that is understandable. But that doesn't mean the guy with the voice didn't have a bit of fun, I swear. On the #21 that runs down a long stretch of Taborstrasse, I noted something a little different about the Karmeliterplatz stop: *"Karmeliterplatz,"* the voice intones, *"Magistratisches Bezirksamt. Krankenhaus der Barmherzigen Brüder. Umsteigen zur der Linie 5A."* That *Fünf Ahh:* the *Ahh* is a tone distinctly lower than the *Fünf.* It registers with me like the opening motif of Beethoven's Fifth: da, da, da, DA.

The *Schaffner* may now be figures of the past, but their legend lives on. This story attributed to Oskar Jan Tauschinski is collected in *Wien von A–Z:*

> While waiting one day at the last stop of the #106, I stood next to a fellow passenger who was wrapped in gauze from head to foot, looking like a walking advertisement for a bandage manufacturer. When the trolley pulled up the driver and conductor greeted the fellow effusively, solicitously inquiring after his health

and engaging him in conversation concerning doctors, hospitals, health insurance and the like. Eventually, the driver returned to his post to start the run and the conductor carried on with his duties. After the fellow got off the trolley, I commented to the conductor, "Well, he must be a good friend of yours. Something terrible must have happened to the poor guy."

"Yes, we're friends, Herr Pieringer and us, the crew of the 106—for two weeks now. That was when he was run over—look, just at this spot—and then dragged for about 30 meters, besides."

"Terrible," I cried out, "Who was it that ran him over?"

"Well, us, naturally—who else?" he said irritably, as if he wanted to make himself understood to someone hard of hearing.

And then he added in a more congenial tone, "Yeah, funny how people get acquainted."[34]

News Item

From the on-line English edition of *Die Presse,* July 8, 2002:

VIENNA.—A 20-year-old man has died after he either fell or mistakenly stepped between two cars of a tram Thursday night in another fatal accident involving Austria's public transportation system. The tram dragged the man some 1.3 kilometres to his death. Police said the man, Alexander P., became lodged between the two cars. The driver, 20-year-old Petra A., said the accident probably happened on the Wiedner Gürtel when she was near the end of her shift at 12:15 a.m., heading in the direction of the Remise in Favoriten. Johann Ehrengruber, a spokesman for Wiener Linien,

Vienna's public transportation operator, said that the "man would only have had a chance if a passenger had noticed the accident and immediately pulled the emergency brake. But, given the hour of the accident, the tram was empty." The man's mutilated body was discovered by mechanics and cleaning staff only after the tram had returned to its depot. His severed foot was discovered on the tracks where the accident occurred. All those involved in the incident are reported to be in shock. According to Ehrengruber, the tram driver "is not doing well at all." The spokesman said that it would not have been possible for her to notice the accident due to the loud noise of the tram. The last accident involving a tram happned in Graz, Styria, earlier in the year when a tram colllided with an oncoming truck, killing one passenger and leaving five injured. And just last month a woman was killed in the underground after falling between two cars of a U6 train as it was approaching the station.[35]

COBENZL

The Viennese like to talk about the unique character of the various *Bezirke*. Each is, in fact, a kind of mini-municipality in its own right, with its own *Amt* or town office and civic associations. Many of the districts were villages or suburbs that were gradually absorbed into Vienna as it grew outward from the old walls, a process facilitated by the creation of the Ringstrasse.

One of the best known of these villages is Grinzing, which lies northwest of the city center in the nineteenth *Bezirk*, easily reached by the #38 that leaves from the Schottentor, on the Ring. At the end of the line, there you are, in the middle of a fairy tale. A short stroll from the village center takes you past

Hansel-and-Gretel houses and their adjoining vineyards, past the wine taverns called *Heurige,* where Viennese go to relax, have a breath of country air, and enjoy a glass of young wine.

From Grinzing you can hop on the #38A (the "A" is for *Autobus*) and travel upwards along narrow, twisty roads to the city's hills: Cobenzl (1,260 ft.), Leopoldsberg (1,388 ft.), and Kahlenberg (1,585 ft.). At any of these lookout points you can, of course, enjoy coffee and cake, or a glass of wine and a meal, while searching the hazy city below for landmarks: the great bell tower of St. Stephen's, the greenish dome of the Karlskirche, the Millennium Tower, the giant wheel at the Volksprater, the Gasometer—the old city gas works—and the legendary river itself, the Danube.

Then, if you're a true blue Wiener, you take a good long walk along one of the myriad footpaths through the woods. Not alone, of course. A Sunday walk in the Wienerwald is a communal, not a solitary, activity. Our friend Lisl used to detest this ritual family outing she endured weekly as a child: "Every Sunday, rain or shine, we had to take a walk. I hated it—I would rather be reading a book." Very likely she was not alone in this sentiment, but you would never know it by the numbers of folks, by no means all tourists, who squeezed into the #38A on a recent Sunday. True, it was a glorious September day and perhaps there was some urgency about enjoying the last of the mild summer weather. Up to Cobenzl G. J. and I went, hanging on to the 38A's overhead straps for dear life, I getting sideswiped repeatedly by a backpack, whose owner's face I couldn't even see, so tightly packed in were we. Out into the golden light we stumbled, I a bit rattled by the ride, and stepped out onto a paved path that was, within moments, nearly deserted. Where had those dozens of bus riders gone? They evaporated into the woods, all but two women just ahead of us, decked out in gorgeous dirndls—some Viennese don traditional dress on such Sunday outings—stopping in quick succession to answer their respective cell phones, the trill of which broke the pastoral spell. *Halllooo?*

The Strassenbahn Museum

Vienna has often been called a Museum City, but I am a little uncertain whether this is a compliment or not. There does seem to be a museum for everything, including tobacco, teddy bears, funeral practices, anatomical specimens, Esperanto, papyrus, and, yes, the *Bim*. It is located in the third district in an old *Remise,* quaintly translated in my *Duden* as "coach house," where the trolleys go home to rest each night.

G. J. and I took a wander through the museum one Saturday morning, looking at a collection of old streetcars and buses, utility vehicles, and signaling devices that extends for acres. Each is labeled with an excruciatingly precise set of specs: the 1901 Type G Electric powered trolley, for instance, is 10.5 m. long, 3.6 m. tall, and weighs 11.3 tons. Reconstructed in 1930, it contains two "Tatzlager" motors and has manual handbrakes plus an electric emergency brake. But this beauty is by no means the oldest specimen in the museum. Decades before there was an electric streetcar system, people got around Vienna on the *Pferdetramway,* the horse drawn tram, established in 1865. The first route carried passengers from the Ringstrasse (the Schottenring to be precise) to the district of Hernals. The museum's green "summer" carriage, with a red and white striped awning and no windows, belongs to that period, built in 1868. It is 7.25 m. long, 1.9 m. tall, and weighs 3.1 tons, and looks like a mere surrey with a fringe compared to the bulkier *Bim*.

We were astonished to learn, too, that the *Bim* has a Connecticut connection. As part of the post-war reconstruction effort, New York City sent the city of Vienna some of its streetcars to fill out its damaged fleet. One of these was a 1939 42-seater Brill 39EX model that served in both Manhattan and the Bronx until it was shipped to Vienna in 1949, where it was used until 1966. Vienna returned it to the States, and it wound up in the collection of the Shore Line Trolley Museum in East Haven, Connecticut.[36]

Another connection we discovered at the museum intrigued us even more. While peeking inside an old "N" type trolley from the 1950s and 60s, G. J. spotted an advertisement for Litega, a chain of retail stores selling linoleum, carpeting, and other home textiles. Litega, we know very well, was the post-war reincarnation of the Wilhelm Weinberger firm, which had first been "aryanized," then sold under duress in 1938.

"Our Pride: Special Inlaid Linoleum by Weinberger"

Ludwig once mentioned to G. J. and me that the Weinberger firm used to advertise in the *Elektrische.* He could remember clearly only one such ad: it depicted a puppy who had made a little puddle on a linoleum floor. The caption, he thought, read something like "Oh, it doesn't matter!" The idea, of course, was to tout the easy cleanup of the product, which was still relatively new to Austria in the 1920s and 1930s. This wasn't quite the sort of advertising campaign we would have imagined for the Weinberger chain, but apparently it got results.

G. J. and I decided to find out whether any of these advertisements, called *Plakate,* still existed and after some investigation via internet and telephone, we discovered—not that it should have surprised us—that the City of Vienna owns an extensive collection of them, including some from the Weinberger stores. The collection curator, Dr. Gerda Barth, told us over the phone that we were welcome to come in and take a look.

It was not particularly easy to find Dr. Barth's quarters in the City Hall, the architectural style of which is referred to as Flemish-Gothic. Byzantine-Gothic seems more apt. But we eventually found her one morning as she was in the midst of putting on a pot of coffee and answering the persistently ringing phone. We had been in and out of offices and archives all week long, but this one was truly a mess: piles and piles

of paper everywhere, big clunky microfilm machines overwhelmed their desktops, and the usual file cabinets, office
equipment, computers seemed haphazardly arranged. But Dr.
Barth was unflappable and unapologetic and clearly Queen of
her Domain. We liked her immediately. Within minutes she
verified that the collection held samples of Weinberger *Strassenbahn* advertisements and began plucking them from her
microfilm files for us to view. The originals, we learned, were
housed elsewhere, too fragile to be handled.

G. J. and I sat before a behemoth of a whirring machine
and when the first image snapped into view, a whole forgotten world seemed suddenly revealed. There was a peacock fill-
ing the screen, its tail feathers extended, touched with red,
green, and sapphire blue: *"Unser Stolz,"* it reads: "Our Pride."
The stylized "S" of *Stolz* extends down the ad to form the "S"
of *Special. Special Inlaid—Linoleum.* The Weinberger logo
stretches across the bottom of the advertisement, flanked by
the addresses of the branch stores: Favoritenstrasse 98, Wallensteinstrasse 16, and so on.

"The Diamond of Flooring Is Special Inlaid-Linoleum"
reads another, illustrated with a lady's elegant hand, gold
bracelets on her wrist, holding between thumb and forefinger
a sparking diamond against a strip of blue floral linoleum.

One by one, we looked at some fifty advertisements, frequently beckoning Dr. Barth to come look. She good-natured-
ly obliged us in our enthusiasm and tolerated our periodic
outbursts. We are stepping into Vienna's trolleys circa 1922 to
1937, examining the evidence of Wilhelm Weinberger's empire, marveling at the creative sensibility reflected in the ads,
and discovering—reclaiming—fragments of family history.

And then there was the naughty puppy that Ludwig remembered: *"'s kann nichts gescheh'n—ist ja: Inlaid—Linoleum
von Weinberger"* it reads, a black spotted pooch glancing behind at the mess he left on the red and blue checkered linoleum. "No big deal—it is, after all, inlaid linoleum from
Weinberger." That certainly must have caused quite a buzz
among the *Hausfrauen* on the *Bim.*

The Strassenbahnfest

It took Vienna two days in September 2003, to throw an anniversary party for the *Bim*. Technically, it was a celebration of the centenary of the Wiener Linien, the city-owned company that operates all public transportation: streetcars, buses, commuter trains, and subways. But, really, this was a *Bim-fest,* complete with stage shows in front of the Rathaus and Burgtheater, little food stalls selling *Bratwurst,* beer, and cheese strudel, and a parade of old trolleys and buses on the Ringstrasse.

It was all in full swing when I arrived early Sunday afternoon: The Nockalm Quintett was on stage in front of the Rathaus playing what G. J. calls "faux-folk," Austria's kitsch country-pop, very easy listening. The crowd was into it, their arms swaying, the hard core fans singing along. There wasn't a seat left at the long picnic tables, so I milled about for a while until I spotted a small booth marked "Flohmarkt." My heart began to race because I could see this flea market had only one category of junk for sale: old signs, filthy dirty, chipped and fading metal trolley and bus signs, *Schilder,* that announced the end stations of the route.

I had to have one. So, it seemed, did everyone else, and elbowing my way to the booth took a while. There were half a dozen or so stacks of signs propped up against it, so I had to get close enough to rifle through a stack and see what was there before getting bumped out of the way. Four times I went in and then retreated, unsuccessful in finding the right one, preferably one that read "Mariahilferstrasse," where my late mother-in-law Jula had grown up or "Favoritenstrasse," where the Weinberger firm got its start. I did spot a "Mariahilferstrasse," but it was from a bus line, and way too big to lug home in my suitcase, and, besides, I wanted an authentic *Bim Schild.*

By the time I found The One, I was sure the Wiener Linien employees inside the booth were eyeing me. Why did this American tourist keep coming back to look? When I finally forked over my four euros, which would be donated to charity, clutching my sign for dear life, I got a smile—or was it a smirk?—out of one of the guys. I think he said something like, "I hope you're having fun." No doubt he was wondering, "Does she know what that sign says?"

Of course I did. My big score, my best Vienna souvenir ever, is my *Bim Schild* from the #71. End of the line: Zentralfriedhof, the Central Cemetery.

THE BEETHOVENGANG

The nineteenth *Bezirk,* Döbling, lies northwest of the *innere Stadt* and stretches out well into the hills of the Vienna Woods. In a section called the Cottage District, "cottage" being a euphemism for villa, the Weinberger family had its last home before fleeing the Nazis in 1938. A little farther north and east of the Cottage District lie the wine villages of Heiligenstadt and Nussdorf, where a century before Wilhelm Weinberger moved from the Moravian town of Mikulschitz to Vienna, Ludwig van Beethoven roamed the woods and meadows, inspired by their beauty to write his "Pastoral Symphony" and, grieving over his inevitable decline into deafness, to write his Heiligenstadt Testament.

The day after the *Bim*-fest on the Rathausplatz, I set out for Nussdorf to walk the Beethovengang, a path through the woods dedicated to the memory of the composer. I would then ride the "D" trolley line from end to end, from Nussdorf all the way to the South Railway Station at the edge of the tenth *Bezirk,* Favoriten.

By the time I reached Nussdorf, I felt as if I had already passed through several centuries' worth of Vienna city and landscape, but not necessarily in chronological order. Picking up the trolley at the Ring, I traveled down the elegant Porzellangasse, with its eighteenth- and nineteenth-century mansions, some lavishly painted and decorated with pilasters, cornices, and modillions; past the shiny, post-modern Franz-Josefs Railway Station; past the *Müllverbrennung-Fernwärme-*

Heizwerk, the city incinerator designed by Friedensreich Hundertwasser, a confection of a building dominated by a blue chimney bulging at midpoint with a shiny gold-tiled ball; past the kilometer-long Karl-Marx-Hof, a housing complex built in the 1920s by the city's first Socialist regime, a relic of a period known as "Red Vienna."

When the trolley finally pulled into Nussdorf there was hardly a soul on board—but why would there be on a Monday morning? On a warm summer weekend day, sure, the *Bim* would be packed with hikers, picnickers, wine drinkers heading towards a favorite *Heuriger* or tourists like me on a Beethoven pilgrimage. I am a poor tourist, though, missing the signpost and heading in the wrong direction down the hill on rough old pavers, only to join up with one or two old ladies headed for the local Spar market. There was nothing much else around, except a coffeehouse.

I knew my presence there would occasion some discreet looks from the regulars, and it certainly did. But the waitress was nice enough and brought me a piping hot *Melange.* In such situations, when I am feeling self-conscious, I cover up by pulling out a small notebook and taking down the details: the Beach Boys' "Surfin' USA" is playing on the radio, the best looking pastries in the case are the raisin-studded *Schnecken,* and so on. Then I spotted . . . a *Bim Schild* propped up against the counter. It was a beauty, quite an old one by the looks of it, from the "D" line: "Südbahnhof-Prinz-Eugenstrasse–Ring–Porzellangasse-Franz-Josefs Bhf–Heiligenstadtstrasse–Nussdorf." Someone here—the waitress? the owner?—had also been at the Rathausplatz yesterday, perhaps elbowing me out of the way to claim her trophy. I wanted to start up a conversation with the waitress, ask her if she had bought it, tell her about my own triumphant purchase, bond over it with her and become friends, even a *Stammgast* in her little establishment whenever I come to Vienna. It was such a happy fantasy that I held on to it a while. But *"Zahlen, bitte,"* "Check, please," was all I managed actually to say before I left.

The Beethovengang was not at all difficult to find; I simply had not paid enough attention earlier. I am struck by its prettiness, its quiet. There is absolutely no one about.

Beethoven Celebration

Forbear if I'm not able, upon request,
To join in celebrating one divinely blessed.
I'd rather enter the temple without a sound
And—if you will allow—with no one else around.

Arthur Schnitzler, *Aphorismen und Betrachtungen*[37]

The path follows the course of the Schreiberbach, not much of a brook, really, but considering we are within a city of one and a half million, it evokes well enough the former rural character of this now well-to-do neighborhood. The signs of suburbia are here: streetlamps, a railing, benches. One bench has been defiled: "Nazis Jagen" has been crudely painted on its slats. I puzzled over the translation: "Jagen" means to hunt, chase, drive away. What is the message, then? Drive out the Nazis? Who are they now? Where are they?

I found it difficult, too, to ignore the backyards of the expensive looking real estate lining the other side of the path, so I concentrate on listening, trying to hear strains of the "Pastoral," the water rushing, the chestnuts plopping to the ground. I hear something mechanical—not the faint noise of traffic from the city that lies not so very distant, but something closer by. Peeking through a hedge, I spot a *Hausfrau,* or more likely the *Hausfrau's* cleaning lady, vacuuming her balcony railings, actually bending over the wrought iron balustrade with a mini-vac and zipping up and down. That is devotion to the virtue of cleanliness bordering, in the city of Freud, on the neurotic.

The trolley ride back, all the way to the end station at the South Railway Station, was wonderfully eventful: an Australian got on at the Ring, sat down beside me and hesitantly asked if I spoke English. How satisfying was the very question! He was seeking his way to the Belvedere and I had to rein in my enthusiasm at being able to direct him, otherwise I am sure I would have scared him off—the weird woman of the "D" line. Then, a troupe of young ballerinas was shepherded onto the trolley by their "Professorin." Darling and dainty girls of eight or nine, their hair pulled back into neat buns, but little prisses all, their pecking order clearly discernible. The one with glasses was in charge, and I just bet there was woe to whomever dared called her "Four Eyes." You go, *Fräulein.*

4 From Favoriten to Döbling: Wilhelm's Vienna Journey

MIGRATION

My father's family came from Moravia. There the Jewish communities lived in small country villages on friendly terms with the peasants and the petty bourgeoisie. They were entirely free both of the sense of inferiority and of the smooth pushing impatience of the Galician or Eastern Jews. Strong and powerful, owing to their life in the country, they went their way quietly and surely, as the peasants of their homeland strode over the fields. Early emancipated from their orthodox religion, they were passionate followers of the religion of the time, "progress," and in the political era of liberalism they supported the most esteemed representatives in parliament. When they moved from their home to Vienna, they adapted themselves to the higher cultural sphere with phenomenal rapidity, and their personal rise was organically bound up with the general rise of the times.

Stefan Zweig, *The World of Yesterday* (1943)[38]

FAVORITEN

"Here you are, *die Herrschaften*," said the butcher's wife, setting down on our tiny tabletop the day's lunch special of pork

Schnitzel and buttery parsley potatoes. An old lady in an apron finishing up her own meal at the next table turned around and wished us *"Mahlzeit!"* She was as wizened and wrinkled as the butcher's wife was plain and plump. Both women could see we were outsiders in this tiny market bistro, where our meal hardly added up to 10 euros; all the more reason to be grateful for their easy cordiality. I wanted to pick up the old lady's tab but G. J. shook his head. That wouldn't do.

I like this workaday market on the Viktor-Adler-Platz in the heart of Favoriten, Vienna's tenth district. It isn't all gussied up like the famous Naschmarkt, but rather littered with cabbage leaves and stray green beans, crowded with butchers' stalls and vegetable stands piled high with cauliflowers, apples, beets. The Naschmarkt has all that and then some for it is considerably larger, but it also attracts busloads of tourists and lots of upmarket local customers, some with attitudes. No one wished me *Mahlzeit—Bon appetit*—the last time I ate there. On this Saturday noon the Favoriten market is noisy with strolling neighborhood families, competing pitchmen, and older housewives in hard negotiation. You can eat well here, have a Döner Kebab or *Bratwurst,* a beer or a glass of wine—and you can get a decent pastry and a good cup of coffee at half of Ringstrasse prices.

Favoriten played a crucial role in the Weinberger family fortunes and so our outing—just a few stops on the *U-Bahn* from the inner city—is for G. J. a return to the family's Vienna roots. The district is named for an old Habsburg retreat, the Schloss Favorita, built outside the city walls. The palace still exists, but now houses the Theresianum, founded by the Empress Maria Theresa in 1746, and arguably the best, certainly the most prestigious, *Gymnasium* in the city. But despite the royal reference and evidence of recent gentrification, Favoriten remains very much what it has been for generations, a respectable middle-class district of small shops and moderate rents. *"Proletarisch,"* Ludwig describes it. We note a few political slogans in the neighorhood, scrawled in red, evidence, perhaps, of a still active proletarian sensibility:

"Anarchie statt Österreich," *" Keine Wand Bleibt Grau,"* and *"Bündelt die Kräfte gegen Kapitalismus und Faschismus."* Anarchy instead of Austria! No wall remains gray! Unite the forces against capitalism and fascism!

G. J.'s grandfather, Wilhelm Weinberger, decidedly one of the capitalists, moved to Favoriten in 1911, four years after arriving in Vienna as a 24-year-old from a small Moravian town called Mikulschitz (Mikulčice), the son of a schoolteacher and his wife, Bernhard and Rosa Wiesner Weinberger. His is a familiar story, one enacted thousands of times over by young men who streamed out of the provinces of the Empire to seek a secure job or ply a trade in the capital. Among those who also arrived in 1907 was the 18-year-old Adolf Hitler, who left his village near Linz to study art. His residence in Vienna lasted several years and produced no material success or security, nor even admission to the Academy of Fine Arts, but contributed significantly to a slowly evolving political ideology. I cannot help but wonder if young Wilhelm and Adolph, whose fates were to become inextricably linked, ever crossed paths in their early years in Vienna, at a train station, a marketplace, on the Ringstrasse. I suppose it is an absurd notion. In 1907 Hitler lived in a rooming house in the sixth district, on Stumpergasse, down the street from where G. J.'s second cousin Louis Mieses lives now, waiting in line for standing-room-only admission to the opera, avidly reading the nationalist and anti-Semitic press, and seeming generally averse to hard work.

Although I know less about Wilhelm's early years than I do about Hitler's, thanks to Brigitte Hamann's *Hitler's Vienna: A Dictator's Apprenticeship,* the prevailing stereotype suggested that as a Czech Jew, Wilhelm would have had industry and cleverness as assets, and perhaps even a contact or two to help him launch his business selling hardware and household goods. Before he was thirty, he had opened up his first retail shop in Favoriten, while Hitler wound up in a series of men's shelters, arguing politics into the night, fleeing to Munich in

1913 to avoid being drafted into the Austrian Army. The rest, as they say, is history.

Favoritenstrasse is one of the major thoroughfares through the *Bezirk*. It was pedestrianized in the early 1990s, and is now a pleasant shopping street dotted with benches and potted shrubs, sausage stands and flower vendors. On this Saturday, G. J. and I emerge from the subway at the Südtirolerplatz and walk south, past appliance shops, clothing stores, and bakeries. All the familiar local retail franchises are here— an Anker bakery, a Schöps clothing store, an Eduscho coffee shop—and so Favoritenstrasse looks pretty much like any other district main street. We look for number 98, the first of the Weinberger stores[39], and as Ludwig had told us we would, we find there a branch of an Austrian bank, Bawag. We can easily see the outlines of the old store in the large plate glass windows. In the 1920s and 1930s, window shoppers could peruse the latest in home fashions, take in the eye-catching displays of linoleum, carpets, and draperies. *"Nur Schönstes vom Schönsten"* read one of the firm's advertisements: "Only the Prettiest of the Prettiest." Wilhelm kept a critical eye on those store windows, having his driver, Miksche, periodically take him round to all the branches after hours, then delivering his critique to Ludwig, who had the unpleasant task of passing on his father's criticisms to the store managers.

Finding Favoritenstrasse 130, the location of another branch store, proves more problematical. Ludwig recalled it had been situated on the corner of Gudrunstrasse, but the numbering doesn't work out. Favoriten had been bombed during the war—the nearby South Train Station a target of the Allies—and it is possible that subsequent urban renewal resulted in a renumbering of the buildings that simply does not correspond to pre-war addresses. A betting parlor-cum-bar, the Admiral Sportwetten, looks a likely prospect, but when we ask a cashier the establishment's street number, she stares blankly and shrugs, finally gesturing to the bartender—"Ask him." He was more obliging, and we gave his bar patrons something other than the soccer match to talk about after we left, but the number he gave us was not 130. We wonder, then, if the flashy "New Yorker" clothing shop facing us on the opposite corner could be the right spot. Its racks of cheap tank tops and polyester trousers dragged out onto the sidewalk, however, are certainly not the prettiest of the prettiest. We continue on, eventually finding a whole block bearing the number 130 perched on one edge of the Reumannplatz and kitty-corner to the Amalienbad. The Weinberger branch could have been situated at either end of the block, where now we find another bank and an empty shop, whose interior is littered and dirty and forlorn.

On our way back to the subway, we detour off Favoritenstrasse onto Raaberbahngasse, and look for #12, a Weinberger address for some 24 years, from 1914 to 1938. Wilhelm would eventually move across the city to well-to-do Döbling, which he no doubt found more befitting his status as *Kommerzialrat*. His wife, Alice Fürth Weinberger, remained here until the end—the *Anschluss*—in the home the couple had created as newlyweds, where they had raised their children, Ludwig and Nora. Raaberbahngasse was a convenient place for the family, only blocks away from two of the Weinberger retail stores and from the Adlerplatz, where Alice did her marketing. There was a synagogue in the neighborhood, destroyed during the Nazi era, and an *Elektrische* the children rode to their respective schools. Ludwig says Alice was happy here, content to stay in Favoriten. Unlike her husband, she was not eager to display the family's growing prosperity.

"She always said, 'You don't show off,'" Ludwig tells me. "She didn't like us to do this."

G. J. and I loiter around the building entrance, snapping a few pictures of this attractive, four-story, late nineteenth-century apartment house, reading the dozen or so names on its buzzer box. No Weinbergers listed, and if there had been, it would have been purely coincidental; it is, after all, a common name in this part of the world. The family lived on the first floor (that is, the second floor in American usage), in a corner apartment. Eventually, they acquired a second flat to enlarge their living quarters and accommodate the firm's offices. At street level a pub, the Bierochs, invites patrons into its corner entrance ringed by barrel staves. We do not venture through them. Maybe next time. We'll order the day's special ("*Heute: Spaghetti Bolognese!!*"), a glass of beer, then look upward and toast the ancestral home.

"Dearest Father"

Ludwig once told me that if I wanted to understand his feelings about Wilhelm, I should read Kafka's "Letter to His Father." I did, and found it an eloquent but painful parsing of the parent-child relationship. To be sure, I recognized the outlines of Ludwig's case on nearly every page. Like Kafka, my father-in-law was born into an upwardly mobile, German-speaking Jewish family of the Austrian Empire, the disaffected only son of a dynamic, ambitious, and powerful businessman. He, too, was bookish and rather shy, at least in the presence of his father, and aspired to something other than having a ready made fiefdom handed to him. He, too, loved his father and desired his approval, but tension born of incompatible temperaments—and dreams—resulted in a silence that over time seems to have defined their relationship. Kafka, though, at least writes his way out of it:

> The impossibility of getting on calmly to-gether had one more result, actually a very natural one: I lost the capacity to talk. I dare say I would never have been a very eloquent person in any case, but I would, after all, have had the usual fluency of human language at my command. But at a very early stage you forbade me to talk. Your threat: 'Not a word of contradiction!' and the raised hand that accompanied it have gone with me ever since. What I got from you—and you are, as

soon as it is a matter of your own affairs, an excellent talker—was a hesitant, stammering mode of speech, and even that was still too much for you, and finally I kept silent, at first perhaps from defiance, and then because I couldn't either think or speak in your presence. And because you were the person who really brought me up, this has had its repercussions throughout my life. It is altogether a remarkable mistake for you to believe I never fell in with your wishes. 'Always agin you' was really not my basic principle where you were concerned, as you believe and as you reproach me. On the contrary: if I had obeyed you less, I am sure you would have been much better pleased with me.[40]

Even today, Ludwig finds the subject of his relationship with his father almost too painful to discuss, and so I must settle for a few parceled out and oft repeated phrases: "We had very bad communications, my father and I," or "I had to kiss his hand and call him Herr Vater." His voice trails off, and he steers off course, admiring Wilhelm's business acumen or applauding his achievements. "He started with nothing," he says with obvious pride. But he seems unable to sustain even a paragraph's worth of conversation about Wilhelm as father, except to suggest that he followed the prevailing, that is to say nineteenth-century, convention of childrearing, that children should be seen and not heard. Ludwig's silence has become a lifelong habit, and I have seen how it has complicated all his human dealings. He is an introvert, often uneasy with the give-and-take of conversation, preferring to preserve the safe and perfectly cordial surfaces of discourse and disappearing when more is asked of him. I offer this observation to G. J.

"Yes," he concurs. "How very Viennese."

I wonder whether Ludwig is angry, still, at Wilhelm, who fled Vienna in 1938 and died of a heart attack in 1939, aged

55. The Nazis came, and the house, the business, the bank accounts were lost, the family dispersed or murdered. Ludwig says that if his father had confided in him, trusted him more, he might have by now recovered some of what was lost: "But he thought, 'children don't need to know about these things.'" Ludwig means things like life insurance policies and bank account numbers and safety deposit box keys. More's the pity he cannot recover what he never had—a voice with which to tell his father he was his own man, to tell him he loved him as well as respected him. The Nazis stole that precious time he and Wilhelm needed to find their way to one another, to replace the silence between them with honest and, perhaps, loving words. There are no reparations for that.

A FAMILY FIRM

"I tell you frankly, they hated me," says Ludwig, referring to his Aunt Luise Weinberger Wiesner and her two sons, his cousins, Ernst and Heinrich. "Whatever she said to my father about me was right."

And apparently whatever she said tended to tout her sons' superiority to their cousin Viki in matters regarding the family business, in which they were all employed during the 1930s. As manager of the drapery department of the Wilhelm Weinberger firm, overseeing the Wallensteinstrasse workshop where made-to-order curtains and draperies were sewn, Tante Luise was in a position not only to see and hear the goings-on in the business, but to whisper her opinions in her brother's ear—although perhaps "whisper" is not exactly the right word. Every account G. J. and I have heard of her suggests she was as formidable a presence as Wilhelm himself, confident, assertive, and highly competent at her job. If Ludwig today has little lingering affection for her, he readily summons up respect for her energy and talent. "She did beautiful work," he says, for when the firm was young, Tante Luise, a skilled seamstress, *was* the drapery department.

When he speaks of his cousins, the late Heini and the 90-year-old Ernst, who lives in Florida, a tinge of bitterness remains. They gave him a tough time back in Vienna, he says, especially Heini, who once threw him out of the Schönbrunnerstrasse store after Ludwig passed on some criticism from Wilhelm about the appearance of a window display: "You don't tell *me* what to do." Heini was older and apparently not about to take any orders from the boss's son, cousin or no cousin.

And therein lies an interesting point: Wilhelm may have mixed business with family, but he did not mix family with family. Throughout most of their childhood and adolescence, Ludwig and his sister Nora remained unacquainted with their first cousins, although they all lived in Vienna. Ludwig never met Ernst and Heini until he went to work for his father. He and Ernst even attended the same business school, Vienna's Handelsakademie, at more or less the same time, but they neither recognized nor sought out one another. Neither did Ludwig know Gretl Fischer, of whom he was so fond later in life, or her brother Leo, although he knew their mother, his Tante Rudi. Why was this, I ask him, if your father was so family-minded as to provide a livelihood for a number of his relations? Ludwig says, "It was a question of status," pronouncing the latter as "stat-tous." Wilhelm did not want him and Nora to get too friendly with cousins who did not stand on the same rung of the social and economic ladder. Gretl and Leo's mother, Tante Rudi Fischer, ran a tavern catering to the working classes, after all. Tante Luise was a widow and lived with her children in what Ernst tells me were quite modest circumstances. Wilhelm wanted his children to cultivate the "right" sort of associates. But he apparently wasn't loath to toss his son and nephews into the simmering cauldron of ego and competition that was the family firm to see what they were made of. And Ernst and Heini, according to Ludwig, had the sterner stuff on which commerce thrives.[41]

Tante Luise and her boys were by no means the only relatives to work for Wilhelm. A cousin, Otto Wiesner (the surname Wiesner is prominent within the family), was the Herr Direktor, second in command of the firm. Wilhelm's brother, Julius Weinberger, to whom Ludwig bears a striking resemblance, was the firm Prokura, in charge of inventory. Egon Fürth, Wilhelm's left-leaning brother-in-law, was employed as an accountant, and Aladar Fischer, Aunt Rudi's husband, managed the Favoriten 130 store. Even Nora, Ludwig's sister, worked for the firm, but only for a short time, Ludwig tells me: "She had always problems with my father."

Tucked into a batch of old documents Ludwig had gathered years ago with Gretl's help, G. J. and I recently found a list of Weinberger employees neatly typed on company letterhead, undated, but presumably drawn up post-March 1938. The employees, it states, are all Aryan: *Die gesamte Gefolgschaft ist arisch.* Among the 58 names listed, from Adolf Abt to Josef Wendel, there is not a Weinberger, nor Wiesner, nor Fischer, nor Fürth among them. The company built upon a foundation of family connection, however self-serving the loyalties or complicated the relationships, was soon after the *Anschluss* stripped of its greatest assets. It was then handed over to a trio of new owners, certifiably Aryan, and therefore deemed by the Third Reich to be far more suitable as purveyors of textiles, carpets, linoleum, and draperies to the good citizens of Vienna.

Fräulein Herta, Cashier

Herta Schwartz is a jolly soul, an eighty-something with a voice that is one part gravel and three parts good will. When G. J. and I saw her last it was in Florida, where she and some others of Ludwig's circle spend the winter. We asked her what she recalled of working for the Weinberger firm over coffee at Helly Kohn's North Miami rental—a penthouse with wind-swept views of the Intracoastal and a clock that on the hour chimed out "Home on the Range."

"I became friendly with his brother," she said, nodding towards Ernst Wiesner, who was sitting with his wife, Irene, across the table. "Heini and our young friends, teenaged friends, you know, we spent New Year's together and I was very upset about losing my job, and he said, 'Don't worry, I'll get you a job.'"

"Ah, *Protektion!*" G. J. laughed, using the German term for patronage or influence.

"So I wrote my resume and I sent it to Direktor [Otto] Wiesner. Ernst I only knew from sight, not that we were ever talking to each other, but I knew him. And Ernst took my resume and—he wouldn't remember, but I remember—and he gave it to Dr. Wiesner. And Dr. Wiesner right away hired me and said, 'In the Währingerstrasse you are going to be a cashier.' This was the beginning of 1937. It was a good job. It was a nice job."

"She could sleep all day there," said Ernst.

Herta took that on the chin: "We had not much to do and we were talking the whole day, and in the evening the secretary from the office called and asked for the figures, and whatever the figure was I gave him."

"I know by what you took in they should close the store," said Ernst.

"That was not a big store," agreed Herta. "And when Hitler came I had to leave and Heini had to leave, so they put us in the other Währingerstrasse store, the smaller one, the two of us, and we had nothing to do. Our friends came. There was nothing to do because it was a Jewish store. And in the evening they called up, and they asked for the figures and we couldn't give them any figures because nobody came."

"What was your salary?" I asked.

"I think I made 120 dollars—I mean schillings"

"A week?"

"No, a month, a month! And then, at the end, Direktor Wiesner gave us extra, a bonus. Then Hitler came."

"Managers of the stores made the equivalent of about $300 a month," Ernst noted.

"Do you recall how the store looked?" I asked. "Can you describe the interior?"

"It was modern, up-to-date for that time."

Ernst offered to make a sketch, and with a fine-point pen he made a rough schematic on a page of my notebook, not of Herta's Währingerstrasse store but of Wallensteinstrasse 16 and Floridsdorfer Hauptstrasse 44, two other branches. He blocked off and neatly labeled the places where the cashier station was located, also the carpet section, the display windows—"show windows," he called them—and the stairs. He noted the dimensions of the Floridsdorf store: 80-feet deep from front to back, and 24-feet across. It has been 66 years since he worked for his Onkel Willy in the family business, and he is 90 years old. I am awed as always at the capacity of all these old folks—Ernst, and Herta, and Ludwig—to recall with such precision so many of the details of their lives in Vienna just before the *Anschluss.*

I asked Herta about Wilhelm Weinberger. She and Ernst number among the precious few still alive who knew him, or in Herta's case, had met him.

"I only saw him twice, but he came to talk to people. See, when he came into the store I was right there next to the door, you know, at the cashiers.' He came and put his cane on the desk and asked 'How are you?' and 'What is your name?'"

"You were a very important person," said Helly.

"No, no, I was a cashier, we didn't make much money."

"How did you address him?" I asked.

"Herr Kommerzialrat," said Herta.

"From what I've heard," said G. J., "If you didn't call him Herr Kommerzialrat, you had a problem."

"Well Deserved Recognition"

The President of the Association of Carpet Dealers, Herr Wilhelm Weinberger, was recognized by the Bundespresident[42] through the conferral of the title of Kommerzialrat. Kommerzialrat Weinberger is the model of a thoroughly modern, enterprising

and circumspect businessman, who has understood
how to turn his business into an international concern which enjoys the best of reputations far beyond
Austria's borders. Kommerzialrat Weinberger will
have the opportunity to put his wealth of knowledge
and his great business experience at the disposal of
the public in numerous ways.

Wiener Handelsblatt, June 4, 1926

HERR KOMMERZIALRAT

In his book, *The Viennese: Splendor, Twilight, and Exile,* Paul
Hofmann writes of Vienna's "Byzantine mania for titles," a
passion not necessarily relegated to the Habsburg past: "Out
of nineteen resounding bureaucratic titles listed in the 1910
issue of the Civil Service Directory," he writes in 1988, "fif-
teen are still officially in use."

> Almost every day the Official Gazette an-
> nounces that the Federal President has be-
> stowed the title Professor on a painter who
> has reached his sixtieth birthday or of Com-
> mercial Counselor [Kommerzialrat] on some
> business owner who has never been in bank-
> ruptcy court and has shelled out money for
> worthy causes. Wives share all the honors.
> The titles Mrs. Lieutenant Colonel and Mrs.
> Veterinary Counsel do not mean that the
> ladies so addressed command an army bat-
> talion or deliver foals but only that their hus-
> bands do or did. Viennese take their titles to
> the grave, as innumerable headstones in the
> local cemeteries prove.[43]

"Frau Doktor" this, *"Frau Doktor"* that: I have long been accustomed to being so addressed in Austria by virtue of G. J.'s
academic credentials. Early on in our travels, we made a point
of using his PhD on correspondence—to hotels, mainly, be-

fore the e-mail era, when we still had to write for reservations and include a reply coupon to get a confirmation—to see if we would be greeted in a formal, deferential manner when we checked in, which we invariably were: *Grüss Gott, Herr Professor Doktor, Frau Doktor!* It was a bit of fun, especially for me, who finds such European trappings both fascinating and, good democrat that I am, a little horrifying. G. J. claims he never liked it (I am not so sure of this) and was glad when I had my fill of such games, which came when I earned my own academic credentials. It began to rankle that although I was now a Frau Professorin Doktorin in my own right, I was *still* "wife of," *still* Frau Doktor.

Wilhelm Weinberger's pursuit of a title was no bit of silliness; but we continue to puzzle over whether, as Hofmann suggests, he might have somehow bought it. Opinions were divided at our Florida *Jause,* Herta insisting it had to be earned, the others more skeptical.

"A title meant a lot, a *lot.* But no, you could buy it, whatever the cost," said her friend, Didi.

On our next trip to Vienna, G. J. and I paid an unannounced visit to the Austrian Chamber of Commerce, a glaringly modern building on the Wiedner Hauptstrasse, to see if there existed any Weinberger firm records. There was the usual confusion with the receptionist over what we wanted and whom we should see. Eventually, she put us on the lobby phone with Frau Magister Rita Tezzele, of the Legal and Commercial Organizations Section of the Chamber's Archive of Commercial History, who promised to conduct a search for us.

She was as good as her word, and a few days later, we sat in her office sifting through a small stack of records that she attempted to decipher for us. Petite, blonde, efficient, Frau Tezzele was clearly pleased over her find, but despite her efforts and our momentary awe at the sight of documents with Wilhelm's name on them, the copies of the papers she showed us have proven baffling, reinforcing for us the stereotype of Austria as a nation once, and perhaps still, burdened by excessive bureaucracy. Among the documents were several titled *Zählblatt IV,* "Register for Changes in Existing Businesses," which were meant, we believe, to record periodic additions to the goods in which the Weinberger firm traded. But the notations of these remain the same from the earliest document, dated 1909, to the latest, dated 1920: linoleum, oilcloth, rubber goods, and one or two other items noted in completely unreadable handwriting. A copy of a 1918 *Zählblatt I*–a licensing document—contains, however, a surprising notation, that the firm is registered also to sell "Art Objects, Glassware, Leather Goods, and Toys." Did Wilhelm envision a one-stop home furnishings shopping empire, a Viennese Pottery Barn or Crate & Barrel?

Frau Tezzele's face lit up—*Why didn't you tell me this before?*—when G. J. mentioned that Wilhelm had been a *Kommerzialrat.* There *must* be records, she said, and promised to launch another search, sending to Connecticut in short order a cache of correspondence pertaining to Wilhelm's application. A few surprises emerge from these documents, chief of which is that he was rebuffed in his, as it turns out, premature bid for the title in 1922, at age 39, a move that Herr Friedrich Elsinger, in a letter addressed to the Presidium of the Chamber of Commerce and Industry, called "an example of a crass instance wherein people push themselves forward for this professional title, which in view of its high value should only be granted for special merit in the relevant profession or in the public domain."

Herr Elsinger, whose position and title are not noted, clearly had other issues with Wilhelm's application, which he implies is tainted by a whiff of *Protektion:*

> Herr Weinberger is certainly a decent man, but he is neither a linoleum, oilcloth, nor leather manufacturer, only a relatively new merchant in these articles; and only in recent times, after the war, has he acquired a sizeable fortune through the purchase of large

quantities of synthetic linen and jute yard goods, cheaply bought and then imprinted with various patterns, as well as through other lucky chances. His company has only been in existence a few years and he has not earned further merit in any other context. As far as I've been able to find out, he has himself requested the granting of this title and paid for the stamp on the application; and the recommendation of Herr Singer, which you have attached, would in any case be attributed to a personal acquaintance. There are no grounds at all for the Chamber to make a positive recommendation in this case, and it would draw notice if that were to follow. I therefore ask the Chamber to take a similar position in the matter.

Wilhelm's name was put forth again for the title three years later, but by whom is unclear. This time, the Chamber of Commerce solicited a recommendation from one Arnold Friedmann, "Well-born Chamber Counselor" (*Hochwohlgeboren Herr Kammerrat*). Wilhelm, it appears, had had a very busy three years building his resume.

To the Honorable Presidium of the Chamber of Commerce and Industry

In response to the esteemed request of 5 October 1925 that I provide a recommendation concerning the bestowal of the professional title of Kommerzialrat on Wilhelm Weinberger, I offer the following statement:

Herr Wilhelm Weinberger was born in Göding, Moravia[44]; he is 43 years old, married, has lived in Vienna for 25 years, and is competent and respectable.

After graduating from business school (Volks-Bürger- und Handelsschule), he devoted himself to commerce, especially in the carpet and linoleum line. He trained in different stores and established himself 20 years ago as a carpet and linoleum dealer.

Through extreme diligence and hard work, characteristics which gained him special trust and credit in the trade, he was, after a time, able to expand his business significantly.

The business consists at present of five locations in Vienna, one of which is located in a building on Wallensteinstrasse that he owns, as well as two locations in Pilzen.

In Vienna, he employs a staff of 50, in addition to 15 home workers, who work exclusively for his company. In Pilzen, he has 20 employees.

His wholesale purchases are only by the wagonload; his yearly gross receipts amount to circa 40 billion kronen. In 1923, he made a net profit of circa 1 billion kronen.

In his own automobile he inspects daily several branches, wonderful shops, which are equipped in an exemplary fashion and are truly worth seeing; the office is managed by a retired military officer.

He spends roughly a billion kronen a year in advertising, proof of the profitability of the business.

Herr Weinberger is also busy in the public arena. He founded the Rug Dealers Association, of which he is President, and to which the most important companies, such as the Orendi, Schein, Koppel & Wagner, and others belong.

He organized the oil cloth dealers and established the Oil Cloth Dealers Association in the Presidium of which he serves as Secretary.

In both of these organizations he works for the benefit of his colleagues in the trade, and he has repeatedly been sent as delegate to official business and tax meetings. He has always participated in these in a competent manner.

He also participates wholeheartedly in charitable events of all kinds and is always willing to help distressed colleagues with his own means.

As a firm pillar of the state and its order, Herr Weinberger is held in special esteem in the tax administrations of Bezirke IV (Wieden), V (Margareten), and X (Favoriten), where he has been active for 12 years as a member and an expert of the tax commission. Even though I work with Herr Weinberger in the tax commission and know him as an upstanding person who has a devoted love for our unfortunately impoverished fatherland, for which he is at all times ready to sacrifice everything, I have nevertheless asked the Privy Counselors Dr. Singer, Dr. Suppantschitsch, and Dr. Platzeriano of the above named tax administration for confidential information about Herr Weinberger.

It is difficult to portray with what delight the above named Counselors spoke about this man and how brilliantly their information sounded out.

Herr Weinberger is described as a person of especially excellent character who not only gladly gives the state what belongs to the state, but who would also like to educate all his fellow citizens by example; although in this matter he is always concerned about endangering the businesses of his colleagues through excessive tax burdens.

In particular, the conduct of his own business is designated in every sense as first class.

I also questioned an entire group of respected companies and everywhere the most favorable information about Herr Weinberger was given to me; in addition, praise in recognition of his public effectiveness was expressed.

Since the information as presented comes from mostly official but also from other trustworthy sources and offers a very favorable opinion, which fully justifies the request before you, I make this request:

The honorable presidium should present the proposal to the Minister for Business and Commerce to grant to Herr Wilhelm Weinberger the professional title of Kommerzialrat in view of his meritorious work for state and society and his improvement of commerce and industry.

Should this request be too far reaching, I would ask on the basis of the above statement to present to the Minister for Business and Commerce a report that the granting of the professional title of Kommerzialrat to Herr Wilhelm Weinberger is most warmly recommended on the part of this honorable Chamber of Commerce and Industry.

Vienna 10 October 1925

Arnold Friedmann

NO-THANK-YOU NOTE

In 1926, Wilhelm Weinberger was a newly minted *Kommerzialrat,* and thereafter affixed the title to his signature. Viennese etiquette required that his associates address him as such: Herr Kommerzialrat Weinberger. It surely has a certain heft.

One of his more established peers, however, seemed decidedly unimpressed by Wilhelm, and was clearly offended by his penchant for overstepping the bounds, offended enough to send a copy of the following letter to the Chamber of Commerce:

June 9 1926

Honored Kommerzialrat:

Yesterday I found in my apartment a package and a letter containing your calling card.

I am asking you to have the package, which I have not opened, picked up. I have only met you twice, in passing, and therefore stand in no relationship to you which permits me to accept a gift. It is obvious that the sending of this package is connected to your recent naming as Kommerzialrat.

I find it necessary, therefore, to call to your attention an entirely false picture of the position of a public official, and that I am obligated in a most emphatic manner to reject the acceptance of a gift relating to official business.

I repeat my request that you have the package picked up from my apartment immediately.

Respectfully,
Dr. Witz-Oberlin

BEFORE THE FALL

I have seen my grandfather-in-law Wilhelm Weinberger in the coffeehouses and at the theatre, and, once, at Steirereck, one of Vienna's most elegant restaurants. He sat two tables away and, after serious consultation with the cigar man, selected a specimen from the cart that is wheeled round after dinner. There was Wilhelm, soon wreathed in savory smoke, a short, portly man large in presence, his dark wavy hair combed back to expose his high brow and curving hairline, his features at fiftyish rather florid. The eyes are restive, however, and his expression is unsmiling but not unkind, a face intelligent and alert. No, not a handsome man, but his polish and self-assuredness render him attractive, a little *Kaiser* attired in custom-made suit and tie.

My image of Wilhelm in his halcyon years of the mid-1930s is pieced together out of the odd scraps I have been able to gather, the old photographs and family anecdotes, my own musings and wanderings about the city of his dreams. Certain places evoke his spirit, places like the Steirereck and the older, traditional coffeehouses (the Tirolerhof, for one) where middle-aged businessmen lose themselves in the daily *Handelsblatt,* nod discreetly at or shake hands with acquaintances who go on to separate tables. Wilhelm could be found every weekday afternoon at his coffeehouse, the Carlton, driven there by Miksche. He sat at a corner table, his *Stammtisch* or regular spot, where he read the papers and no doubt enjoyed the solicitations of the staff: *"Herr Kommerzialrat, how are you today? The usual, Herr Kommerzialrat?"*

Every afternoon at 6:00, he expected Ludwig to come by with the day's sales figures, a chore Ludwig dreaded: could they ever be high enough? The interview was usually short.

Wilhelm was a man who demanded orderliness and liked routine, not only in business but at home. Ludwig told me how he commanded Marie, the family housemaid, to fetch a ladder one day at the family's midday meal. *Go on, climb up and look at the table. Tell me what is missing!* A single soup spoon was absent from its assigned place.

Wilhelm had a Swiss bank account or two, began to collect paintings for his new home in Döbling, and with some trepidation asked his literature-loving son to fill the bookshelves. He enjoyed winter visits to Nice and to Luxor, escaping for a few weeks Vienna's dreary winters. It would surprise no one, certainly not his son, if he had a mistress, perhaps an attractive traveling companion with whom to share balmy evenings under a star-filled Egyptian sky. He did not live with his wife,

Alice, who was very much taller than he and growing increasingly deaf, but he saw to it that she had what she needed—at least in the material sense.

Herr Vater did not trust his children's judgment regarding personal attachments. Nora, especially, worried him as a potential victim of unscrupulous young rakes after her money; he kept her on a tight leash, but permitted her to join her cousin Heini and his friends at the five o'clock tea dances. Miksche drove her. Wilhelm even set up a date for Nora, but when Nora fell in love with the boy, that was that. And even the young man about town, Ludwig, found himself at odds with his father over Erika, his first serious girlfriend. It is difficult to imagine Wilhelm's objection; Erika was Jewish and her family well-to-do. Ludwig had to tell her he could not marry her and their courtship faltered. Wilhelm never met his son's future wife, Jula Mieses, who lived on the Mariahilferstrasse and whose father traded in furs.

Wilhelm actually arranged a marriage for his own father, Bernhard, after his mother, Rosa, passed away. He wanted someone to look after the old fellow and keep him company, to cook for him and keep house. He found a suitable woman, Hermine, about whom we know little, except that she was a widow born in Hungary and that she died in Auschwitz. Was the marriage an act of love by a caring son? Or just another machination to keep his world tidy? One thing is certain: Wilhelm's world would not remain tidy for very much longer.

Der Künstler
(The Artist)

By the mid-1930s the Weinberger firm encompassed seven branch stores throughout Vienna, two more in the Czech city of Pilzen, a warehouse or two, and at least one factory that manufactured linoleum. In all likelihood, this was not the full extent of Wilhelm's business interests, and so between running the firm, keeping up his various professional and civic activities, and holding the reins over the lives of his extended family, one has to wonder how he made room in his life for art.

Wilhelm was not just a budding collector, but a sculptor. He kept a small studio in the fourth *Bezirk,* where after donning a white smock, he modeled clay and chipped away at blocks of marble under the guidance, according to Ludwig, of an artist named Weiss.[45]

"I remember one of his first pieces was a bust of Dante— for a long time that was in the Raaberbahngasse," Ludwig recalls. He doesn't know what became of it or the other sculptures.

Two old photos of Wilhelm in his studio have survived, however, and provide glimpses into his work. In one, he is shown working on a study of a hand. The other depicts a trio of faces: Wilhelm and Ludwig, sculptor and model, a bust of Ludwig between them. Ludwig is seated, dressed in three-piece suit and striped tie, one hand shoved into his trouser pocket, the other semi-clenched. He is wretchedly bored, nearly pouting, yet astonishingly dapper and handsome. Standing, Wilhelm is only as tall as his seated son; he takes a casual stance, leaning an elbow on the platform with the bust, a sculpting tool in hand. Chin up, he looks straight into the camera.

I asked my friend, Jim DeCesare, a portrait painter, what he saw in this photo. The bust of Ludwig, he said, shows good technique, but is weirdly big, outsized, not human scaled. And while it conforms to the general outline of the model's head and features, some of the details aren't accurately rendered.

"The mouth is good, but did you notice the eyes? They're just not right," Jim said, squinting at the picture. The eyes bother him.

"You know what it is?" he finally asked. "They're not the model's eyes, they're the sculptor's."

Wilhelm the artist rendered Ludwig in his own image.

THE HOUSE IN DÖBLING

Many times over the years, G. J. and I have taken the trolley to Döbling and strolled the peaceful enclave known as the Cottage District. As the Viennese say, this is *eine gute Adresse,* a good address, and indeed the neighborhood is pervaded by an atmosphere of quiet privilege. No McMansions here, but rather ivy-covered, gated, discreet and solid villas. In the late nineteenth and early twentieth centuries the district attracted many of the city's wealthy and famous: Arthur Schnitzler lived on Sternwartestrasse, in a home he bought from the Burgtheater and film actress Hedwig Bleibtreu; another resident was operetta composer Emmerich Kálmán (*Gräfin Maritza*), whom Ludwig often saw out for a stroll in the neighborhood. Wilhelm Weinberger owned a house on Blaasstrasse, where in the mid-1930s he installed the headquarters of his flourishing business and took up residence with his son. Alice and Nora, however, remained across town in Favoriten, in the family's apartment on the Raaberbahngasse.

Blaasstrasse was Wilhelm's last address in Vienna, and his villa there represented the apogee of his rise from *Kaufmann,* small businessman, to *Kommerzialrat.* Although it took him nearly 30 years to reach the Cottage District, his tenure there was short. He and Ludwig moved first into a rented house on Felix-Mottlstrasse, then, as we know from the Notification of Residency (*Meldezettel*) obtained from the Vienna City and State Archives, he occupied the house on Blaasstrasse for only three years, from April 1935 until March 1938, until the day after the *Anschluss.*

Whether the house simply remained empty for the duration of the war we are unsure; we do know, however, that in 1939 a self-employed Vienna businessman named Ernst Koreska attempted to purchase it. Records obtained by Gretl Frisch shortly before her last illness in 2000 tell the following story. On July 20, 1939, Koreska filed a Request for Authorization to Purchase (*Ansuchen um Genehmigung der Erwerbung*) with the Office of Transfer of Assets (*Vermögensverkehrsstelle*). The document states he was prepared to offer 60,000 reichsmark for the house on Blaasstrasse to its owner, Wilhelm Weinberger. Koreska, aged 39, lived on Blechturmgasse in Vienna's fourth district, an expectant father who affirmed that both he and his wife were Aryan. He lists his employment and educational history on the back of the form; like Ludwig, he was a graduate of Vienna's Handelsakademie.

In a follow up letter two weeks later, Ernst Koreska wrote:

> Regarding my humble petition, with six supporting documents, from the 20th of the previous month, for permission to purchase the house at Blaasstrasse—in Vienna 19 from the Jewish owner Wilhelm Weinberger who has emigrated to Palestine. Unfortunately, I cannot furnish a sales contract since neither his sister, Frau Meier [sic], nor his legal representative, Herr Dr. Thurn-Zallinger, has power of attorney from Herr Weinberger to sell the house.
>
> Therefore, I most courteously ask, since this case concerns an abandoned Jewish property, whether it would be possible to appoint a trustee with whom a sales contract could be concluded.
>
> For your gracious reply, I thank you in advance and greet you with
>
> Heil Hitler!

Koreska waited nearly four months before receiving the following response, initialed, but not signed:

14. Nov. 1939

Appointment of a Trustee for Wilhelm Weinberger

> In response to your petition of 4. August
> 1939 in the above mentioned case, I inform
> you that the appointment of a trustee for
> Jewish property, insofar as it is not required
> by the public interest, is at this time out of
> the question.
>
> It is however anticipated that trustees for
> absent persons, who are empowered to dis-
> pose of property, will in the future be ap-
> pointed on request by a lower court that has
> relevant jurisdiction. Exactly when this will
> become possible I cannot tell you at this time.
> When it does, I will revisit your request.
>
> Heil Hitler!

The Manager of the Property Department

The remaining document in this exchange is dated August
24, 1942:

> Since according to the legal regulations
> there is no longer any prospect of the grant-
> ing of my request [to purchase the house on
> Blaasstrasse], I am herewith withdrawing
> the same, and request most courteously the
> return of five supporting documents (my
> property title, excerpt from the land regis-
> try, rent receipts, real estate tax receipt and
> declaration of Aryan descent) to my above
> mentioned request.
>
> Heil Hitler!
> Ernst Koreska

What particular regulation forestalled Koreska's acquisition
of the house is unknown to us. After the war, Rudolfine
Weinberger Fischer, one of Wilhelm's sisters and one of his
three named heirs, took possession of the house. Their young-

est sister, Frieda Weinberger Mayer, who is referred to in Koreska's 1939 letter, had perished along with her husband in Auschwitz. Rudi and Aladar Fischer, together with their daughter and son-in-law, Gretl and Erich Frisch, and grand-daughter, Eva, lived in the Blaasstrasse house until the mid-1950s. Around that time Ludwig signed over his share of the property to his mother, who had not been provided for in Wilhelm's handwritten last will. The house was then sold to an Austrian family and has remained in their possession ever since.

In September 2003, more than 45 years after any member of the Weinberger family had set foot in the house, I rang the buzzer at the gate. This was not quite as bold—or as brave—as it may sound. I was expected, invited by one of the occupants to see the house, or at least some rooms. I had merely jotted down the name from the gate and searched the Internet. It took only seconds to find the right e-mail address, but some-what longer to write my message. It took my correspondent still longer to respond:

> Dear Prof. Weinberger,
>
> You wrote me a few days ago. My husband tells me, that it ist right, the house was in your familys property. Now the owner is my father in law. . . . If you make a date, you are welcome to see my rooms here. Please call me, so we can arrange. my best wishes [. . .]

Accompanied by my friend Barbara, I set forth on the jour-ney from Leopoldstadt to Blaasstrasse, suddenly filled with misgivings. What did I hope to learn? I had explained in my e-mail that I was researching family history, adding my aca-demic credentials in the hope these would legitimize my re-quest to see the house. (But I also heard Ludwig's voice in the background: "Call yourself Professor Doctor, it impresses these people.") I suppose any decent sort of person would feel obligated to honor such a request, but who, really, would want to admit to her home a stranger dredging up the Nazi past?

A slim dark-haired woman in her mid-thirties extended her hand in welcome, addressing me as "Professor Weinberger," and ushering us into the house and past a workman in overalls. Drop cloths covered the narrow entry hall that was strewn with other evidence of renovation work—tools, a ladder. Our host apologized for the mess in passable English, and led us into a suite of rooms she uses professionally. Sky-high ceilings, burnished wood trim, Palladian-style windows flooding the rooms with September sunlight . . . it took no more than these to conjure an image of Wilhelm, impeccable and imperial, sitting behind a desk in what was once his private study. Five minutes into the visit and I was ready to go. I did not wish to see any more.

Barbara is certain that my welling eyes and silence did not go unnoticed by our host, who had her own story to tell of her husband's family's suffering during the Nazi times. They lost their business holdings in the Czech Republic and, if I understood correctly, had to make a painful decision to sell off a beloved family estate in the south of Austria in order to purchase this villa in Vienna. She pointed to a few pieces of antique furniture that looked as if they belonged to a manor house, or to a museum.

I did not expect to see more, only these few rooms on the first floor, although I asked if we could step into the back yard, as it is not at all visible from the street. Barbara and I were astonished at its generous size and artful landscaping, the particular hobby of one of the family's elders. The grounds, thank heavens, were nothing approaching manicured, but cool, shady, serene. Barbara is an avid gardener and I could see how captivated she was. "A haven," she called it and later told me this was where she could best imagine the Weinbergers relaxing on a warm fall afternoon. That is a nice image, but not one I share. It is just too difficult to imagine either ambitious Wilhelm or nervous Ludwig in a state of relaxation.

Ludwig. The longer we stayed and looked, the more intense my sympathy towards him. This was not the same as standing across the street with G. J., looking up at the three-storied villa, heaving a sigh or two, then moving on. I was inside now, occupying a space where Ludwig had trembled before his father, joked with the office staff, eaten lonely meals, cultivated his friendship with Pudi, who lived around the corner on Lannerstrasse, and lived his life as a well-to-do young man who had every expectation of living out the rest of his life here, as a son, a husband, a father, the eventual head of the family firm and superintendent of its fortune. In this very house. He may have had other dreams, but he never doubted his destiny.

I was ready to go when our host extended an invitation to visit the second floor where she resides with her husband and children. (The third floor, the former offices of the Weinberger firm, had long since been converted into yet another flat that is rented out.) Barbara and I are certain this was a spur of the moment decision on her part, but a gracious gesture nonetheless. We walked through a modern flat that bore no resemblance to the first floor—white walls, Scandinavian-type cabinetry, comfortably messy, so much like the homes of all our friends with young children.

We thanked our host and said our goodbyes, no doubt to mutual relief.

"That was rather sad," Barbara said later, "like visiting a gravesite."

5 The True Lover of Books

PENMANSHIP

The capital A was good. So was the capital and the small M. He was dissatisfied with the capital R—it must bulge in the second, not in the first bend. Even a capital R has its development.

Ernst Lothar, *The Door Opens* (1945)[46]

I have only one photo of my father-in-law as a boy, a 1926 postcard-style Christmas card of eleven-year-old Ludwig bundled up in a double breasted coat with big shiny buttons, his striped sailor suit collar neatly arrayed over his shoulders. But, are those white pinpoints dotting the sepia image meant to evoke snow? Hard to tell if this is a bit of photo fakery or just poor film development, although the Weitzmann studio on the Keplerplatz in Favoriten where it was taken called itself, more than a little pretentiously, a *Kunst,* or art, *Atelier.* Ludwig is wearing a hat, its fur visor pushed up and framing his long face, a smiling boy with winter pleasures on his mind. Yes, it must be "snow."

On the back, the card is addressed to his aunt, Rudolfine Fischer, and bears the family's Christmas and New Year's greetings to her:

Liebe Rudi! Allseits frohe Weihnachten u.
ein glückliches neues Jahr wünscht.

Familie W. Weinberger 12./XII. 26

(Dear Rudi! Merry Christmas and Happy
New Year wishes from the Weinberger family)

The year before, Tante Rudi received a New Year's card, dated
January 1, 1925, with Nora's picture: a chubby nine-year-old
in a striped frock she lifts slightly as if she were about to curtsy.
Underneath a heavy fringe of cropped hair, she wears a sweet,
sober expression, eyes steady on the camera. No hint of winter
in this shot, only the suggestion of spring in the short ruffled
sleeves and white anklets and pretty pose. A new year and a
new beginning for the family of Wilhelm Weinberger.

> Prosit Neujahr wünscht dir liebe Tante!
> Deine Nichte, Nora
> (Happy New Year to you, dear Aunt. Your
> niece, Nora)

One night at dinner, I showed the cards to Ludwig. He did
not, at first, even recognize the boy in the picture, but turning
over the cards he instantly responded to his mother's handwriting. The sight of it brought a few tears to his eyes. It reminded him, he said, of how she used to chide him about his
Schönschreiben or penmanship: "'Don't smear, do it right,' she
would say."

"She was very Austrian," he said. *"Bodenständig."* He explained the term as a sort of joke, ironically suggesting that
she was a real native, a daughter of Austria, instead of one
who had merely adopted the customs and manners of Vienna.
Alice Fürth Weinberger had been born in Susiçe, in the region
known as the Sudetenland, now part of the Czech Republic.
She came to Vienna as a child, the daughter of a lawyer, Ludwig Fürth, for whom my father-in-law is named, and his wife,
Regina.

All I know about Alice are the bits and pieces offered by
Ludwig from time to time. To talk about her "hurts a little,"
he tells me, adding one time, "We weren't nice to her, my sister and I." He has, perhaps, *Butter am Kopf.*

Alice Weinberger played chess in Vienna's coffeehouses, and taught Ludwig and Nora to play. She would not let them win, and they cried when they lost. She read the papers assiduously, sent money to poor Jews in Palestine, and took holidays in Tyrol or Switzerland, where she could take long walks. She was several inches taller than Wilhelm, and grew substantially deaf, both conditions, perhaps, rendering a social life with her prominent husband difficult, if not impossible, to conduct, to say nothing of a marital life. Eventually, they obtained a legal separation, the signatures on the document no doubt neatly signed in the parties' best hand.

Dummkopf

Ludwig once told me that Wilhelm wanted him to attend the prestigious Theresianum, but that he didn't qualify because his marks weren't high enough.

"Ich war ein Dummkopf," he said. "I was a dummy."

Ludwig was not, it appears, academically gifted, an admission he makes without particular embarrassment and even with a hint of amusement. He knows we know he was no *Dummkopf.* But his is an old story: the bookish boy, sometimes a little lost in his own thoughts and not paying enough attention to the teacher, parents with high expectations. And when G. J. and I went searching for his Vienna school records, we discovered Ludwig was not a horrible student, just an average one.

The records are incomplete, as are Ludwig's recollections of his school days. He has been able to offer us a few specifics about his high school and business school days, but only vague impressions of grammar school. He went first to a *Volksschule,* a primary school, a private one, he thinks, but he is uncertain of its location, although it seems likely to have been in Favoriten.

From 1926 to 1929, Ludwig attended what is now called a *Bundes-Realgymnasium* (he simply calls it the *Realschule*) on Waltergasse, in the fourth district, a block or so off the

Wiedner Hauptstrasse.[47] It is a pleasant, ordinary blue and
white building on a quiet, shady street. There, one September
morning, a school secretary greeted G. J. and me and handed over copies of records recovered from the old ledger-style
books stored in the basement. No questions asked, no iden-
tification required, no permission slip demanded: G. J. had
merely called up the school a few days before, given the secretary Ludwig's name and a range of dates, and that was that.
We had expected resistance, suspicion, annoyance, and a very
long wait.

"Ring back on Monday," she had told G. J. "I'll let you
know what we find."

We had, therefore, little reason to linger, although I wanted to wander around the school, peek into classrooms and
eavesdrop outside their doors. Just stepping into this school
with its neat bulletin boards and faint institutional smell pro-
voked an ache that caught me off guard. I missed teaching.

We sat in the schoolyard examining the records, basically
report cards, although they note other information as well:
Ludwig's mother tongue is German, his religion is *"Mosaic,"*
his father is a *Grosskaufmann,* which I gather means not just
an ordinary businessman, but a substantial one. Numbers
rather than letter grades denote academic achievement, 1 assigned to excellent work and 5 to failing. Like other period
records we've examined, much of the handwriting does not
rise up to Alice Weinberger's standards. We cannot make out
most of the few additional teachers' remarks.

But we do learn that as an eleven-year-old in 1926/27,
Ludwig took instruction in religion, German language, history and geography (his best subjects, all 2's) and mathematics,
science, business, drawing, penmanship, physical education,
and singing (all 3's).

Genügend—satisfactory—was his overall evaluation. Little
Viki's conduct, his *Betragen,* however, was exemplary: a 1 for
the year. And so it continued for the next two years: mostly
3's, a sprinkling of 2's, a lot of *"genügend"*s. The curriculum
remained largely consistent, although instruction in English

was introduced the following year, as well as physics and earth science. His conduct suffered a bit in the 1927/28 school year, dipping down to the merely good, although restored to excellent in 1928/29.

Ludwig's school history begins to blur when he transferred to the Albertgasse *Realschule* the following school year, 1929/30, where no records from those days have survived. Why he transferred is unclear, but he thinks he was asked to leave Waltergasse on account of his poor performance. Perhaps those 3's were in fact what the Ivy League used to call "gentlemen's C's," a lovely euphemism that spared the feelings of underachieving sons of "good" families.

Yet, when Ludwig talks about his high school days, it is about life at the Albertgasse school, located across town in the eighth *Bezirk* and where he spent only one year before entering the Handelsakademie, a commercial business school. He remembers rising early on the Raaberbahngasse to catch the *Bim* to the Margaretengürtel, then another to the Josefstädterstrasse, and walking the two blocks to the school, where classes commenced promptly at 8. It was the midday break, however, that he cherished.

"I took a lunch along," Ludwig says, "and also bought something to eat or drink in school. But every day I went to the Josefstädterstrasse to a very famous bookstore, Steckel, next to the theatre. I can see it now. It was a Jewish store, it doesn't exist anymore. They were one of the first publishers of Freud. I became, not a friend, but a . . . a. . . ."

"A *Stammkunde?*" I ask, a regular customer?

"Sure. I browsed around. They knew me. I bought the paper and the magazine, *Die literarische Welt.* I bought books and they sent the bills to the office."

Ludwig often lent the books—novels, works of history, politics, biography—to his father's employees, especially the office staff.

"Did Wilhelm approve?" I asked him once.

"No. But he did not forbid this. He thought I was probably too left [politically], and that maybe the staff was too and the books would encourage this thinking."

As a teenager, Ludwig's tastes ran to Thomas Mann and Stefan Zweig. Nothing much for a conservative capitalist father to worry about.

It must have been difficult for Ludwig to tear himself away from Steckel's shelves on those school days, but afternoon classes awaited. And then, the trolley ride back to Favoriten with its tantalizing glimpses of a city chock full of more books.

VIENNA AWAITS OUTSIDE THE SCHOOLYARD

Until our fourteenth or fifteenth year we still felt ourselves perfectly at home in school. We made fun of the teachers and we learned our lessons with cold curiosity. But then the hour struck when school began to bore and disturb us. A remarkable phenomenon had quietly taken place: we, who had entered the Gymnasium as ten-year-olds, had intellectually outgrown the school already, in the first four of our eight years. We felt instinctively that there was nothing more of importance to be learned from it, and that in many of the subjects which interested us we knew more than our poor teachers, who had not opened a book out of personal interest since their own student years. But there was another contrast which became more apparent from day to day: on the benches, where no more of us than our breeches was sitting, we heard nothing new or nothing that to us seemed worth knowing, and outside there was a city of a thousand attractions, a city with theaters, museums, bookstores, universities, music, a city in which each day brought new surprises. And so our pent-up desire for knowledge, our intellectual, artistic and sensuous inquisitiveness, which found no nourishment in school, passionately yearned for all that went on outside of school.

Stefan Zweig, *The World of Yesterday* (1943)[48]

PROFESSORS OF NATIONAL SOCIALISM

During Ludwig's brief attendance at the Albertgasse school, he took classes from two notable professors of German literature, Franz Spunda and Robert Hohlbaum.

"They both wrote a lot of books. I had these books, I read them," says Ludwig. "But they [the professors] were far right. Not the center, but the far right. And later on, '*Sieg Heil.*'"

The thought of Nazi-sympathizing teachers lecturing in the early 1930s to impressionable Viennese teenagers, Jewish or otherwise, and Ludwig among them, gives me a serious case of the creeps. No wonder his grades were bad.

I have yet to find any of Spunda's or Hohlbaum's books or any literary criticism of their work in English. At best, I find the briefest of biographical data and a notation or two about their respective subject matters. Spunda (1889–1963) wrote novels and nonfiction on occult and historical themes, with bits of the mythological, religious, and erotic thrown in; Hohlbaum (1886–1955) produced historical and religious novels of a nationalistic and Roman Catholic bent. He also wrote poetry, bad poetry, G. J. tells me after having read the few samples I found on the Internet.

"Writer and grammar school teacher" Spunda, states the *aeiou* online encyclopedia of all things Austrian, "turned National Socialist."[49] Hohlbaum's entry notes he "spoke against democracy and in favour of annexation of the German Reich," and that he wrote "'Führer-novels' heroising [sic] the Führer," and "worked for the then illegal NSDAP on cultural and educational policies."[50]

In the Internet universe Spunda's name pops up on occult, science fiction, and fantasy-themed sites, where, after a glimpse or two, I fear to tread. But a series of links once led me to the memoir of a Vienna-born, self-proclaimed psychic investigator named Hans Holzer, whom Spunda also taught, although a few years later than Ludwig. Holzer recalls him vividly, describing him as "a taciturn, dour man who seldom joked or said an unnecessary word and whose scholastic behavior was stern and uncompromising."[51] Holzer recounts his efforts to impress his teacher by writing a paper on parapsychology entitled "Dr. von Schrenck-Nötzing's Theory of the Telekinetic, Teleplastic Ideoplasticity." He was rewarded only with Spunda's disdain for his sloppy research.

Holzer paid the Herr Professor a visit after the war, and claims Spunda repented his earlier National Socialist zeal:

> We talked freely of the past and he admitted his errors of a political nature: Spunda had welcomed the Hitler movement at first with the unrealistic emotional optimism of a Wagnerian revivalist of Pan-Germanic days, only to find the bitter truth difficult to accept. Essentially a religious man, he realized in the later war years that the German cause had been betrayed by the Third Reich, but he had a difficult time cleansing himself of his association with it for many years after.[52]

If only Holzer had left it at that, instead of turning apologist: "And yet, he had never done anything overt, and never denied his mistakes." I click off-line.

Another day I checked the German site of the on-line bookseller Amazon to see which of Spunda's works are still in print. Up sprang 13 titles, among them *Baphomet: A Novel of Alchemy, The Mystical Life of Jakob Böhme, Magical Tales from France, Legends and Frescoes of Mount Athos,* and *Journey to the Ancient Gods.* His most controversial book is *The Magical Instructions of Philippi Theophrasti Bombasti von Hohenheim* (1923), an alleged translation of Hohenheim's own alchemy handbook.[53] Hohenheim is better known as Paracelsus, the

16th century Swiss-born enigma—part scientist, part philosopher, part wizard—whose hold on the popular and literary imagination seems eternal. (A colleague reminded me recently that Mary Shelley evoked his name in her novel *Frankenstein*.)

Spunda claimed to have drawn upon Paracelsus's own handwritten manuscripts, which he said he stumbled across in the Vienna Court Library, texts previously unknown to scholars. For that reason alone, some doubt was cast upon the authenticity of the book.[54] Only a few hundred copies were originally printed, but in 1980, *The Magic Instructions* went back into print.

Hohlbaum's work also continues to attract a German-reading audience. There were 15 titles available on Amazon Deutschland when last I checked, and three or four were up for bid on German eBay. A seller from the pretty Bavarian village of Dinkelsbühl placed a starting price of three *euros* (about $4.00) on Hohlbaum's *Himmlisches Orchester* (*Heavenly Orchestra*). I tracked it for a couple of days: there were no bids.

Like Spunda, Hohlbaum seems to have had a strong religious bent, reflected in such book titles as *Tedeum, The Road to Emaeus, Good Friday,* and *Jesus Legends.* But according to a German website devoted to literature during the National Socialist period, Hohlbaum "heroicized German history and propagated the 'Führer principle' with an unconditional loyalty."[55] The *Führerprinzip,* allegedly deeply ingrained in the Germanic cultures and oversimplified as a longing for a strong leader, was one aspect of the, shall we say, collective unconscious Hitler manipulated in his rise to power. Hohlbaum seized on the theme in such books as *The Man from Chaos: A Novel of Napoleon* and *Stein: The Novel of a Führer.*

Once, when G. J. and I were in the University of Vienna library, looking at old issues of the notoriously anti-Semitic newspaper, *Völkischer Beobachter,* to see if there were any notices of the aryanization of the Weinberger firm, we ran across an article by Robert Hohlbaum. The byline leapt off the page at us, as did the boldfaced title, printed in the old Gothic-style font called *Schrift* in German:

HOW I CAME TO GRILLPARZER . . .

The Pan-German Significance of the Austrian Dramatist.

"The famous Austrian writer Robert Hohlbaum writes here about his relationship to the Austrian author, Franz Grillparzer. We present these remarks in view of the world political events of recent days and as a sign of the solidarity of pan-German culture."[56]

We looked at the date: March 22, 1938. Austria had been annexed by Hitler only ten days before, but attempts at cultural integration were clearly in full swing. Grillparzer, Austria's greatest nineteenth-century writer, must have heaved mightily in his grave. Breaking up the text of Hohlbaum's article, positioned squarely in the middle of the page, the editors of the *Völkischer Beobachter* inserted a four-stanza, twenty-line poem by Heinrich Anacker, who borrowed for its title a popular Nazi slogan: "*Ein Volk—ein Reich—ein Führer!*" "One People—one Realm—one Leader!"

We found that day in the library no announcement about the Weinberger firm; its aryanization had not yet begun. I am still searching for a statement by Professor Hohlbaum, who survived a decade beyond the war's end, that he, perhaps like his colleague Franz Spunda, came to regret his embrace of Nazi ideology. I would like to think his and Spunda's last years were haunted by such regret and by silence, the silence of the defeated, of war-weary citizens, but most of all by the silence of empty classroom chairs facing their lecterns in the Albertgasse school.

The University Cloister

The works of a Palladio and Scamozzi, a Sangallo and Michaelangelo, stood before the spirit of the master dur-

> *ing its creation, especially in his design of the grand*
> *interior courtyard and the staircases. At the same time,*
> *however, like all Ferstel's works, the building is to be*
> *credited with a note of natural gracefulness, a breath of*
> *genuine Viennese character, something of that music of*
> *language which resounds from Grillparzer's verses.*
>
> Carl von Lützow (1884)[57]

I tiptoe not only past Freud, but Billroth, Hebra, Semmelweiss, Doppler, and a cleaning lady swabbing with some vigor the marble pavers of the central courtyard of the University of Vienna. It is quiet this Friday morning in February—and cold. A few dots of snow lazily float out of the grey sky, forming a slick film on the "Spring of Wisdom," the fountain that dominates the center of this secular cloister. A sort of pilgrim, I circle the arcade, protected from the snow but not the winter air, meeting more stone cold eyes of the legendary men of this professors' pantheon: Kraft-Ebbing, Boltzmann, Popper, Kaposi, Mach, van Swieten.

My walk inspires thoughts of the small university back in Connecticut where I teach, and its lovely, drafty, echo-y old Founder's Hall, a model of New England architectural restraint, as elegantly plain as any small-town Congregational church. Oil portraits of past presidents preside over guest lecturers and Faculty Senate meetings, thoughtful looking men in suits and ties devoted to the egalitarian principles of public higher education and to the teaching of the art of teaching.

Eventually, I encounter Marie von Ebner-Eschenbach, the sole female face among the 150 or more busts and sculptures of the University of Vienna's notable scholars that line its courtyard. She is a welcome sight but, I remember, she is here not as a former faculty member, but because in 1900 she was awarded an honorary doctorate, which read, in part:

> Marie von Ebner-Eschenbach is indisputably
> the first German woman writer today, not
> only in Austria, but also in Germany; and

> even among the women writers of the past
> her rank could be challenged by [Annette]
> Droste alone [. . .] In intellectual power, in
> comprehensive and deep knowledge of men
> and the world, few are comparable to her in
> contemporary literature, none superior.[58]

Doppler gave us radar (sort of); Boltzmann, atomic theories
and laws of thermodynamics; and Kraft-Ebbing, a catalogue
of sexual perversion, but Ebner-Eschenbach did something extraordinary, too, for an aristocratic nineteenth-century woman of the Austro-Hungarian empire. She became a writer. Not
only did she face discouragement from her family—women
did not engage in such pursuits—but persisted through her
failures as a dramatist before cultivating her talent in narrative
prose. Her story reminds me a little of Edith Wharton's (and,
come to think of it, of many another nineteenth- and early
twentieth-century American woman writer). As a New York
blue blood, Wharton was treated with disdain and suspicion
among her family and social circle over her literary ambitions.
Both women developed a clean, crisp prose style in the mode
of literary realism, their stories and novels depicting the hypocrisies and failings of a hierarchical, status-conscious society, especially as they affected women. And both cultivated
and enfolded themselves within a rich cultural milieu—a network of relationships with the like-minded—that sustained
them into old age. Eventually, too, came critical and popular
acclaim for the work they had begun in middle age.

I remember an old German reader that I found at my own
university library, a 1930 *Crofts German Series* that offered a
few Ebner-Eschenbach stories and homework exercises. The
introduction in English was hilarious, in a maddening kind
of way:

> To the drama Marie Ebner had devoted half
> a lifetime. After such a failure a less resolute
> nature would have given up all attempts at
> writing. But Marie Ebner was not to be de-

terred. Beginning her work in the novel and
story at an age when the creative effort of
many artists is on the decline, she now found
her true field and was able to turn the apparently wasted years of effort into a rich harvest of fulfillment and achievement.[59]

I'd like to know how old Professor Clifford E. Gates of Colgate
University was when he wrote that because I cannot quite tell
whether he was an arrogant young scholar (the worst sort) or
merely a doddering old idiot. Ebner-Eschenbach was all of 45
when she switched to prose, and Wharton was 42 when her
breakthrough novel, *The House of Mirth,* was published.

The fact that Ebner-Eschenbach is the only woman honored in the university cloister is not surprising. It took this institution (founded in 1365) 532 years before it even admitted
women as fully matriculating students. Now, the women out-
number the men by a fraction or so. The very first woman to
receive a faculty appointment as *Dozent,* or lecturer, was Elise
Richter. That was in 1907, ten years after the first females
were admitted. Professor Richter was head of the University's
Institute of Phonetics, widely published in her field of linguistics, and founder of the Association of Austrian Academic
Women. She hit the glass ceiling, however, failing to gain appointment as a full or "Ordinary" professor. Her story gets
worse, though. After the *Anschluss,* all Jews were purged from
the faculty, and Richter eventually ended up in the Theresienstadt concentration camp, where she was murdered. Surely the
University of Vienna owes her a place in the courtyard.[60]

The nineteenth-century Viennese architect, Heinrich Ferstel, created in the 1880s what was then called the "new" university on the Ringstrasse, drawing inspiration from one of
the great palaces of the Renaissance, the Palazzo Farnese in
Rome. As I stroll around its courtyard this morning, I think
I hear the music in its beautiful stones that Ferstel's admirer von Lützow described; and it is, so typically of Vienna, a
sound that is as melancholy as it is sweet.

MEDICINE MEN

The faculty of the University of Vienna Medical School were renowned in the late nineteenth and early twentieth centuries not only for the brilliance of their research and groundbreaking innovations in the science and practice of medicine, but also for their correspondingly great egos. The diagnostician Josef Skoda (1805–81), for example, best known for his development of auscultation and percussion, was called upon one day to treat a sick member of the royal family. He appeared at the palace in a suit. A valet quietly pointed out to him that court etiquette required he wear formal dress, that is, tails, in the presence of royalty. Offended, the doctor took his leave, replying, "I thought what was required was Skoda. But I'll send over my tuxedo right away."[61]

Ferdinand von Hebra (1816–1880), was another of Vienna's great physician professors, a specialist in dermatology. A story recounted in the memoirs of Adolph Lorenz, a student of Hebra's and himself a pioneer in orthopedics, tells of an elegantly dressed gentleman who appeared in Hebra's clinic, greeting the doctor as an old acquaintance.

"Unfortunately, I haven't had the pleasure," Hebra replied coolly. "But do get undressed."

The gentleman did so, leaving on only his undershirt and extending his rear end towards the Herr Professor. Interested, Hebra bent over and called out, "Oh, beg your pardon, Herr Baron. Now I recognize you."[62]

BUSINESS SCHOOL

The #62 *Bim* passes right by the handsome portico of the Handelsakademie, which is flanked by two impressive sandstone sculptures, one of Adam Smith and the other of that global venture capitalist from Genoa, Christopher Columbus. As G. J. and I hop off the trolley and get our bearings we realize we are just a few yards away from the Ringstrasse and a stone's throw from the Hotel Imperial, the Musikverein, the

Technical University, the Künstlerhaus, and the Karlsplatz. This is a busy corner of the city, an intersection of its cultural, academic, and commercial realms.

The Handelsakademie, or "Vienna Business School," as it also calls itself these days, is yet another example of Ringstrasse-era architecture, done up in neo-Renaissance style, but not so grand as the University of Vienna. Then again, it is a relative newcomer so far as city schools go, founded only in 1857. We step into its lobby and find ourselves suddenly engulfed by students. They look more high school than college-aged, sporting the universal uniform of jeans and sweatshirts, their *Handys* or CD-player earphones glued to their heads. We later learn that students as young as 14 may earn here their *Matura,* roughly equivalent to our high school diploma. Ludwig was only 15 when he enrolled.

The porter's booth is populated by chain smokers in blue overalls, one of whom points the way upstairs to Frau Schuster's office. All in all, this is not the atmosphere we expected from Ludwig's *alma mater.* He speaks of his years at the Handelsakademie with some pride. No, it was not the same, in terms of prestige, as attending the University of Vienna, but it was nonetheless a most respectable alternative, a solid training ground for Vienna's young entrepreneurs.

Frau Luise Schuster was dealing with another swarm of students in that no-nonsense, unsentimental way characteristic of venerable school secretaries everywhere. She knew of our mission to collect Ludwig's transcripts but hadn't made it down to the archive yet. We followed her back to the lobby, where we sat next to the porter's lodge wreathed in second-hand smoke, while she and one of her burly colleagues went searching. Eventually, they reappeared lugging a big, dusty leather-bound record book. We offered Frau Schuster the permission slip she had requested, signed by Ludwig before we left home, but she waved it away.

"Let's just see what we've got here," she said, obviously as curious as we.

Out of this book came two of Ludwig's transcripts, for 1932/33 and 1933/34, when he was aged 17 and 18. There should exist records for 1930/31 and 1931/32, but Frau Schuster was unable to produce them. No matter. We are struck by the impressive organization of each page, the school subjects marching across two pages: German Language, French Language and Correspondence, English Language and Correspondence, Business Geography, General and Commercial History, Mathematics, Business Mathematics, Bookkeeping, Merchandising and Mechanical Technology, Physics. And those were only the subjects Ludwig took out of the extensive curriculum. Others might have studied Natural History, Business Law, Stenography, Physical Education, Penmanship, Typewriting, and Analytical Chemistry. At one time the school had a particularly strong chemistry department, the result of close ties and shared lab space with the nearby Technical High School, later to become the Technical University.

Looking at Ludwig's transcript, I see the many 3s and 4s and recognize the *genügend*s (satisfactory) that sum up Ludwig's yearly performance. But what are all those zeros sprinkled across the pages?

"Well, they might indicate missed assignments," said Frau Schuster. "He seems to have had a lot of absences." She pointed to the *entschuldigt* or "excused" column (there is also an "unexcused" column). Ludwig accumulated 261 hours of absences during the 1932/33 school year. Yet, he performed "satisfactorily."

G. J. squinted at a teacher's comment, dated June 17: *ben. sich Lausb.!*

"I think this means '*benimmt sich Lausbübisch*'—he was acting up, being a bad boy. Here's another, same handwriting, looks like a week earlier. All I can make out is '*stört.*' He may have caused a disturbance in class."

Ludwig behaving like a *Lausbub,* a ruffian? He denies it, and I have difficulty imagining it. Perhaps all he did was talk back to the wrong teacher.

"I was really a lousy student," he says. "If it hadn't been for my father, they would have kicked me out."

LINOLEUM

Ludwig's favorite Handelsakademie story goes like this: he was doing dreadfully in some class or other, whether Mechanical Technology or Physics or his Practicum in Marketing he is no longer sure.

"The professor said to me, 'Okay, you will give a talk about linoleum.'"

This, of course, worked out beautifully. Ludwig had at his disposal the resources of the entire Weinberger firm, the first and biggest importers and retailers of linoleum in Austria. The firm manager, Direktor Wiesner, wrote up a report explaining all about its manufacture, which Ludwig studied and then delivered—to the complete approbation of his professor.

PROFESSOR KOMORZYNSKI

On Ludwig's 1933/34 Handelsakademie transcript there is a clearly written notation that as of March 1, 1934, he became a "*Privatist*," which we take to mean a privately tutored matriculant. Wilhelm and Alice Weinberger withdrew their son from school because of a serious lung ailment, and packed him off to Swiss sanatoria in Arosa and Davos for several months during 1934. It was a lonely time for the 19-year-old. He has often told me that no one came to visit him, except Herr Direktor Wiesner, who was on a skiing holiday nearby.

But his tutor sent him books. Of all the teachers throughout his school years, he remembers best and speaks most affectionately of Professor Egon Komorzynski, who not only taught classes in German Language and Literature at the Handelsakademie, but tutored Ludwig before and after his illness. Like so many Viennese professors, Komorzynski had a whole other life—in his case, as a theatre critic and musicologist. He wrote several books, including *Mozart: The Mission and Fate of an Artist* (1941), *Pamina: Mozart's Last Love* (1941), and *Genius Between Two Worlds: A Novel of Schubert* (1944). But like all great teachers, he offered lessons beyond the classroom. Ludwig tells me,

> He was very helpful. He gave me books and magazines to read. I learned a lot from him, just about life. The daily life in Vienna, it was not so rosy for most people. My parents didn't want me to know about these things. I really appreciated what he did because it made things a little easier for me later on, when things in Austria got bad. During the war, I sent him care packages, and I visited him the first time I went to London after the war. He was a refugee, too, and lived on the Edgeware Road. I brought him cigarettes— he was a chain smoker.

Komorzynski eventually went back to Vienna and lived there until he died in 1963.

"I guess we were both survivors," Ludwig says.

GIRLS AND BOOKS

Just the other day, Ludwig was sitting in Walgreen's on his "Cadillac," his bright blue cardiac walker, resting while G. J. stood in the checkout line. What remote association called to his mind his time in Arosa, some 70 years earlier?

"I had a girlfriend there. She was from Essen."

This is the first I've heard of any German girlfriend from Essen, but not all that long ago I learned for the first time about his girlfriend in Scotland, where his father had sent him to study linoleum manufacture.

"What was her name?" I asked.

"I don't remember, but she lived on Richard-Wagner-Strasse, this I remember. A nice girl, she was in the next room in the sanatorium. I gave her *The Magic Mountain*—Thomas Mann. Komorzynski sent me this."

He cannot remember her name, this companion in his loneliness, but he remembers the book he lent her.

Later, I asked if anyone had come to visit her. Or was she as alone as he had been?

"Just her brother. He was in the Hitler Youth."

Did he come in uniform?

"No, it was Switzerland. He was not allowed to wear this."

Did you write to her?

"No, we couldn't. I was Jewish."

Books, I suspect, have played a part in all of Ludwig's courtships. My mother-in-law, Jula, loved to tell how the day after their first date in 1937, Ludwig dispatched his father's chauffeur, Miksche, to her family's apartment on the Maria-hilferstrasse with a small stack of books and a calling card:

12 April [1937]

Dear Jula,

Here are a few books; I hope that this small selection will appeal to you.

Kindest regards,
Viki

She kept the card in its tiny envelope, managing, somehow, to preserve it on her journey from Vienna, across Europe, to Marseilles, to Uruguay, to New York, to Connecticut.

And what were the books, I ask Ludwig, probably for the fiftieth time?

"Something from Stefan Zweig, that I am sure. What else, I don't know. But for sure, Zweig."

Jula bought Viki a book, too. But that was the following year, in 1938. It was the German version of Dale Carnegie's *How to Win Friends and Influence People*. He read it on the voyage from Marseilles to Montevideo.

"There wasn't much else to do," he said.

Of all the books he might have taken on this, the epic journey of his life—of all the precious few items of his now dismantled life he was even able to take—he chose the one that Jula had chosen for him.

FOR THE FUTURE

Ludwig is ingenious at finding ways to store his hundreds of books in his tiny retirement home apartment: he has them stacked on the floor, wedged behind other volumes in the bookcases, positioned on every inch of available surface. He now spends most of his days enthroned on his power-lift chair, surveying like some ancient *Kaiser* his own private Book Land. This is both a comfort and a trial. He can no longer read as he would like. Not only are books heavy for him to hold or even to cradle in his lap, but cataracts obscure his vision and make reading a slow, exhausting task.

"It takes me all day just to read the paper," he complains.

When he moved from New York to Connecticut at age 87, one of his great concerns was whether or not he could take all his books with him. Of course he could, we told him (with some trepidation). Into dozens of boxes went German language literary classics, histories, reference books, biographies, travel books, Judaica, Austriaca, and his beloved *Exilliteratur,* works by such exiled writers as Elias Canetti, Franz Werfel, and Robert Musil.

There were a few English works, too, including one I am periodically tempted to throw out because it causes him, and us, so much grief—his *PDR Guide to Prescription Medicines.* If he reads about a potential side-effect stemming from any of the ever-changing cocktail of drugs keeping him alive, he is certain to develop it.

Along with Ludwig's books, we packed a small frame containing "an inspiration," as he quite rightly calls it. G. J. translated into English a quote from Umberto Eco that Ludwig had once come across, and printed both it and the German version in large bold type:

The true lover of books does not need to have read them all. The important thing is to know that this or that book exists and that it is available—for the future.

Figure 1. Wilhelm Weinberger, circa. 1935.

Figure 2. Undated photograph of Weinberger store at Währingerstrasse 61.

Figure 3. "For 25 years the company management has guaranteed quality and taste."

Figure 4. Ludwig Weinberger, age 11, 1926.

Figure 5. Nora Weinberger, age 9, 1925.

Figure 6. Wilhelm and Ludwig Weinberger in Wilhelm's atelier, circa 1935.

Figure 7. Ludwig Weinberger, early 1930s.

Figure 8. "Forget me not," wrote Jula Mieses on the back of this photo, 1937 or 1938.

Figure 9. Paris, July 1937: Ludwig and Jula, with friends Wilfred Lederer and Trudi Baerenfeld.

Figure 10. Jula outside the Café Casa Piccola, whose window bears the Nazi swastika.

Figure 11. Gretl Fischer Frisch, 1995.

6 Searching for Schnitzler

"WE ARE ALWAYS PLAYING"
("WIR SPIELEN IMMER")

It was play! What should it be otherwise?
What do we do on earth that isn't play,
May it seem ever so great and profound.
One man plays with wild mercenary bands,
Another with mad, superstitious fools.
Somebody else perhaps with suns or stars.
I play with human souls. Meaning is found
Only by him who searches for it.
Dreaming and waking, truth and lie mingle.
There's no certainty anywhere. We know
Nothing of others, nothing of ourselves;
We are always playing. Wise is the man who
knows it.

Arthur Schnitzler, *Paracelsus* (1899)[63]

AMBIVALENCE

My husband, G. J., the son of Vienna-born parents, the grandson of a successful and ambitious Vienna businessman, a scholar and translator of the quintessentially Viennese writer, Arthur Schnitzler, a student of the city and a speaker of its language, sums up all his feelings about Vienna in one word: ambivalent.

It is a word I encounter over and over in connection with Vienna, one that economically sums up a typically Viennese world view, an assumption of impending disaster in the midst of present pleasure. "Ambivalence," Paul Hofmann writes, "overshadows everything: like the double-headed Imperial Eagle, the true Viennese manages to gaze in opposite directions at the same time."[64]

Over the past 20 years, I have watched as G. J. periodically delights in Vienna's splendor. Whenever we return to the city, he takes particular pleasure in our first stroll through the *innere Stadt,* our first glimpse of the Stephansdom and its wavy reflection in the mirrored façade of the Haas Haus, our first turning-the-corner from Graben onto Kohlmarkt that startles us once again into awe at the looming Hofburg, its patinated dome touched with gold.

In Vienna, G. J. loiters before the Loos House, admiring its clean straight lines that so horrified the Emperor Franz Joseph, who couldn't very well avoid looking at it when he peeped out the Hofburg windows. G. J. admires, too, the curving Jugendstil motifs of architect Otto Wagner, and Olbrich's revolutionary Sezession building, inscribed with the motto: "To every age, its art; to art, its freedom." In Vienna, he seeks out the portraits of Klimt, and the paintings of Schiele and Kokoschka, the furniture of Josef Hofmann. He is a thoroughgoing modernist, but he shares, too, my fondness for small doses of bourgeois Biedermeier—the paintings of Waldmüller, the *Gemütlichkeit* of the wine taverns, the old sentimental ballads.

And G. J. loves Vienna's *gut bürgerliche Küche,* its homey, hearty, comfort foods: the crispy *Wiener Schnitzel;* the pot-roast-like *Tafelspitz* accented with horseradish; the *Zwiebelrostbraten,* onion-smothered beef steak; and *Kaiserschmarrn,* the "Emperor's omelette" served with sweet-tart plum compote. He finds the baked goods delectable, from the simplest crisp and yeasty *Kaisersemmel* to the showiest of Gerstner's layer cakes. He enjoys a good bottle of Zweigelt or Blauer Portugieser, the local red wines, and the strong coffee and old coffeehouses, especially the Tirolerhof, the Griensteidl, and the Sperl.

G. J. loves the stamp shops, especially Herr Taferner's in the Opernpassage, and a good walk in the Augarten early in the morning. He loves going to the theatre, especially if Schnitzler is playing, and to the Volksoper, especially if Strauss is playing. He loves most of all, he says, the Morawa bookstore on Wollzeile, for a browse through the latest editions of Austrian writers and the new works on Vienna history and culture.

This adds up to a lot of love, and yet G. J. won't admit to loving Vienna.

What doesn't he love? I ask occasionally. Some of the faces he sees, he tells me, especially those of elderly folks; the vague uneasiness that sometimes sneaks up on him; the hair-trigger temper he develops the moment he enters city limits. A certain look or a particular tone of voice from a waiter, a store clerk, a trolley passenger, a bank teller and to the surface rises an anger that startles and dismays me. The Viennese, G. J. admits, put him on edge, make him guarded, mistrustful. He is reluctant to engage with locals we don't already know, suspicious of unsolicited acts of kindness.

I can easily persuade G. J. to go to Vienna, but not to stay there for very long.

Schnitzler would have understood, despite his utter devotion to the city. Perhaps that is why G. J. is attracted to his work. In his study hangs a framed poster from an old Schnitzler exhibit held years ago at the Palais Pallavicini. It shows the author clad in tweed, a photo probably taken in Semmering or some other Alpine retreat in the 1920s. "*Sicherheit ist Nirgends,*" the poster reads, borrowing for the exhibition title a line from his 1899 play, *Paracelsus:* "Certainty is Nowhere." It is a condition the Weinbergers have long understood.

FOUND IN TRANSLATION

Arthur Schnitzler came into G. J.'s life only shortly after I did. Given Ludwig's worship of Austrian and German literature, not to mention his collection of books, this strikes me as remarkable. In grad school G. J. was drawn to British literature, especially sixteenth and seventeenth-century drama and poetry. He felt an affinity for the metaphysical poets, writing his doctoral dissertation on John Donne's "The Progress of the Soule" and the mock-encomium tradition. He loved Donne's wordplay, his rascally seduction poems, his embrace of science, the delicious conundrum of a poet who was both clergyman and skeptic.

In his late thirties G. J. started listening to Mozart, and through Mozart found his way to Vienna, the place from which his parents had fled, a place about which he knew everything and nothing. Vienna had always been in the backdrop of his life, spoken about in snatches, visited once with his parents in 1959, but only briefly, a place probably best avoided, an enigma he had no particular desire to examine. But having entered Vienna on a trail of music, he found his way to Schnitzler—and to Schnitzler's Vienna.

Schnitzler, who was born in 1862 and died in 1931, came of age in a city experiencing what historian Frederic Morton called "a nervous splendor," in a gold-tinged epoch that collapsed with the First World War. His plays and stories captured the creative fury and artistic tensions of *fin-de-siècle* Vienna, its end-of-empire fragmentation and heady nostalgia, its hypocrisies and decadence.

"Illusion and reality, uncertainty, ambiguity, loneliness, religious antagonism," G. J. once told me. "He was my guy, witty and melancholy at the same time."

A guy who spoke his language.

"His German is *my* German," G. J. says. "Familiar, comfortable."

For more than a decade, G. J. devoted his working life to Schnitzler and his Vienna, producing five volumes of translations, a critical study of the late plays, and scholarly articles with titles like "The Bacchusfest Motif in Arthur Schnitzler's Later Plays" and "Of Social Change and Woman's Autonomy: Schnitzler's *Spiel im Morgengrauen.*"

The days of Schnitzler's obscurity to an English-speaking audience are long past, and everyone, it seems, wants to take a crack at him—even people who don't speak German, like Tom Stoppard (*Undiscovered Country*), David Hare (*The Blue Room*), and Stanley Kubrick (*Eyes Wide Shut*).

They discovered, as did G. J., that translation is less a linguistic exercise than a collaboration of souls.

To the Coffeehouse!

In Schnitzler's day, as now, Vienna's coffeehouses—some 700 of them![65]—contributed greatly to the city's *Gemütlichkeit*, its intimate atmosphere. Through the institution of the coffeehouse, everybody who was anybody in Vienna had at least a nodding acquaintance with each other. True, individual establishments attracted a particular clientele—writers gravitated to the Griensteidl and Central, politicians to the Landtmann, musicians to the Imperial, artists to the Museum, and so on—yet the coffeehouse was neutral territory and open to all (except, in some cases, unescorted women) for the price of a cup of coffee. Here, men of even the most modest credentials might be addressed as *Herr Baron, Herr Direktor, Herr Doktor* by that most quirky and yet circumspect species of human being, the Viennese coffeehouse waiter.

Schnitzler's friend Peter Altenberg (1859–1919) may have been the ultimate Vienna coffeehouse habitué. He practically lived at the Café Central on the Herrengasse. If the Post Office is the ultimate authority on who lives where, well, there you have it: mail posted to Altenberg at the Central was duly delivered. He lives there still, in effigy at least, seated at a tiny table by the front door, his bald head, brushy mustache, and large expressive eyes greeting each patron who walks through the door seeking a few moments—or hours—of coffeehouse community.

Altenberg was a master of *Kleinkunst* or "little art." His gift was for short prose and verse, sketches, portraits, aphorisms—forms, Andrew Barker writes, "meant to portray a person in a sentence, a spiritual experience on a page, a landscape in a word."[66] If not precisely born in the coffeehouses, the genre, as well as the souls of its writers, was certainly nourished by them:

> You have worries of this kind or that—to the coffeehouse!
>
> She can't come to see you for some reason, be it ever so plausible—to the coffeehouse!
>
> You have holes in your boots—Coffeehouse!
>
> Your salary is 400 Kronen and you spend 500—coffeehouse!
>
> You are properly frugal and permit yourself nothing—coffeehouse!
>
> You're a civil servant but would like to have been a physician—coffeehouse!
>
> You can't find the woman who suits you—coffeehouse!
>
> You stand spiritually on the brink of suicide—coffeehouse!
>
> You detest and despise people and yet can't do without them—coffeehouse!
>
> Your credit has run out everywhere—coffeehouse![67]

LITERATURE ON TOUR

One autumn afternoon, G. J. and I joined the small crowd congregating outside the Café Griensteidl for a tour of Vienna's most famous literary coffeehouses. We were greeted by a tall, attractive woman strikingly dressed in a men's-style suit. Elisabeth-Joe Harriet asked us to wait while she continued her lively conversation with the others. We soon realized these other folks were not literary pilgrims awaiting an afternoon of amusing anecdotes and coffeehouse lore, but disgruntled local tour guides vigorously taking exception to Frau Harriet's lack of credentials. Whether she lacked a license required by the city or simply a membership in their professional association,

I am not sure; however, they were throwing down the gauntlet in a tour guide turf war.

She stood her ground—this was a mere skirmish—and dismissing the complaints, whisked G. J. and me into the Griensteidl to a reserved table, where she attributed the incident to nothing more than a tempest in a teapot.

"Typical Viennese theatrics," she said.

She should know, this Austro-American actress. While it was true we would walk with her around the *innere Stadt,* her program was called "Literature-Theatre-On-The Move." This was no mere walking tour, but a one-woman show, a program of dramatic readings of her own translations of Vienna's coffeehouse literature, performed against the backdrop of the historic cafes.

For the next two-and-a-half hours, we meandered from the Griensteidl to the Central, to the Korb, to the Hawelka, to the Bräunerhof, and back to the Griensteidl for our well-earned coffee and strudel, having done our best to digest a stunning array of *bon mots* from writers and artists, past and present, who formed the cream of Vienna's coffeehouse society. Frau Harriet heroically channeled Arthur Schnitzler and Karl Kraus, literary miniaturist Alfred Polgar and journalist and raconteur Anton Kuh, theatre critic Hermann Bahr and arch-Bohemian Peter Altenberg, painter and writer Oscar Kokoschka and historian Egon Friedell, and contemporary writers such as Thomas Bernhard, Elfriede Jellinek and H. C. Artmann. Along her coffeehouse trail she quoted their aphorisms, related their anecdotes, recited their poems, and even sang a few bars of Kraus's satiric version of the Austrian national anthem.

A few months later, G. J. conducted his own Vienna coffeehouse tour for a small group of students he and a colleague—not me this time—shepherded abroad during Spring Break. I have a snapshot of him standing outside the Griensteidl, one arm extended, no doubt in emphasis of some fascinating aspect of coffeehouse culture, while the students are gathered round in rapt attention. But he tells me that for a few minutes, he kept looking around, unsettled by the prospect that an angry mob of tour guides, perhaps spearheaded this time by our Frau Harriet, would demand to see his license.

CAFÉ MEGALOMANIA

I hear many Viennese say that the Griensteidl is just for tourists now. It is not, after all, the original establishment, the legendary gathering place for the *Jung Wien* or "Young Vienna" writers who formed the vanguard of literary modernism in the late nineteenth and early twentieth centuries. In its heyday of the 1890s, Arthur Schnitzler, Hermann Bahr, Hugo von Hofmannsthal, Karl Kraus, Felix Salten and others congregated at the Griensteidl to write, read, escape their day jobs, their homes, their wives. Most of all, they came together to talk, argue, discuss, feud, and philosophize about literature, language, art, politics, themselves, and Vienna. They drank coffee, too, "that sumptuous coffeehouse coffee," as Mark Twain called it, "compared with which all other European coffee and all American hotel coffee is mere fluid poverty."[68]

So powerful were the personalities, so brilliant the conversations, that Karl Kraus took to calling the Griensteidl "Café Megalomania." When the coffeehouse closed its doors and submitted to the wrecking ball in 1897, Kraus marked the occasion with one of his most famous essays, *Die demolirte Literatur*—"The Demolished Literature." Kraus became disenchanted with the *Jung Wien* crowd over their individual and collective personal, literary, and linguistic foibles. While his essay takes aim at the city's coffeehouse culture generally, it ridicules the literary aesthetic of *Jung Wien* in particular, at the same time eulogizing the passing of a Vienna institution:

> Our literature is bracing itself for a period of homelessness; the threads of artistic creativity are being cruelly severed. Men of letters might henceforth abandon themselves to pleasant sociability at home. But profession-

al life, work with its manifold nervous crises
and upsets, took place in that coffeehouse,
which like no other appeared suited to repre-
sent the true center of literary activity.[69]

He then "demolishes" that very literary activity. Kraus does not
name names, but he doesn't have to; so well-known in Vienna
was the Griensteidl cast of characters that he avoided libel
through allusion. "The gentleman from Linz" is Hermann
Bahr, the shaggy bearded *Vater*-figure of the lot, without
whom, Kraus noted, "many a young nontalent would have
run aground and been forgotten."[70] Richard Beer-Hofmann's
penchant for smart attire comes under scrutiny, along with his
prose: "Here is a writer who has so much success to show in
the area of fashion that he can confidently enter a competition
with the prettiest of his readers. For years he has been working
on the third line of a novel, since he ponders every word in
several changes of dress."[71] And Felix Salten, author of the beloved tale *Bambi,* was treated by Kraus, famous for his loving
obsession with the German language, to a blistering analysis of his grammatical shortcomings. His remark that Salten
"still succeeds in confusing the dative and the accusative cases
with undiminished youthful enthusiasm" is among the more
translatable, not to mention kinder.[72] (Salten eventually paid
him back—with a slap.)

When their beloved coffeehouse folded, the Griensteidl
writers headed a few blocks down the Herrengasse to take up
residence at the Central, shifting the locus of literary Vienna
to a grander arena of a vague Oriental decor within the Palais
Ferstel. With them went their nemesis Karl Kraus. Eventually,
he defected to the Café Imperial, which he claimed was less
noisy. For the time being, though, he continued his watch on
"Young Vienna," but always at a remove of several tables.

Banned in Vienna (and Berlin)

*There may be no illegitimate children on stage, fathers
and sons cannot have a falling out, kings must always
be excellent, bad presidents and ministers demoted,
and however the list of utter nonsense goes on, the good
Vienna audience accepts it.*

Karl Gutzkow, "Reiseeindrücke aus Deutschland,
der Schweiz, Holland und Italien" (1876)[73]

In *Die demolirte Literatur*, Karl Kraus spared Arthur Schnitzler
much of the meanness that characterized his commentary on
the others. He objected, however, to Schnitzler's shallow characters:

> He who plunges deepest into such shallow-
> ness and is the most absorbed in this vacuity,
> the writer who made "the sweet young girl"
> suitable for the Burgtheater, knew how to
> preserve a quiet unpretentiousness of mega-
> lomania amid deafening surroundings. Too
> good-natured to approach a problem head
> on, he concocted a little world of gay blades
> and pleasure-loving working girls to ascend
> once in a while from these depths to false
> tragedy.[74]

The implied sexual play of those "gay blades" and "sweet
young girls" more than irritated the censors of "Kakania," the
playfully scatological term for the Habsburg realm coined by
Robert Musil (drawn from the royal prefix *K und K, Kaiserlich
und Königlich*). Schnitzler's most famous play, *Reigen*, was
banned from production in Vienna until after the collapse of
the monarchy and caused scandal when it was finally staged.
Best known to English speaking audiences by its French title,
La Ronde, the play has ten scenes, a kind of "round dance"
in which each player moves from one dalliance to the next

until the circle is complete: whore and soldier, soldier and house maid, house maid and young gentleman, young gentleman and young wife, young wife and husband, husband and sweet young thing (*das süsse Mädel*), sweet young thing and poet, poet and actress, actress and count, count and whore. When the play, written in 1896–97, premiered in Vienna on February 1, 1921, it caused an uproar. There ensued riots and denunciations (especially from the anti-Semitic press which had long reviled the Jewish Schnitzler), until the production was shut down. Viewed as pornographic in its time, the play today, critic Egon Schwarz notes, is understood "not at all as a celebration of free sex but as a denunciation of lovelessness in a corrupt society."[75]

This was not the first time Schnitzler had run afoul of both the censors and the public. The first scandal of his career resulted from his 1900 short story, *Leutnant Gustl.* For its unflattering portrayal of the military, the Royal and Imperial Army stripped Schnitzler of his reserve commission, citing his violation of "professional honor."[76] His play *Professor Bernhardi,* a weighty medical-ethics drama, although Schnitzler called it a comedy, was banned by the Habsburg censors in 1912, ostensibly for its portrayal of a Jewish doctor who out of compassion for his dying patient prevents a priest from administering to her the last rites. The play finally premiered at Vienna's Volkstheater only a few weeks after the end of the First World War, and although Schnitzler worried about a possible demonstration, none materialized. Indeed, between acts, Schnitzler took several bows, much to his satisfaction. "It is," he wrote, "the greatest success I've ever had."[77]

The "Burg"

Mark Twain admired no Vienna institution more than the Burgtheater, which he called, in an article in the *Neue Freie Presse,* "the most beautiful theater in the world."[78] He attended performances often during his two-year stay in the city, and particularly admired the now obscure drama *Master of*

Palmyra by von Wilbrandt, using its example to castigate the New York theater world for its meager pleasures. He recommended establishing

> a Burg in New York, with Burg scenery, and a
> great company like the Burg company. Then,
> with a tragedy tonic once or twice a month,
> we shall enjoy the comedies all the better.[79]

An enterprising producer brought the play to New York, where it soon closed. While the Viennese audience sat through the play "rapt and silent—fascinated," as Twain reported, New Yorkers apparently had little appetite for the story of a man who bargains for immortality, then begs for death.

Despite his disastrous experience working with Bret Harte on their play *Ah, Sin,* Twain decided to have another go at writing plays, this time in collaboration with a Viennese writer, Siegmund Schlesinger. This, too, came to naught, and Twain suffered the disappointment of taking no author's bow at his beloved Burg.

The royal court theater, established by Joseph II in 1776, had moved out of its old Michaelerplatz location—an appendage of the Hofburg—to its new home on the Ringstrasse only nine years before Twain arrived in Vienna. In keeping with Ringstrasse Historicism, the new Burg was designed in Renaissance style by the architects Gottfried Semper and Carl von Hasenauer, who also built the twin Fine Arts and Natural History museums. Aesthetically, the building was, and remains, a true temple of art with its frescoes by Makart and Klimt and statuary of Goethe, Schiller, Shakespeare, and Grillparzer. It should have represented state-of-the-art theater technology, and largely did, according to Twain, who was impressed by all the backstage machinery. But in one crucial aspect the house fell short—the acoustics were terrible, as noted by the actor Hugo Thimig:

> It is devastating to act on the new stage.
> There's an echoing and thundering before

> an indifferent audience. All my colleagues
> are deeply saddened. This house is a splen-
> did crypt. And to think with a tenth of the
> expenditure a practical, beautiful and sacred
> home for our art could have been created!
> One could go mad. Nothing but splendor,
> luxury, wastefulness and distracting frippery
> [. . .][80]

Schnitzler's *Liebelei* premiered here in 1895 and its *süsse Mädel*
about whom Kraus writes so derisively took her place on the
stage alongside Juliet, Joan of Arc, and Medea. The sweet girl
of modest means, who lived in the outlying neighborhoods of
the city and was vulnerable to the attentions of the well-to-do
young man (who wants merely a dalliance), caused a bit of a
sensation. It wasn't exactly Schiller, and it wouldn't be the last
time Vienna would face itself upon the boards of its beloved
Burg and shudder at its reflected image.

HEARTTHROB

There is a junk shop on the Himmelpfortgasse in the *innere Stadt* in which G. J. and I like occasionally to browse,
just down the street from the great baroque "winter" home
of Prince Eugene of Savoy, whose "summer" place was the
Belvedere, now one of Vienna's great art museums. Dark and
cave-like, the shop is crammed floor to ceiling with "Old
Austrian Curiosities." Its proprietors are two ladies of late
middle age, one of whom always seems to be knitting, the
other smoking.

Among its hodgepodge of rusty shop signs and bronze
doorknockers and heaps of buttons and remnants of uniforms and frocks is a large cache of theatrical memorabilia.
Movie and theater posters hang crookedly on the walls or
are propped up on shelves along with playbills, dusty record
albums, knick-knacks. And postcards—thousands of postcards—fill dozens of boxes. That is why we come here, to

thumb through the picture postcards of the legendary actors of the Vienna stage and screen. Some are of recent vintage: Klaus Maria Brandauer, Austria's most famous living dramatic actor, Oskar Werner, Romy Schneider, all of whom crossed over into Hollywood fame. Other stars of the German speaking world are here as well: Maximilian Schell, Curd Jürgens, Gert Frober. I have found pictures of Peter Lorre, whose real name was Löwenstein and who came from what is now Slovakia, and of Fred Astaire, whose name was Austerlitz, and whose family came from Hungary. One day I will buy a card of Hedy Lamarr; she was a favorite actress of my late father's, an odd choice for a Connecticut farm boy, but perhaps it was her exoticism, her lovely accent that attracted him.

Mostly, G. J. and I root around in the boxes searching for those familiar names and faces of the stage actors who made Vienna in the nineteenth century and into the twentieth one of the greatest of theater cities. And we find them: Alexander Girardi, Josephine Gallmeyer, Adolph Sonnenthal, Marie Geistinger, Fanny Elsser, Josef Kainz.

On our last visit to the shop, we purchased a postcard of Kainz, who played the huge dramatic roles, among them Hamlet, Romeo, and Mephisto. But asked once why he never played Faust, why he considered this role so difficult, he replied, "Faust can only be played by a truly significant human being and a truly significant human being does not become an actor."[81] Humble, as well as incredibly handsome. A 1903 photograph of him as Hamlet, holding the skull of poor Yorick, evokes the brooding sensitivity of Olivier. He must have made his audiences swoon not only on account of his looks, but his voice, which Stefan Zweig described in *The World of Yesterday:*

> Every word, even in private conversation, had its purest outline, every consonant its sharp-cut precision, every vowel vibrated fully and clear. Even now, I cannot read such poems as I had once heard him recite, with-

> out his voice speaking at the same time, with
> its measured power, its perfect rhythm, its
> heroic vibration; never since has it been such
> a joy to hear the German language.[82]

Our postcard of Kainz portrays him in a rakish ruffled shirt
and beret for his role in Schnitzler's *Der grüne Kakadu,* a
production of which we had just seen the week before at the
Josefstädtertheater. "The Green Cockatoo" premiered in 1899
at the Burgtheater, and presumably this picture of Kainz is a
souvenir of that production. Although the play became one
of Schnitzler's most enduring, it was shut down by the censors after only a few performances because of its revolutionary theme and unflattering portrayal of the aristocracy. Set
in a Paris tavern, "The Green Cockatoo," on July 14, 1789,
the day the Bastille was stormed and the French Revolution
launched, the one-acter revolves around the tavern owner/the-
ater producer who attracts a high class clientele by allowing
them to hobnob with actors portraying thieves and murder-
ers. Quickly the lines of the fiction blur until there is no clar-
ity as to what is real and what is illusion.

Our postcard had been mailed on October 1, 1917, and
still bears its green five-heller stamp bearing Franz Joseph's
image. (Interesting that seven years after Kainz's death, such
a picture postcard was still in circulation.) It is addressed to
the *Hochwohlgeborene* or "Well-born" Fräulein Lotte Steiner,
Teacher, Kaiser-Franz-Josefs-School, Baden bei Wien. "*Heartfelt wishes and kisses*" reads the greeting, although I am taking
a liberty with the translation; the writer, whose name is illeg-
ible, actually sends a *Handkuss*—a hand kiss—along with his
good wishes. I wonder, though, which made Fräulein Lotte's
heart beat the faster, the kiss sent through the post from her
admirer, or the dreamy eyes of Josef Kainz.

A Rake's Progress

Arthur Schnitzler was a ladies' man who kept a "kiss and tell"
diary. These *early* diaries, G. J. wishes me to stress, recorded

his intimacies with his women friends; that is, the number of intimacies. A random sampling of his diary of August, 1890, for example, indicates the 28-year old Schnitzler was seeing quite a lot of the 23-year-old actress Mizi Glümer:

> August 5. Mizi, afternoon, my place (5).
> August 17. Evening, Mizi, my place (3)
> August 31. Mizi, morning, my place (4). Afternoon, my place (3).[83]

How economically he noted the when, who, where, and the how many. G. J. thinks Schnitzler has suffered too long from the impression that he *was* Anatol, the most notorious of his playboy characters (*Anatol,* 1893) who has become synonymous with *fin-de-siècle* decadence and *carpe diem* attitude. Schnitzler, he argues, respected women as well as desired them (often), and his plays and fictions expose Vienna's hypocritical social mores and their sometimes devastating consequences. A rake turned feminist? Probably not, although that would be progress.

TINGELTANGEL

Once when G. J. and I were driving about close to home we passed a small carnival, the kind that seems to crop up in church parking lots and empty suburban fields with some regularity over the summer months.

"*Ein Tingeltangel,*" noted G. J.

A wonderfully euphonious word, *Tingeltangel,* a word I must remember to share with my friend Barbara, one that needs no precise definition, I think, although for the record my *Oxford Duden* says that it means "cheap nightclub/dance hall; honky-tonk." Perhaps it isn't quite the correct translation of a traveling carnival, but the *sense* of it is right: noisy, lively, public entertainment.

The Wurstelprater is Vienna's permanent *Tingeltangel,* an amusement park which at night becomes a raucous playground of thrill rides and unwinnable games, of *Heurigen* and beer gardens pungent with the smells of grilling chickens and sausages and red cabbage. The place is all hubbub, populated by overstimulated children and their tired parents, packs of young immigrant men, girls in tight jeans, and overweight couples tucking into huge portions of *Schnitzel* or *Knödel.*

And in the backdrop of this scene is a giant Ferris wheel, the *Riesenrad,* slowly, slowly revolving from day into night.

The Wurstelprater is carved out of a corner of the green Prater, the huge public park of some 3,000 acres, once Habsburg hunting grounds. Joseph II, Maria Theresa's reform-minded son, opened it to the citizens of Vienna in 1766 and it became as integral to city life as Central Park would become to Manhattan. Its main promenade, the *Hauptallee,* lined with chestnut trees, is a favorite place for Sunday strolls, away from the crowded inner city or the noisy neighborhoods, away from the *Tingeltangel* of the Wurstelprater.

When I first visited the Wurstelprater I assumed, to G. J.'s profound amusement, that it had derived its name from the word for sausage, *Wurst.* The *Wurstelstand*—call it a hot dog stand—is a Vienna institution in its own right. But the relevant word is *Wurstel,* meaning "muddle." And making a muddle of every situation is Hanswurst, a puppet character beloved by generations of Viennese. The Wurstelprater was so-called because of its many puppet theaters, the earliest of which dated back to the 1830s.

The "Hanswurst" tradition, however, originated in the eighteenth century and has its roots in both English puppet plays and *commedia dell'arte.* Hanswurst, also known as Kasperl, is really the more familiar Punch (of Punch and Judy fame), both the hapless instigator and victim of all manner of puppet mayhem. So beloved was Kasperl that even Joseph II, founder of the Burgtheater, acted the part in a court entertainment. One anecdote has it that he asked a courtier how he liked his performance, putting the fellow on the spot, for Kasperl is not the most admirable of characters. After an awkward pause, he tells the Emperor, "Your Majesty was Kasperl incarnate, the true Kasperl!"[84] He got it right. All actors, even if they are emperors by day, crave praise.

One can still see a puppet show at the Wurstelprater, these days more commonly called the Volksprater, but in Schnitzler's time, their popularity was at its peak. One of his Jung Wien circle, Felix Salten, wrote a book called *Wurstelprater,* in which he describes a typical Hanswurst/Kasperl show:

> "Kling, kling, kling." The Kasperl appears, ring-
> ing a bell. The children laugh at this start to the
> performance, and the piece to be performed is
> as old as the folksong. The Kasperl rings, runs
> swiftly around the stage, shakes his head, bows,
> claps his hands. At the same time his wife comes
> in; Kasperl embraces her, they kiss, and press
> each other breast to breast so hard that they totter
> back and forth. Kasperl has found something. He
> drags up a small anvil and a hammer and starts
> banging away. His wife likes this; she also gets
> a hammer and starts banging. Now they both
> bang as if possessed, but Frau Kasperl is clumsy
> and Herr Kasperl too. Bang! He hits her on the
> head and now she's lying there, stone cold dead.
> Kasperl shakes her, listens at her breast and cries.
> She is quite dead. Quickly he leaves and returns
> with a serious man wearing a pointy hat. This is
> the coroner. He sniffs around the corpse, then
> turns angrily to Kasperl and demands an expla-
> nation. Kasperl denies responsibility. He wants
> to show how the misfortune happened, grabs the
> hammer and kills the coroner. Now Kasperl has
> become a criminal. He fetches a crate and throws
> both corpses in it. Now the Jew appears. Kasperl
> wants to sell him the crate, but the Jew is bar-
> gaining, at which Kasperl becomes angry. And
> because he is now a madman, he kills the Jew
> too. His tragic fate is sealed. Kasperl has three

murders on his conscience and now the devil enters with his long red tongue and black horns.
Kasperl begs, pleads, defends himself, but already Lucifer has him by the collar, upon which
an angel appears and saves him. Kasperl leaps up
and dances. Suddenly, Frau Kasperl appears and
dances, and their joy is great. . . . Down below
there is a nice audience, an incomparable, good,
attentive and charmed public. How it listens,
how it gets scared, how it is joyful, how it cheers.
In no other theater do you find such an atten-
tiveness, rapt listening, on all faces. Such admiration, such amazement in all the eyes, such tire-
less pleasure [. . .] Who would not want such an
audience? The greatest actors and greatest writers would scramble for it. Only Kasperl has this
audience, no one else. Of course, he makes sure
that all plays in which he performs have a good
ending; that has to be. He couldn't possibly allow
a terrible murder or a spectacle to end badly. No.
That he really can't do to the audience.[85]

But Arthur Schnitzler could. He drew upon the Hanswurst
tradition to create his own puppet plays, many of which G.
J. has translated into English, including *The Transformation
of Pierrot, The Veil of Pierrette* and *Marionettes,* a collection
of three short one-acts. They proved a worthy vehicle to pose
some of the "big" questions: what is reality, what is illusion?
Who pulls the strings of fate? One of the *Marionettes* trilogy is
The Great Puppet Show (called *Zum grossen Wurstel* in German
and written between 1901 and 1904), a rollicking, unsettling
play-within-a-play (within-a-play?) set in the Wurstelprater.
Not one, but two marionette theaters occupy the stage upon
which an audience awaits and then watches and comments
upon the action. All manner of character types appear, ref-
erencing, G. J. says, Schnitzler's more conventional theater
pieces: the sweet young girl, the writer, the aristocrat. The

well-born and the lowly interact, sometimes in the "performance," sometimes as "audience." Eventually, the "audience" is revealed as being, too, merely a collection of puppets, whose strings are cut by The Unknown Man. But who is *he?*

> You ask too many questions. I don't know
> What I signify. Many an earthly day
> Have I been doomed to wander here below,
> A puzzle to me and all I meet on my way.
> This sword, however, is sure to impart
> Who's had a puppet's, who merely a human heart.
> This blade severs invisible strings as well,
> As many grieving puppeteers can tell!
>
> *He swings his sword over the entire stage; all
> the lights go out and every character except him
> collapses*
>
> You too? . . . *Seeing the author collapse*
>   And you? I shudder at my might!
> Is it truth I bring you, or darkest night?
> Is it heaven's . . . or hell's bidding I fulfill?
> Did Law create me–Or Arbitrary Will?
> Am I a god . . . a fool . . . or the same as you?
> Am I really I—or just a symbol too?[86]

A tangle, yes, but a *Tingeltangel?* Well, that too.

DOPPELGÄNGER

Berggasse 19, in Vienna's ninth *Bezirk,* is one of the world's most famous addresses. This ordinary-looking apartment building on an ordinary-looking city street is as much a Vienna shrine as the State Opera House, the Musikverein, Demel's pastry shop and the Sacher Hotel. For 47 years, Sigmund Freud lived here as a husband to Martha, father to Mathilde, Martin, Oliver, Ernst, Sophie, and Anna. He worked here as a physician and psychoanalyst, as founder of the Wednesday Night Club, as collector of antiquities, as researcher and writer who exposed our unconscious selves, our dreams, our desires. From these rooms that anchored him for nearly half a century an 82-year-old Freud was forced into a reluctant exile when the Nazis arrived in Vienna in 1938.

I try to remember all of this when I visit Berggasse 19 because the home the Freuds created is now merely a museum, an interesting one, to be sure, but a little soulless with its lecture room, optional film presentation, library and gift shop. The couch where Anna O and Dora might have lain isn't the original, which remains in England, where Freud fled. Only a few pieces of the family's furniture are here, replaced by a stupefying collection of memorabilia—books, clippings, articles—that line the walls or fill glass cases. I find greatest pleasure in looking at Freud's ancient statues. Now here are some interesting faces: Osiris, Horus, Buddha, Imhotep, Amun-Re. A passionate collector, Freud once wrote to Stefan Zweig that he had "read more archeology than psychology."[87]

In a relatively small city with a lively intellectual community, it is not surprising that Arthur Schnitzler and Sigmund Freud knew each other. What is surprising is that they cultivated no great friendship. They had much in common, both as physicians and assimilated Jews. But perhaps as Freud suggests, they were too much alike, working the same territory of the human soul, analysts in their different ways of the unconscious mind. In a letter to Schnitzler on his sixtieth birthday, Freud wrote:

> I think I have avoided you from a kind of shyness in the face of my own double. Not that I am easily inclined to identify myself with another or that I mean to overlook the difference in talent that separates me from you but time and again when I get deeply absorbed in your beautiful creations I seem to find beneath their poetic surface the very presuppositions, interests and conclusions which I know to be my own.[88]

Schnitzler simply noted in his diary that he had received a "nice" birthday letter from Freud, followed a month later by an invitation to Berggasse.

> Afternoon at Prof. Freud's. (His congratulations for my birthday, my reply, his invitation.) Wife and daughter Anna (who was Lili's teacher for a few months last year).—had only spoken fleetingly to him a few times until now.–He was very cordial. Conversation about hospital and military times, chiefs we had in common, etc.—Lieutenant Gustl etc.–Then he showed me his library—his own books, translations, works by his students;—all sorts of small antique bronze figures, etc.; -he no longer keeps office hours (or sees patients) but only trains students who allow themselves to be analyzed for this purpose. He made me a present of an attractive new edition of his lectures. Accompanied at a late hour from the Berggasse all the way to my house.—Our conversation grew warmer and more personal; about growing old and dying; he confessed having certain Solness-feelings (which are totally alien to me).[89]

Halvard Solness, Ibsen's *Master Builder,* is such a rich character, one that, dare I say, lends itself handily to Freudian analysis (not yet entirely out of fashion in the halls of academe). But was it Solness's midlife crisis with which Freud empathized—his joyless marriage, his attraction to a young woman? His supression of desire? His feelings of guilt? His manipulation of others to realize his own ambition? Or perhaps the facet of Solness that struck a chord with Freud was his fear of being surpassed by a younger man, the next generation of builders of towers. Sometimes a tower is just a tower, though probably not in this case.

DREAMS, DISGUISED AND UNDISGUISED

In the case of dreams which are intelligible and have a meaning, we have found that they are undisguised wish-fulfillments; that is, that in their case the dream-situation represents as fulfilled a wish which is known to consciousness, which is left over from daytime life, and which is deservedly of interest. Analysis has taught us something entirely analogous in the case of obscure and confused dreams: once again the dream-situation represents a wish as fulfilled—a wish which invariably arises from the dream-thoughts, but one which is represented in an unrecognizable form and can only be explained when it has been traced back in analysis. The wish in such cases is either itself a repressed one and alien to consciousness, or it is intimately connected with repressed thoughts and is based upon them. Thus the formula for such dreams is as follows: they are disguised fulfillments of repressed wishes. It is interesting in this connection to observe that the popular belief that dreams always foretell the future is confirmed. Actually the future which the dream shows us is not the one which will occur but the one which we should like to occur. The popular mind is behaving here as it usually does: what it wishes, it believes.

Sigmund Freud, "On Dreams" (1911)[90]

G. J.'s DREAM

One morning in Vienna G.J. related to me a dream that, remarkably for him, he remembered most vividly. He was a young, 30-ish, English teacher at our university, but his parents owned the Hotel Imperial on the Ringstrasse. G. J. was in charge of its operation. He had two computers, one for school, one for the hotel business. So, he had to go to Vienna, to the Imperial, and a young woman employee looked at a document he signed and said, "Ah, you are also a Weinberger," to which G. J. replied, "I am not *a* Weinberger, I am *the* Weinberger."

That dream brought out the Wilhelm in him, I said. He said the dream had reminded him of a Schnitzler play, *Der Schleier der Beatrice* (*The Veil of Beatrice*).

"There's a line in it," he said. "'Dreams are desires without courage.' But I don't remember the rest."

> But Dreams are desires without courage,
> Insolent desires which the light of day
> Chases back into the corners of our soul
> Out of which they dare creep only at night.[91]

7 Schöne Post

The Stamp

The postage stamp felt a thrill
As he found himself affixed.
A princess had touched him with her lips.
And his love then rose to the quick.

He wanted to return her kiss,
But that would tear his being.
And so he loved her quite in vain.
Life's certain tragedy ever to be feeling!

Joachim Ringelnatz, *Der Briefmark* (1912)[92]

Lovely Mail

"Die schöne Post ist da!" is the *cri de coeur* of the Weinberger household. G. J. awaits the daily arrival of the mail with the same sense of urgency with which I imagine Queen Elizabeth II awaits her royal dispatches, and has long since infected me with a similar, although less intense, sense of anticipation. Rarely, however, does our mail yield riches or documents of national import; but it does arrive from the four corners of the earth decorated with little works of art we know as postage stamps. Each of a long line of mail carriers has told us we receive the most interesting mail on the route, sent from such places as China, Abu Dhabi, Albania, by equally philateli-

cally-minded people who, like us, loathe metered mail. Our *Post* is indeed *schön*, lovely.

G. J. is a triple threat in this arena: philatelist, postage stamp dealer, and aficionado of post offices both domestic and foreign. Thus our marriage for me has been one long education in all things philatelic and postal. Invariably, when we travel to Vienna or elsewhere in the world, our first outing is to the nearest post office, whether or not we have packages or letters to send. *Schöne Post*, then, can mean (although not literally) "Great mail today" but also "Here we are at the beautiful post office where I can mail packages and browse at the philatelic window and check the rates for sending a postcard to. . . ." Such trips to the post office have become a part of our traveling life, and so I have come to know the Vienna Krugerstrasse branch of the Austrian Post as well as I know our own small town post office here in Connecticut. Maybe even better, because I pay more attention to it, to the patient citizens queuing up, to their invariably complicated transactions and often heated conversations with the folks behind the counter, to the nervous tourists hoping they will get the right number of stamps for their postcards, to the employees who smile sparingly and who, until recently, smoked on the job. I, who still hardly know how to register a letter at home, admit to feeling a little awed when G. J. steps up to the Krugerstrasse counter and dazzles some bored bloke who's been doling out pretty stamps to tourists all day with his precise instructions and command of post office lingo—and *auf Deutsch*, at that.

The Conversion of the Stamps

One steadfast employee of the Krugerstrasse post office, the kind of plodding middle-aged fellow G. J. is apt to call an *Esel* (donkey), was clearly unimpressed by G. J. and his command of post-office-ese. We had been sent to him in order to exchange a handful of old Schilling stamps for new euro-denominated ones. Here it was, May 31, and the deadline was coming up shortly in June. He looked at us rather suspiciously, I thought, as G. J. pushed towards him a pile of stamps.

"Make a list of the number of stamps—by face value," he ordered. When we couldn't produce a piece of paper, he handed us one, delivered with a withering look.

G. J. and I took ourselves to an empty counter and sprinkled out our stamps, sorting them into piles and writing out our list: 13 @ 5 schillings, 18 @ 2 schillings, 10 @ 1 schilling, and so on. The face value added up to about 250 schillings (at the time about $20).

That was Step One. Our next task was to paste all the stamps onto another sheet of paper, arranged of course by denomination (now that they were jumbled back in their envelope).

"You mean lick them onto a sheet of paper?" G. J. asked. "Why?"

"Regulations," said the Donkey.

The little sponge dishes placed at the service counters were mostly dry. We licked stamps enough to fill five pages, and handed them in, watching while our civil servant scrutinized our tally, then counted each stamp, once, then twice, then a third time. Then he did his multiplication: 13 @ 5 schillings equals 65 schillings, 18 @ 2 schillings equals 36 schillings. . . . We held our breath.

"*Stimmt*," he finally said. Our schilling totals were in agreement.

Now came the currency conversion, so many schillings worth so many euros. And once he determined the euro figure, he could issue us new stamps in that amount. But in what denominations?

"Do what's easiest," pleaded G. J.

He counted out into two tidy piles one-euro and half-euro stamps, striving mightily, we could see, to make them come out even. Then he counted them again. *Stimmt.*

News Item

From the on-line English Edition of *Die Presse*. July 15, 2002:

> VIENNA. Over 20,000 hoarded letters have been discovered in the home of an Austrian pensioner. The retired postal clerk had 23 sacks worth of packages, letters and junkmail stashed at his house in Perchtoldsdorf. 50 year-old Helmut T. blamed the stockpile on years of alcoholism in the past, leaving him unable to deliver the mail. The collection was discovered when a neighbour suspected a fire and called the local fire department. As Helmut T. was not home the firemen went in through an open window—and discovered the huge piles of post.[93]

Postage Stamps and Cinnamon Meringues

"It isn't so often a young woman comes into this shop smiling," said Herr Walter Taferner, proprietor of the stamp shop in Vienna's Opernpassage, an underground shopping and transportation hub in the vicinity of the State Opera House.

I cannot help but smile. A visit to Herr Taferner's establishment can perk up the worst of my Vienna days. He and G. J. go back some years in their stamp dealings, occasions upon which I have always tagged along to listen to his slangy and thus mostly incomprehensible German and to reap certain rewards, especially the extravagant compliments and the rum-filled chocolate bonbons he keeps behind the counter. His impossibly tiny enclosed kiosk of a shop is always lively, a theater in the round of which he is the undisputed and ever-affable impresario.

When we dropped in one recent afternoon, the shop was typically crowded, although two people standing at his counter constitute a crowd, and now we make four and the temperature rises. Immediately, Herr Taferner dispatched his helper to fetch us coffee from the nearby café. There's no refusing his hospitality, so we agreed to a *kleiner Mokka,* a single espresso.

"Too soon after lunch," he declared. "*Mokka* is too strong and bad for the stomach. Make it a *Melange.*"

In my experience and observation, stamp dealers as a species tend to be dour, grumpy old men who inhabit cramped quarters and do not suffer fools lightly, fools being those who mistake them for sellers of postage instead of purveyors of stamps—mint, canceled, old, rare, in sheets, blocks, on covers—for collection in albums. Walter Taferner is one of the exceptions. Every day he suffers fools who are drawn to his displays of stamps, coins, and antique postcards that fill up every inch of his shop windows, if not gladly then certainly with a quirky sense of humor. Like Waluliso, he qualifies as a *Wiener Original,* although he isn't Viennese by birth. He was born in the Austrian province of Styria (Steiermark), where, as a boy, he collected, traded and sold stamps—just as G. J. did as a teenager in New York City. We made a little joke with him about "Steirermann," a reference to a popular song, whose dialect lyrics are sprinkled with English. It pokes a bit of fun at Arnold Schwarzenegger, who also hails from Styria, and who had just declared his candidacy for governor of "Kally-*forn*-ya." The refrain goes something like: "*Steirermen san very good, very very good für Hollyvood.*" *Gotteswillen,* Herr Taferner sputtered. Kallyfornyans couldn't be so silly as to elect Ahh-nie as their governor, could they? *Aber nein.*

Chatting all the while, Herr Taferner conducted business, counting up a stack of covers that a customer had been intently scrutinizing. Now here is a specialist, a collector more interested in the postmarks than the stamps. He buys only those covers with cancellation marks from Burgenland, an eastern province once part of Hungary; however, the postmarks must have only the (former) Hungarian name of the (now) Austrian town or village. He found a small cache and handed over a few hundred euros. Other customers came in and out in a steady parade, Herr Taferner addressing them all with exaggerated courtesy: *Herr Direktor* to a young guy browsing and *Herr Doktor* to a man in a threadbare suit. A good looking woman came in and political correctness be damned—*Grüss Gott, Fräulein!* She handed him a large coin.

"What's it worth?" she asked. "Maybe a euro or a dollar," he replied. "But don't sell it—I am sure this one will bring you luck."

During a lull, he brought out a couple of small photo albums. Over the years he has taken pictures of some of his *Stammkunden,* his regulars, including a strange guy who will come in several days in a row and then disappear for months. But he always buys something, whether a cheap set of stamps for a euro or two, or coins, or a religious medallion, or, in one instance, a $500 set of commemorative medals from the Lillehammer Olympics.

"But if you saw this guy on the street, you'd give *him* money," Herr Taferner said. "He's filthy; his clothes are ragged."

The picture in the album bears out his observation—a rotund man wearing a Tyrolean hat, his face and shirt in need of a good scrub. But business is business: when Herr Taferner thinks he might be due for another shopping spree he places something in the window he thinks will tempt him—and it usually does. I think, though, he has a soft spot for such folks. His loyal helper, for instance, is clearly a marginal soul, saying little but remaining at the ready to run the boss's errands. Mainly, though, his male and middle-aged clientele appear by their photos to be perfectly average and respectable. One is a well-known musician, although Herr Taferner declined to give his name. He is a *"Philharmoniker,"* he said, rather proudly, a member of the Vienna Philharmonic Orchestra.

Herr Taferner's own collecting passion isn't for stamps, but for currency. He once showed us his personal album of very fine, bank-fresh, paper notes, including a gorgeous 1,000 kronen note from 1910, the engraving done by one of the great Deco-period artists, Kolo Moser. There was a 1,000 schilling note from the inflationary period of the 1920s that was worth, he said, "a thousand meals" because in those days you could buy a whole meal for one schilling. His World War II curiosities include currency printed by the American military in 1944 in anticipation of victory and as part of the Allied occupation strategy to put some valid currency into immediate circulation.

Although difficult to imagine Walter Taferner outside his tiny shop, so completely does my image of him include a backdrop of stamp albums and stacks of narrow stock boxes, I like to picture him at work in his former career. Before he bought the shop in the Opernpassage, he worked for 20 years as a pastry chef directly above, in the Hotel Bristol, one of Vienna's poshest. In a city that worships its sweets and ritualizes their consumption through the afternoon *Jause,* he earned distinction for his *Zimtnockerln,* cinnamon meringues.

"We sold hundreds of them a week," he told us. "I made the Bristol a lot of money using up all the leftover egg whites."

I would love to have tried one, served up as he described with vanilla sauce and garnished with fresh berries. But I will settle for his rum filled chocolates and a bit of dish every now and then.

Der Brummige Wodak

G. J. and I were disappointed when we arrived last year at Herr Alfred Wodak's stamp shop on the Kärntnerstrasse and discovered it was no longer there. For years we had passed through the modest door in the midst of Vienna's most expensive retail blocks and trudged up a long drab flight of stairs to his first floor shop. Before we got to the top, the *Haushund,* a terrier, would start yapping, and we would hear Herr Wodak say in his deep soothing baritone, "All right now, calm down, calm down." The two-room shop always seemed dim, despite the windows overlooking the Kärntnerstrasse, its fancy, old-fashioned flocked wallpaper dotted with hunting trophies, a startling assortment of antlers. You'd think you were in some *Gasthaus* in a remote valley in Tyrol.

Tall, with wispy white hair, Herr Wodak always dressed in a jacket and tie and was a primary illustration of my stamp-dealers-are-grumpy-old-men notion. G. J. and I took to referring to him as *der brummige Wodak*—the grouch—but with more affection than malice. He was never rude, just taciturn; like most Austrian stamp dealers we've encountered, he was reluctant to do business, that is, to buy items G. J. offered for sale. G. J. might speak the language but he isn't local.

"I already have too many of these," was his standard response to whatever G. J. was selling.

The rare transaction that did take place was not accompanied by much conversation, although I would often egg on G. J. to engage him—efforts that yielded no real success beyond a perfunctory observation about the weather. How profoundly I regretted my lack of fluency that always prevented me from taking a crack at him.

We found him a few days later at his new, spiffier shop just a few blocks away on a side street, rather glad he hadn't yet retired. Philatelic Vienna would not be the same without him and Herr Taferner of the Opernpassage. His new street level store is lighter and airier, but lining the walls are all the mounted horns, and trotting out first thing to greet us was the old terrier.

Herr Wodak was chattier—perhaps the sunnier new place perked him up. I got G. J. to tell him how much we had enjoyed visiting the old shop, and just then I think he might have remembered us. He had made a tremendous profit by selling, and with the faintest gleam of satisfaction he added, "*Ja,* seven figures." We offered up our admiration. He had been there 32 years, he said, and was now aged 83. We offered up further admiration of his obvious good health. His secret?

"*Kein rauchen, kein saufen,*" he said, "No smoking, no tippling." His years of hunting out in the fresh air also had kept him fit.

He seemed eager to buy something, sorting through G. J.'s stock book and visibly disappointed there was nothing for him. I was holding another small box, intended for another dealer.

"Let me see what's in there," he said, despite G. J.'s indication that there was nothing of possible interest. He poked through the bunch of glassine envelopes anyway.

"I know how he felt," G. J. told me later. "You see a ratty old box of stamps and it's like a treasure hunt. You're always hopeful."

SUNDAY STAMP CLUB AT THE DOMMAYER

The Sunday Stamp Club was meeting from 7 to 11 a.m. at the Café Dommayer in Hietzing, Vienna's well-to-do thirteenth *Bezirk,* just a few blocks from Schönbrunn Palace, the former summer home of the Habsburgs. I had visions of genteel old guys in sweater vests and ties looking at one another's stamp albums, discussing their new acquisitions, doing a little trading, complaining—there had to be complaining—about how the grandchildren weren't interested in collecting stamps anymore. Maybe there would even be a short lecture on, say, the Franco-Prussian War balloon post or a tutorial on eBay bidding.

"It says, 'Newcomers Welcome,'" I told G. J., pointing to the events calendar notice.

We went partly to satisfy my curiosity and mostly because we love the Dommayer's excellent breakfast rolls. It made a nice Sunday morning excursion by *Bim.* G. J. took along one small stock book, in the highly unlikely case someone wanted to buy or trade a few stamps.

A sign indicated the section of the café reserved for use by the club, but we saw no club, only a few men (one or two indeed in sweater vests and ties!) seated here and there—each by himself. As we looked around, one fellow looked up.

"This section is reserved."

G. J. told him he was looking for the stamp club.

"Here it is," he said.

He handed G. J. a sheet of paper on which he was to write his name and address. He was then permitted to peruse the stamp albums of any of these half dozen or so gentlemen. If he wished to purchase a stamp, he would negotiate the price, then record the sale on the sheet and return it to the registration table to pay.

While I had my coffee at a table just beyond the stamp club boundaries, I read the paper and spied on G. J. making the rounds. It didn't take long. Each collector took a cursory glance or two at his stock book, only to hand it back with a "*Nein, danke.*" The prices quoted for the one or two items he found of interest were, he said, inflated.

Naturally, I was disappointed that G. J. made no new friends among the stamp collectors of Hietzing. He, however, was quite content to butter up a couple of crisp, fragrant *Kaisersemmeln,* slather them with apricot jam, and sip a big *Mokka.*

FAMILY ALBUM

Ludwig's friend Lisl Lederer told us one day last summer that an old stamp album had turned up in her daughter Judy's basement. When Lisl moved to Summerwood from the Queens apartment where she had lived since the 1950s, some long-forgotten boxes stashed in closets were simply transferred intact to Judy's, and one of these contained the musty Schaubek album. It had belonged to her late brother-in-law, Ernst Lederer, whom she had never met and about whom her husband had rarely spoken. Along with the album, Judy found a small packet of documents: Ernst's Vienna school records; his Austrian passport with its big red J; a few letters to his family posted from Dachau, where he was imprisoned in 1938; the telegram sent from Buchenwald notifying the family of Ernst's death in 1939 from, it stated, a lung ailment.

"I didn't even know this stuff existed," Lisl said.

She asked G. J. to appraise the stamp collection, and we took it home. To me, it seemed a sacred object. This and a few pieces of paper were all that remained of a young Viennese man whose younger brother Wilfred, nicknamed Pudi, had been Ludwig's best friend over a span of 70 years. All 422 pages of this bulky album had been shipped to America—lovingly, if hurriedly—with other of the family's most precious possessions. Its dry, brittle pages, their edges nicked and yellowing, seemed poignantly to evoke a life, a personality, a boy's glimpses of a world beyond Vienna through the window of tiny postage stamps. That album haunted me for days. How, I kept wondering, could a boy who collected stamps become a young man who died in a concentration camp?

G. J. says it is not valuable or unique in terms of philately, but rather a child's collection, missing the most costly stamps in individual sets. Arranged by the world's geography, it begins with Albania in Europe and ends with the United States of America ("Vereinigte Staaten") in the Western Hemisphere. Ernst had only eight U. S. stamps, including an 1870 one-cent Ben Franklin with a Boston cancellation and a 1927 10-cent "Spirit of St. Louis."

The heart of the collection, though, is the Germany and German Colonies stamps that record the all-but-forgotten permutations of a once-powerful colonial empire. Here are German New Guinea, Cameroon, Caroline Islands, the Marianas, Southwest Africa. There are stamps from occupied Belgium and France, German stamps overprinted in Belgian and French currency denominations, circulated during WWI. Here are Romanian stamps marked "German Military Administration." Here are post-World War I plebiscite Territories—Upper Silesia, Saargebiet, Allenstein. There are stamps from the 1923 inflationary period: 500 marks, 100,000 marks, 800,000, 2 million, 10 billion, 50 billion. That's *billion.*

Ernst's last acquisitions are probably the few stamps postmarked Vienna, April, 1938, all bearing Hitler's image, all now put into circulation in the expanding German Reich. One carries the ubiquitous legend *Ein Volk, Ein Reich, Ein Führer;* there is also a block of four stamps—a souvenir sheet, G. J. calls it—issued to commemorate Hitler's birthday, April

20. *Wer ein Volk Retten Will Kann Nur Heroisch Denken,* it reads: "He who wants to save a people can think only heroically." Ernst probably bought it at his local branch post office in Döbling. His *schöne Post.*

On the Postage Stamp: A Hundertwasser Painting in Words

In 1983, Viennese artist Friedensreich Hundertwasser designed a set of six postage stamps for the United Nations to commemorate the thirty-fifth anniversary of the U. N. Declaration of Human Rights. The artist's signature geometry, his swirls and circles and blocks, merge with and into human figures, cheerfully, gloriously, rendered in ripe pinks, oranges, purples and blues. On the occasion of their first day of issue, Hundertwasser composed a meditation, a kind of prose poem on the postage stamp which reads, in part:

> A true postage stamp must feel the tongue of the sender wetting the glue and being stuck on the envelope.
>
> A postage stamp must experience the dark insides of a mailbox
>
> A postage stamp must suffer the rubber stamp of the post office
>
> A postage stamp must travel in company with other letters in mail sacks by ship, by air, by road.
>
> A postage stamp must feel the hand of the mailman delivering the letter to the receiver.
>
> A postage stamp that has not been posted is no postage stamp, it has never lived, it is a fake.
>
> It is a fish that never swam, like a bird that never flew.

8 Grace Notes

An Evening at the Kursalon

Visitors to Vienna may be puzzled at first, although charmed, by the remarkable number of persons strolling about wearing periwigs, frock coats, and buckled shoes. One sees them riding the *U-Bahn* or the *Bim,* having a quick *Mokka* at an espresso bar, young folks, mostly, who marvelously decorate and lend that anachronistic—some would say "theme-park"—touch to the City of Dreams. Although they appear to be loitering about the entrance to St. Stephen's or the Hofburg, or milling about Graben and Kohlmarkt, they are actually working; and while they may very well be the least obnoxious of their species to be found anywhere in the world, they are nonetheless touts, purveyors of Vienna's musical heritage and pitchmen (and women) for the small local orchestras and ensembles competing for tourist dollars. A ticket to the Vienna Philharmonic or the State Opera may be impossible to get or alarmingly expensive, but music for the masses is always available, usually in some delightful formula: a dab of Schubert, a dollop of Beethoven, much Mozart, and a big scoop of Strauss.

These days I seem to attract less attention from the touts, who can spot tourists from fifty paces, but I still get waylaid often enough to feel triumphant over an unmolested passage through the *innere Stadt.* The secret is to hide the camera, look purposeful, and carry the badge of citizenship, the bright yellow and red plastic shopping bag from the ubiquitous local grocery chain, Billa.

Many of the Mozart look-alikes seem to enjoy their work, prompting visitors to listen to the music for which the city is so justly famous, chatting with people from around the world, practicing foreign languages, but I do not think it is such an easy job. One bitter cold and rainy winter morning, for example, I couldn't dodge a tout all bundled up in a burgundy nineteenth-century, regimental-style great coat posted outside Schönbrunn Palace. I shook my head as I passed him, and he sounded weary and exasperated as he called after me, "I'm not selling vacuum cleaners, you know!"

Not long after, I bought a ticket to a Strauss concert from one of his colleagues, a disappointingly brisk and business-like transaction. The program of the Salonorchester "Alt Wien" promised Strauss standards, ballet dancers, opera singers, plus a "hommage to W. A. Mozart." Very "old Vienna" indeed. I had been on a concert spree for the past week, doling out the euros for whatever presented itself, which had turned out to be a rich and heady hodgepodge of an organ recital, a Bach mass, a Strauss operetta, and a program of *Schrammelmusik* featuring the gentle, tuneful, folk-based melodies of the Biedermeier era composed by the brothers Schrammel. G. J., who was at home in Connecticut, would have balked at attending the program of early opera at the Konzerthaus and the modern string quartets at the Musikverein—his loss!—but I loved them, and loved, too, the grandness of these occasions, the dressing up, hopping the *Bim*, checking my coat and buying a program, sitting in these magnificent gilded halls, listening, watching.

The grand peachy-yellow ballroom of the Kursalon at the edge of Vienna's Stadtpark was the venue for the "Alt Wien" concert, and it was lavishly decorated with fancy stuccowork and illuminated by crystal chandeliers. For my $67 I was seated in the front row, separated from the small platform stage by only a few yards of polished wooden dance floor. Swirling around me were fragments of British and American English, Italian, Japanese, French.

The musicians entered: three violinists, flutist, clarinet-
ist, pianist, cellist, bass player. After welcoming remarks in
German and English, the maestro launched them into a rous-
ing march, "Wien bleibt Wien" ("Vienna Remains Vienna").
Strauss Jr.'s "Roses from the South" followed, a gorgeous
waltz (the Strausses wrote only gorgeous waltzes). A slim,
girlish singer then trilled her way through "Mein Herr Mar-
quis" from *Die Fledermaus;* and, dressed in Hungarian folk
costume, the dancers polka'd energetically to "Eljen a Mag-
yar." Through it all, much of the audience nodded, chatted,
and kept time with their fingers or feet. This was a program
tailor-made to offset tourist ennui, delivered with charm, if
not gusto, by musicians and dancers practiced but not passionate. This was the Vienna the audience expected, all late
nineteenth-century romance and gaiety.

At the intermission, I went to the bar for a drink and
found most of the orchestra already there, thoroughly disen-
gaged from the music, laughing, joking, wine glasses in hand.
Back in the ballroom, people were milling about on stage,
one woman seated at the piano while her partner snapped a
picture. She played a few notes. I tried to imagine what would
happen if anyone climbed into the orchestra pit at the State
Opera House and plucked a few strings on the harp or leafed
through the sheet music. Police action, maybe.

The homage to Mozart led off the second half with *Eine
kleine Nachtmusik.* The audience vigorously clapped between
movements. The players, to their credit, did not smirk. They
must be used to it. But perhaps the audience was right: isn't
the customary silence during performances a relatively recent
custom? I have read plenty of accounts of eighteenth-century
Viennese audiences bursting into applause whenever they felt
like it.

The concert's final selection was, not at all surprisingly,
"The Blue Danube Waltz." The encore also was no surprise:
Strauss Father's "The Radetzky March," to which our maestro
invited us to clap along. We did. To the second encore, Le-
hár's "Merry Widow Waltz," our maestro invited us to dance.

Within half a minute the floor was crowded and my knees were brushed by passing couples. I watched as two teenagers, the girl in camouflage pants and tee-shirt, the boy in jeans and sneakers, gamely tried out the basic box step, keeping each other at arm's length and watching their feet. However, the gabby old British couple, who had sat behind me, he with the pink face, she with the sparse hair, seemed to know what they were doing, and glided by me with aplomb. Perhaps all their Vienna holiday hopes and dreams were being realized at this very moment, played out in three-quarter time.

THE CONGRESS DANCES

The waltz exercises an inconceivable power. As soon as the first bars are struck, the faces become milder, the eyes light up, and a hush goes through the crowd. The dancers form into graceful, spinning units, begin moving along the dance floor, cross and pass one another [. . .] You have to see these marvellously beautiful women, covered with flowers and diamonds, drawn on by the irresistible music and molded in the arms of their partners; you must see how the shining silk and mousseline of their gowns follows every movement and forms into beautiful waves, and finally the ecstatic happiness which breathes out of every pore of their faces, when exhaustion forces them to abandon the heavenly regions of the dance floor in order to collect new powers from the earth.

Count August de la Garde, *A Portrait of the Vienna Congress 1814–1815*[94]

THE OPERA BALL

There is an undeniable glamour to Vienna during ball season, although I am still often struck by the fact there *exists* a ball season. Any Viennese, however, has a long and rich historical memory to draw upon when it comes to balls: the lavish court affairs of the Habsburg centuries, the glittering and decadent parties of competing hostesses during the Congress of Vienna, the waltz-mad balls of the Strauss era.

In 2004, more than 300 balls were reportedly held in Vienna,[95] most of them during *Fasching,* the pre-Lent period. (This total would seem incredible if I hadn't read somewhere that in the mid-nineteenth century there were twice as many.) Among this year's events were the Pharmacists' Ball, the Judges' Ball, the Coffeehouse Owners' Ball, the Vienna Philharmonic Ball, the Hunters' Ball, and the Ball of the Atomic Energy Commission. What a blast *that* must have been.

I had almost talked G. J. into booking a trip to attend the Kaiser's Ball at the Hofburg, the official launch of the season, but it seemed a daunting undertaking requiring dancing lessons, a tuxedo rental, and decisions over ticket categories (with or without dinner, with or without a place to sit for the evening). In the end, the whole package looked too geared towards foreign visitors and too expensive. And after all, there is no more Kaiser in Vienna, and a Kaiser Ball without the Kaiser? I think not.

But G. J. and I did witness the spectacle of the *Opernball,* the Opera Ball, the grandest of them all. We watched it unfold on television on a cold and blustery February night, snug in our Darwingasse apartment, sharing a bottle of *Zweigelt* and pastries from Gerstner. It was a bit like watching the Oscars. Stepping carefully out of the limousines and horse-drawn carriages and slowly ascending the red carpeted stairway of the State Opera House were the President and Prime Minister of Austria and their bejeweled spouses, diplomats sporting sashes and medals, socialites and former aristocrats, a minor royal or two, men in uniforms (more medals), and notable figures from the worlds of music, art, literature, film, and sports.

And then there were the Lugners. Richard Lugner is a rich Austrian industrialist who each year invites (the press uses words like "leases" or "rents") a Hollywood star—in this case, Andie MacDowell—to join him and his wife, known as Mausi, at the Opera Ball. Eva Wertheimer had warned me about them, how they were everywhere, crass and irksome and irresistible to watch. And so they were, their faces splashed all over the tabloids the days before and after the ball, their penchant for publicity so great that they even produced their own *The Osbournes*-style reality show that featured Herr Lugner receiving a botox treatment and Mausi fretting over her ball gown.

But for all the hype and glitz surrounding the ball and all the annoying accoutrements of the on-the-scene, play-by-play television reporting—complete with interviews with everyone from the Staatsoper carpenters to the florists to the grandfathers of the debutantes—and for all the explicit theatricality of the evening, I felt nonetheless drawn into its magic, transported into a Viennese fantasy. When the opening ceremonies began and 80 young women wearing white dresses and delicate tiaras began with their escorts the stately *polonaise* into the glowing, golden ballroom, I noticed my heart beating. And when they began the first waltz to *"An der schönen blauen Donau," The Blue Danube Waltz,* my eyes welled. It was simply so beautiful, and the waltz so perfect a union of music and movement.

I know it was all finely choreographed and well-rehearsed, but there remained the touch of innocence to it all, as well as timeless romance. Even when recollecting that evening I have trouble holding on to a healthy cynicism about it, although I know I should. The Opera Ball may now be a staged-for-television event diminished by the vulgarity of celebrity, but it is not bowed by it. Grace, tradition, beauty, civility have not been entirely given over to the Lugners.

"To dance at the Vienna Opera Ball is the dream of all young girls," the Russian soprano Anna Netrebko told reporters from the Vienna daily *Kurier*.[96] And she must be right, because for one February night, I was wrapped in that Cinderella dream, a thirteen-year-old girl once again.

An Irishman in Vienna

The people of Vienna were in my time dancing mad; as the Carnival approached, gayety began to display itself on all sides, and when it really came, nothing could exceed its brilliancy [. . .] For the propensity of the Vienna ladies for dancing and going to carnival masquerades was so determined, that nothing was permitted to interfere with their enjoyment of their favorite amusement—nay, so notorious was it, that for the sake of ladies in the family way, who could not be persuaded to stay at home, there were apartments prepared, with every convenience, for their accouchement, should they be unfortunately required. And I have been gravely told, and almost believe, that there have actually been instances of the utility of the arrangement. The ladies of Vienna are particularly celebrated for their grace and movements in waltzing, of which they never tire. For my own part, I thought waltzing from ten at night until seven in the morning, a continual whirligig; most tiresome to the eye and ear,—to say nothing of any worse consequences.

Michael Kelly, *Reminiscences* (1826)[97]

How Blue Is The Danube?

As a rule, G. J. does not sing. But one June afternoon, as he and I were sitting at a café directly across from Praterstrasse

54, home to both the Johann Strauss, Jr. Memorial Rooms and a McDonald's restaurant, he was inspired to hum the familiar strains of *"An der schönen blauen Donau."* He then added some "lyrics" which I doubt require translation:

> Die Burgers sind fein, so fein, ah fein,
> Die Katze sagt "Nein, oh nein, oh nein!"

G. J.'s are not the first words set to this iconic Viennese waltz, Austria's unofficial anthem, although I have never heard it performed as it was originally intended, as a choral piece. Strauss wrote it for—donated it, in fact, to—the Wiener Männergesang-Verein, the Vienna Male Choral Society, for its annual pre-Lenten bash. Usually, the society held a gala *Narrenabend,* a Fool's Night, where masked partygoers danced and made merry. But in the carnival season following the Empire's defeat at Prussian hands at Königgrätz, a less potentially raucous program was planned. According to John Whitten's account, on the evening of February 15, 1867, the Dianasaal in Vienna's second district was jammed with over 1,200 guests, with hundreds more having been turned away.[98] "The Blue Danube Waltz" opened the second half of the program, performed by the 150-member male chorus and a military orchestra, that of the Infantry Regiment "King of Hanover." Strauss himself did not conduct, was not even present for the debut because of another engagement. Whitten writes:

> It took five hours to perform the enormous program in the overheated ballroom, from 8 p.m. to 1 a.m., with only one intermission. First the orchestra played the Poet and Peasant overture by Franz von Suppé. Then followed about two hours of musical and spoken parodies, and finally came a long intermission, during which one could strengthen oneself at the buffet or at dinner. Right after the intermission, the strains of 'On the beau-

tiful blue Danube' were heard for the first
time ever: the long, lovely orchestral introduction, followed by five waltz sections for
the chorus and orchestral accompaniment
[. . .] In spite of the heat and the late hour,
the audience, applauding loudly, demanded
and got a repetition of the waltz. [99]

Whitten suggests the song, if one can call it merely a song,
was a hit, and to insert a bit of pop-culture trivia, the term
"hit" (*Schlager* in German) to describe a musical work of great
popular acclaim was first used by a journalist in a newspaper
account of the event. But biographer Joseph Wechsberg notes
that a single encore, when the debut of a new Strauss waltz
would typically garner half a dozen or more, indicates a merely polite reception.[100] "The Blue Danube Waltz," he asserts,
was not truly embraced by the public until it was performed a
few months later in Paris, where one critic called it "the waltz
of waltzes."[101]

To honor Strauss's achievement, the Choral Society awarded him a gold ducat. His publisher, Spina, paid him 150 gul-
den for it, a pittance, and then, according to Wechsberg, made
a fortune on the sale of sheet music.[102]

Hardly anyone remembers the lyrics sung on that debut
evening as they were superseded by a text that would more
precisely match the composition's title. In 1890, Franz von
Gerneth wrote the now standard lyrics of celebration of the
legendary river:

Danube so blue,
Through valley and meadow
You flow peacefully past,
Our Vienna greets you,
Your silver band
links nation to nation
and joyful hearts beat
on your beautiful shore.[103]

The original words by the Choral Society's music director, Josef Weyl, reflected an entirely different, and more typically Viennese, theme, an exhortation to set aside present sorrows and celebrate the moment. Weyr's lyrics were topical, meant to comment on the gloom that settled on the city in the aftermath of war. They formed a kind of a dialogue giving voice to that eternal Viennese ambivalence—things are fine, things are horrible:

> *Viennese be glad*
> Oho, how come?
> *Well just look around!*
> Oh please, but why?
> *A shimmer of light*
> We see nothing yet.
> *It's Carnival time!*
> Ah, right, oh well!
> *So, defy the time*
> *Of spiritual gloom.*
> Ah, that would be smart!
> What use is regret
> Or mourning?
> *Then be joyful and glad.*[104]

But Weyr wrote another set of lyrics two years later, the first of a long tradition of parodies. At the dawn of the Ringstrasse era, a time of change and modernization of the city, his new version reflected yet another lamentable reality of Vienna:

> Who hasn't seen our Vienna
> For a good long time
> He'll find no longer any house;
> Because wherever one looks stands
> A palace!
> The Ring is a jewel
> Where lives all Israel,
> Ten years hence they'll build themselves a new
>   Jerusalem.[105]

The Aryanization of Johann Strauss

The Nazis had a problem: Johann Michael Strauss, the paternal great-grandfather of Johann Strauss, Jr., had been born a Jew. A ledger in the archives of St. Stephen's Cathedral noted that on February 11, 1762, Johann Michael, "a baptized Jew," married Rosalia Buschinin.[106]

The "Waltz King" was himself born and raised a Catholic, although he converted to Protestantism late in life in order to marry his third wife, Adele. But according to Strauss genealogist Hanns Jäger-Sustenau,

> If the ancestry of the family Strauss had become known, it would have been a catastrophe for the entire music business in the Third Reich. All Strauss melodies would have to be banned, like the beautiful music of Mendelssohn-Bartholdy and many others. Imagine what that would have done to the repertory in concerts and radio.[107]

After the 1938 *Anschluss,* the Germans took some pains to hide—no, obliterate—the fact of Strauss's Jewish lineage by confiscating Johann Michael's marriage records. The original ledger was secreted away, and a photocopy of it given back to St. Stephen's, minus the Strauss entry. After the war, the fraud was revealed and the original record book returned to its rightful place.

The Strauss family's origins, however, had been no secret in Vienna, where Papa Strauss, Johann Michael's grandson, and the founding musical genius of the family, had been called in his day "the Jew with the fiddle."[108]

Father and Son

In his foreword to the English translation of Arthur Schnitzler's autobiography, *My Youth in Vienna,* Frederic Morton writes:

> The very lives of the Strausses, father and
> son, personified Schnitzler's obsession with
> the intertwisting of canker and rose. Johann
> Strauss, Senior, "magician of the lilt," was a
> pitiful, driven neurotic. It was said of him
> that "he died like a dog and was buried like
> a king." Johann Strauss, Junior, even more
> renowned, a still more glistening and trium-
> phant sower of joy across the world, suffered
> even more from depression and nervous ex-
> haustion, from recurrent despair. "His biog-
> raphy," writes a Viennese critic, "is a case his-
> tory."[109]

The Strausses are legendary among Vienna's dysfunctional
families. The innkeeper's son who married an innkeeper's
daughter, Anna Streim, Johann Strauss, Sr. (referred to by the
Viennese as Strauss Father), rose to prominence as a composer,
orchestra leader, and Royal Court Ball conductor. Moreover,
along with his colleague-turned-rival Josef Lanner, he stan-
dardized the musical structure of the Viennese waltz (orchestral introduction, five waltz sections, coda) and fomented
its wild popularity in Vienna and elsewhere. Strauss Father
was probably the first conductor to form a touring orchestra,
which he took all over Europe in the 1830s, even to London,
where he performed at Queen Victoria's coronation in 1837.

A gifted and enterprising musician he may have been, but
he was a less-than-stellar father. While providing a comfortable middle-class home for his expanding family (he and Anna
had six children), he discouraged—actually forbade—his el-
dest son and namesake to pursue a career in music. Later, he
even attempted to thwart his efforts to obtain a license from
the city to form his own orchestra. His lengthy extramarital
affair with a milliner resulted in seven more children, a divorce suit by Anna, and a custody battle. Somehow, I cannot
quite get over the fact that two of his second crop of children
bore the names of two of his first: Johann and Josef.

With Anna's encouragement, young Johann charted his own musical course, studying piano, violin, and composition, eventually establishing his own orchestra, which debuted on October 15, 1844, at the Dommayer Casino in Hietzing. The program, which included original numbers as well as some by his father, was a great success. A local writer famously proclaimed, "Good night, Lanner! Good night, Strauss Father! Good morning, Strauss Son!"[110]

Although the two reconciled before Strauss Father's untimely death in 1849 at age 45, they were for several years fierce competitors in Vienna's musical marketplace, savvy businessmen whose creativity is in evidence not only in their music but in their marketing strategies. Strauss, Jr. deliberately cultivated a younger audience; mindful of the city's rich array of ethnic groups, he cleverly wove familiar folk tunes into such compositions as *The Serbian Quadrille* and the *Czech Polka*. Strauss, Sr. would include in his programs works by other contemporary composers, like Berlioz, both capitalizing upon and popularizing works already familiar to the public. He served as bandleader of Vienna's First Citizens' Regiment, his son of the Second Citizens' Regiment.

And the rivalry lives on. By custom, the Vienna Philharmonic's New Year's Day concert broadcast around the world from the Golden Hall of the Musikverein closes with "The Blue Danube Waltz." Strauss, Jr. may well have been the true genius of the family and his music the most enduring metaphor of the City of Dreams, but the last sounds the audience hears in the encore are his father's irresistibly catchy, patriotic "The Radetzky March," a tune that supported the doomed Empire's illusion of military might. Father gets in the last note, if not the last laugh.

Strauss Rocks Boston

In 1872, at the height of his career as Vienna's living legend, its superstar, Johann Strauss, Jr. set forth for the New World. He did so most reluctantly as he was a terrible traveler, but the offer of $100,000 plus expenses to conduct in Boston was too good to turn down. Before he left Vienna, however, he made out his last will and testament.

Strauss was accustomed to public acclaim, and although he remained throughout his life a modest man, he had nonetheless cultivated his image as a charismatic conductor, rather dashing with his handsome head of black hair. Women swooned over him and sent him love letters. But nothing prepared him for his reception in Boston, where he was mobbed at every turn by adoring fans. And that was not the worst, for he apparently had not understood exactly the size of the venue, a specially built hall meant to accommodate an audience of 100,000. What is more, he had the daunting task of conducting some 20,000 musicians and singers. He later wrote that after giving a sign,

> my hundred sub-conductors follow me as fast and well as they can. And now there begins a terrific racket which I won't forget as long as I live. Since we all had started at approximately the same time, I did all I could so we would all finish at approximately the same time. Somehow I managed to do it—it was really the only thing I could do. The audience cheered. The noise was fantastic.[111]

The seemingly indefatigable Strauss conducted fourteen of these concerts during his stay in Boston, and somehow squeezed in a brand new composition, "New Jubilee Waltz," which his biographer Wechsberg notes, ends with a waltz arrangement of "The Star Spangled Banner."[112]

The Critic

"Every genius has its limitations," wrote Vienna's most powerful nineteenth-century music critic, Eduard Hanslick (1825–1904). He was referring specifically to Johann Strauss, Jr. (and specifically to his one and only foray into "serious" opera, *Ritter Pasman*). He might, however, have been commenting on any one of the geniuses of the Vienna music scene. Reading Hanslick's reviews is, I admit, an exercise in *Schadenfreude.* Of bad reviews there are many, for he was an unabashed opponent of most innovation, or of what he often called "the music of the future." I have no idea whether he was right or wrong in his assessments of, say, Brahms's *Symphony no. 4* or Verdi's *Otello,* but I delight in the voice that emerges from his writing, so self-assured, so wry, so wonderfully musical. Take, for example, a sentence from his 1858 review of Wagner's *Lohengrin:*

> The despotic degradation of music to a mere
> means of expression accounts, in Lohengrin,
> for those extended scenes in which one takes
> in little more than a continuous fluctuation
> of featureless, fluid tonal matter. [113]

Wagner was not amused by the criticism, nor impressed by Hanslick's writing style, and the two men were ever after at odds. Besides hurling some anti-Semitic slurs at him, Wagner also satirized the critic in the figure of Beckmesser in *Der Meistersinger,* the unlovable fool of a clerk who plays the foil to the hero, Walther. In his review, Hanslick wrote, "A poet of genius [Walther] against a dozen pedantic masters who cannot understand him [Beckmesser, et al] and yet dare to judge him. Do you get it?"[114] Hanslick mostly stuck to the high road, however, and kept his focus on the music, although he once called Wagner "thoroughly uncongenial," adding, "A stranger would have seen in his face not so much an artistic genius as a dry Leipzig professor or lawyer."[115]

To read Hanslick's reviews of works by Brahms, Bruckner, Richard Strauss, Beethoven, Tchaikovsky and performances by Patti, Liszt, Clara Schumann, Anton Rubenstein is to get a heady sense of the astonishingly rich character of Vienna's musical life in the second half of the nineteenth century. Hanslick heard it all, knew them all (not Beethoven, of course), and with courage and verve commented on it all. Of Bruckner's *Symphony no. 8,* he wrote:

> Everything flows, without clarity and with-
> out order, willy-nilly into dismal longwind-
> edness. In each of the four movements, and
> most frequently in the first and third, there
> are interesting passages and flashes of ge-
> nius—if only all the rest were not there![116]

And of Richard Strauss's *Don Juan:*

> He who desires no more from an orchestral
> piece than that it transport him to the dis-
> solute ecstasy of a Don Juan, panting for ev-
> erything feminine, may well find pleasure in
> this music, for with its exquisite skillfulness
> it achieves the desired objective insofar as it
> is musically attainable. The composer may
> thus be compared with a routined [sic] chem-
> ist who well understands how to mix all the
> elements of musical-sensual stimulation to
> produce a stupefying "pleasure gas." [117]

While Hanslick did not spare the beloved Strauss his criti-
cism of his operettas—he notoriously panned even *Die
Fledermaus*—he wrote a loving, elegant tribute to the Waltz
King upon his death in 1899:

> The sources of his melodic invention were as
> fine as they were inexhaustible; his rhythm
> pulsated with animated variety; his harmo-
> nies and his forms were pure and upright.
> He named one of his waltzes "Liebeslieder."
> The designation was applicable to all of
> them: little love stories of bashful courtship,
> impulsive infatuation, radiant happiness,
> and here and there a breath of easily consol-
> able melancholy.[118]

9 The Anschluss and After

BLIND

I was very patriotic. I was an Austrian patriot.

They were running around in the streets. "Juden heraus." We didn't realize it meant something. The police came, they ran. Later on, the police looked away.

We tried to ignore this. That was our mistake."The Jewish are safe." Since Emperor Josef the Second we are safe. It was a mistake. The generation before me, or even before, two, three generations back, they make money, they build up the country. And they were protected by the government, you know. But, in the long run, in the back[ground], they were anti-Jewish. Starting with the mayor, Lueger.

But, we were blind. The Jewish people from Poland, Russia, they know they have no way to exist so they went to the United States, built up the United States, let's face it, a lot, a lot. The big industry, it was all Jewish background. Not all, but a lot. We didn't do this because we were blind. We came home from school, we had a meal on the table. Not everybody had this, not everybody can afford it, to have a meal on the table, on the plate. Not that I was spoiled, I was not spoiled, I mean, I was a little spoiled. But it hits you. We were blind. Then suddenly it hits us as a big surprise. We thought everything is okay. That goes on for a hundred years, another hundred years. Because Emperor

Josef the Second—he wasn't for the Jewish or against them—he was smart enough to see what the Jewish could do for his country.
   That's the way it was. We were blind.

Ludwig Weinberger, July, 2002

HE SAID, SHE SAID

Der Anschluss is a term—an event—that overshadows twentieth-century Viennese history. The contention over its meaning is often reduced to a matter of translation: translate the term as "annexation" and the Austrians become victims of Hitler's grand design to create his "Greater German Reich"; translate it as "union" or "connection" and Austria becomes a partner in the transaction. We have, in other words, a case of linguistic "he said, she said." Was the *Anschluss* rape or was it consensual? At least one historian, Gordon Brook-Shepherd, has worked out a middle ground. In his book, *The Austrians: A Thousand-Year Odyssey,* he titles the chapter on the *Anschluss* "Rape by Consent."

   The story of this political entanglement is both hopelessly complex and endlessly fascinating in its political, ideological, and psychological dimensions, but I am no historian to unravel these Medusa strands. Hitler and his team were diabolically clever in their manipulations of Austria's internal political divisions. Austria's Chancellor, Kurt Schuschnigg, was alternately strong and weak-willed in dealing with the Nazis, and the Austrian people proved remarkably malleable of mood, ready to vote for their independence in March 1938, and for their own subjugation in April. Brook-Shepherd notes there

> was also something very Austrian about the
> sudden switch which applied particularly to
> the Viennese. They had been born with the
> "one eye laughing, the other weeping" which
> came out in Schubert's music. The capital

> of waltzes and operettas was also the city
> of Angst and record suicide rates. There is a
> pendulum built into the Austrian psyche.[119]

In the April 10, 1938, plebiscite, 99.73 percent of eligible voters (which did not include Jews), approved the *Anschluss,*[120] a legacy that spawned a bitter soul-searching, one now passed from generation to generation, continuing to haunt both citizens and the few remaining elderly exiles alike.

HELDENPLATZ

For two golden mid-September days, Vienna's Heroes Square, the Heldenplatz, was transformed into a fairground that would do any small New England town proud. The local farmers—yes, Vienna has farmers—were sponsoring a harvest festival, complete with goats and lambs, giant pumpkins and wagonloads of late summer vegetables, a wood chopping contest, women bursting out of the bodices of their Dirndls and men in Lederhosen displaying fine muscular legs. The young wine was plentiful, dispensed from tiny booths set up by local vintners, and the food! Well, farm-made Bratwurst, grilled to bursting, and homemade apricot or plum *Kuchen* are Austrian soul food. While a local brass band delivered the hearty, tuneful music of the land, it was easy to forget that the Ringstrasse trolleys and tour buses lay yards away, just beyond the Burgtor, the square's monumental archway.

When the music stopped and the speeches began, G. J. and I headed toward the inner courtyards of the Hofburg, stepping carefully through the crowds until we realized that the speaker, a fellow in rustic Austrian garb whom we thought surely was some Farmers' Association official, was actually the Chancellor of Austria, Wolfgang Schüssel. We stopped for a while to listen and to marvel at the intimacy of the setting, the absence of armed guards. A head of state in a post-9/11 world addressing a crowd in a capital city and it was all relaxed, civilized, respectful. People were actually listening as

Schüssel delivered the homespun platitudes one expects to hear on such occasions: farmers are the caretakers of the land, the backbone of the nation.

I have thought often about that afternoon, about the homey, lovely rurality that lies so close to the geographic and spiritual heart of Vienna, of the good-natured crowd sharing food and drink around long picnic tables, of the food stalls and craft booths ringing the equestrian statues of Prince Eugene of Savoy and Archduke Karl—the heroes of Heroes Square—of the parade of flower-trimmed farm vehicles threading through the Michaelertor and into the *innere Stadt*. But such thoughts inevitably inspire a "Vienna moment," a flash of overlying images, those of a 2003 harvest festival and a 1938 Nazi rally, the color of the former fading to the black and white of old newsreel footage of the latter.

Perhaps more than anywhere else in the city, the Heldenplatz, fashioned by the Habsburgs during the Ringstrasse era, serves as emblem of the *Anschluss*. And no peaceful harvest fair, no wine festival, no children's carnival or any of the dozens of other events held there each year can erase the memory of March 15, 1938, when Hitler, who had entered the city the day before, made his triumphal address from a balcony of the Neue Burg. "There are embarrassing, even shaming, episodes in the lives of all nations," writes Brook-Shepherd. "One such, for any Austrian with a glimmer of patriotic conscience, was the spectacle of the huge crowd which filled Vienna's Heldenplatz on the morning of 15 March."[121] Afterwards, Hitler and his cronies expressed not only delight but surprise at the Austrians' warm welcome.

Posted to the Heldenplatz that day was a 22-year-old *Kanonier,* or artilleryman, serving his compulsory military service. I have often wondered whether Ludwig Weinberger was the only Jew present, watching, listening, witnessing what so many have called Hitler's hypnotic effect on crowds. That day he was surely not blind, but mute, reduced to a chilled silence, fearful his uniform would provide no protection from the German troops, from his bunkmates, or from the cheering crowd of Viennese, many of whose basest instincts would be roused within the coming days and weeks.

J

The Patrons' Room of the Austrian National Archives smells just like a high school library and is about as aesthetically pleasing as the one in which I did my homework decades ago, with its beige linoleum floors, long wooden tables, and uncomfortable chairs. I am getting squirmy waiting for Herr Schön—Mr. Beautiful!—to bring forth from the forbidden regions of stacks or vaults or filing cabinets Ludwig Weinberger's military records. The woman at the next table is apparently having more fun, smiling as she reads through a pile of documents, obviously pleased. I am curious as to what she's working on in this place that would prove so amusing, but it wouldn't do to ask.

Herr Schön arrives, all apologies about the delay, and hands to G. J. a yellowing document.

"That's it," he says. "That's all there is."

We cannot, for a moment or two, look beyond its top page, on which has been printed a giant red "J," J for *Jude,* Jew. That was the only fact of Ludwig's life, apparently, that mattered, a life reduced to a symbol, a mark on a piece of paper. My stomach muscles contracted, as if I had been punched in the gut.

"BROTHER, ARE YOU GLAD WE'RE HERE?"

"I had a beautiful uniform, made for me by my father's tailor," Ludwig tells me. "I was only a soldier, but people thought I was a general in that uniform."

For a well-to-do young man who favored silk shirts from the Knize shop on Graben, who wore handmade shoes, who drove a Fiat around town, and met his girlfriend, Jula Mieses, at the coffeehouses, a stint in the Austrian Army, even outfitted in a handsome uniform, could not have been a happy prospect. But on October 1, 1937, Ludwig began his compul-

sory duty with the Artillerieregiment Kaiser Maximilian I at
the Kaisersteinbruch camp northeast of Vienna. He had, he
says, an *Intelligenzknopf,* a button, literally, that denoted his
"higher" educational status as a graduate of the Handelsakademie. His period of service was, therefore, cut in half, but
whether from one year to six months, as he claims, or from
two years to one remains unclear. The record we obtained
from the Staatsarchiv states his obligation as one year, to be
followed by yearly training until age 42, very likely a couple of
summer weeks of calisthenics and target practice.

Ludwig has little to say about the six months of military
training he actually underwent. It is difficult, frankly, to picture him as a soldier, wielding a rifle and marching about.
He merely indicates he toughed it out, without complaint or
distinction, save one.

"I was the only Jewish in my regiment," he says.

Until early March 1938, Ludwig's Army days passed without particular incident, only the threat of a demerit when
he ran into an officer while at the theater one weekend with
Jula—out of uniform. No doubt the officer had other, far
more pressing worries than disciplining an otherwise unob-
jectionable soldier out on the town with his girlfriend. But the
political situation in Austria, Vienna, in particular, had grown
tense. Early the previous month, under pressure from Hitler,
Chancellor Schuschnigg appointed a Nazi, Seyss-Inquart, to
the cabinet, and then defiantly ordered a national referendum:
Vote *Ja* or *Nein* for an independent Austria. Meanwhile, local
Nazi party members vandalized Jewish-owned stores and held
street demonstrations.

On March 11, two days before the vote and uncertain of
its outcome, Hitler made his move, ordering German troops
to cross the border into Austria. Fearful of a bloodbath,
Schuschnigg ordered the military not to resist. Within a day
or two, troops appeared at the Kaisersteinbruch camp. Ludwig was posted to guard duty and had to let them in.

"I was the only Jewish soldier in my company, and I was
the one who had to go open the *Zoll,* the gate, to let them in.

One soldier asked me, *'Bruder, bist du froh dass wir da sind?'* 'Brother, are you glad we're here?' What could I say?"

"What *did* you say?" I ask.

"What *could* I say?"

Within a day or two after the Heldenplatz rally, Ludwig was dismissed from the Army, sent home, he says, because Jews were not permitted to take the loyalty oath to the new Führer. I have read that Hitler wanted no Jew even to utter his name aloud.[122] Ludwig never knew, however, that the Army still had plans for him, suggested by the final notation on his military record, dated 31 March 1938: *"Transferred to the reserve as a Werksoldat as a consequence of his profession of the mosaic faith, in keeping with the regulations Erl. 54.002—Erg/38, Nr. 295/St fg/38, R.T.B. 20/38/ St.bfl. 6/38."* He was spared, at least, an undoubtedly miserable fate and almost certain death as a laborer, and simply walked away from the Army. But whether he was allowed to do so out of compassion or bureaucratic confusion, the typically Austrian incompetence called *Schlamperei*, we will never know.

Unfurnished Tales

Ludwig told me once about his uncle, Egon Fürth, who remained in Vienna during the war, hidden by his Gentile wife and her family.

"I saw him after the war. I gave him money."

"Did he tell you what it was like, how he managed to survive?" I ask. "It must have been horrible."

"No. You don't talk about these things."

Details. I ask my father-in-law for details, but he gives me outlines in return, mere sketches and bare storylines of the Weinbergers during the years 1938 to 1945. Their movements, machinations, and motives as they attempted to cope with the nightmare of the Nazi era are vague, unverifiable, or simply lost as the generation who lived through it all passes away. Ludwig struggles to answer my questions, faltering as he attempts both to remember and to communicate accurately. Dates are especially difficult for him, and so the timeline wavers as much as his 90-year-old voice. His sister Nora went to England, but when? His father stayed in Switzerland, but for how long? Ludwig cannot say, although he can tell me with absolute certainty that he met Jula at the airport in Zurich on August 18, 1938, and that he paid the fine she owed for landing without a visa.

"How did your mother get out of Vienna?" I ask.

"I don't know," he replies, and for a moment I think he feels bad admitting it. They may never have discussed it after the war. She got out, survived, that was the point. And I can well believe that for Ludwig *not* asking for details was a part of his own survival, carrying on, and creating a new family, in a new culture, in a new language.

Even his own story is a synopsis, a telescoping of what must have been agonizing, danger-fraught weeks and months into a straightforward paragraph delivered in measured phrases. "I was lucky," he says. "I always say, 'it's a miracle I sit here today.'" There is no denying that Ludwig was lucky, luckier than most, that his and Jula's departure from Austria and from Europe was accomplished rather efficiently. Somehow, I had always had the impression that Ludwig escaped Austria by train. I have watched too many movie scenes, perhaps, of disguised and perspiring passengers avoiding sharp-eyed Gestapo as they coolly paced the aisles of trains just waiting to seize them. In fact, Ludwig flew to Paris from Vienna without incident, although nervous that his new Czech passport would arouse suspicion during the stopover in Prague, and fearful of being hauled off the plane and sent back to Vienna.

He stayed in Paris only for two weeks, then traveled to Zurich, where he met Wilhelm and secured some funds. In a convoluted scheme they arranged, an Italian linoleum factory near Lake Como with ties to the Weinberger firm sent invoices to a Zurich bank, which were paid out to Ludwig in British pounds.

"I wanted to get as far away from Vienna as possible, I told my father," says Ludwig. "I wanted to go to Buenos Aires." He did not tell Wilhelm that along with his passage out of Europe, he intended to buy two wedding rings.

While Ludwig was in Zurich, Jula obtained her exit permit in Vienna. She was free to leave Austria, but without a visa had no guarantee she would be welcome elsewhere. Switzerland was merely imposing fines in 1938 and ordering most refugees who sought asylum there to leave within six months. Later, the country would turn away Jewish immigrants altogether. Jula boarded a plane to Zurich on August 18, and was reunited with Ludwig, who paid the Swiss government their fee with the money Wilhelm had helped him obtain. Ludwig never introduced her, though, to her future father-in-law.

They never made it to Argentina. The embassy in Zurich refused to grant them visas, and so they applied to Paraguay, which did. They also obtained transit visas to travel through Uruguay to Asuncion. Their plan in place, Jula and Ludwig made their way to Marseilles, where they married and booked passage on a French boat, the *Florida*. The voyage to Montevideo took three weeks.

"I read a little," Ludwig says, and little else.

When they arrived in Montevideo, they were met by acquaintances of Jula's father, Lazar Mieses, and with their help, disappeared into the city, now illegal immigrants. They found a small but cohesive German-speaking Jewish community ready to help the young couple get started. From a distance of 8,000 miles, they read, listened for, and awaited news of the family and of Vienna, the *alte Heimat*, the place they would never again call home.

OPERATION ACTION

Among the 386 young Jews gathered at the train station in Vienna on June 9, 1938, were Ludwig's cousin and his wife, the newly married Ernst and Irene Wiesner. They had been instructed to bring nothing but a knapsack and a set of sheets, and to wear the uniforms of the Betar, the youth group of the militant organization, the Zionist Revisionists. They were permitted little money, only a few Reichmarks, although Ernst smuggled on board a pair of diamond earrings his mother gave him, earrings that Irene still wears today.

They were setting off on a journey through Yugoslavia and Romania to Athens, where they would board a ship, the Artemisia III, bound for what was then British-controlled Palestine. It was an illegal voyage, as the British had restricted severely the immigration of Jews to their Biblical homeland and had blockaded its shores.

Dr. Willy Perl was a young Viennese lawyer with an office on the Stubenring who was, as Irene says, "one of the brains" behind the operation, nicknamed *die Aktion,* or *die Perl Aktion.* During Hitler's rise to power in the 1930s, Perl and a handful of Zionists had devised a scheme to transport illegally to Palestine young, activist, eastern European Jews, who would work toward founding a Jewish state, with weapons, if need be. When the *Anschluss* occurred, the plan took on urgency as a rescue mission, and was the only successful operation to assist significant numbers of Jews out of Austria. After surviving arrest by the Gestapo and a trip to Berlin to obtain Nazi sanction of the plan, after outmaneuvering uncooperative diplomats and shady opportunists, and without the blessing of local and international Jewish organizations, Perl's group managed to send off Ernst, Irene, and the others under the watchful eye of Adolph Eichmann, the fast-rising star of Vienna's Gestapo, who came to witness their departure. Over the next six years, some 40,000 Jews would leave the City of Dreams in this fashion to reach the next Promised Land. In his account of *Die Aktion,* Perl wrote:

> In all our ships, the starved, decrepit, almost dying people were singing and praying the words which are part of the Jewish national anthem, "to return to the land of our fathers." This anthem is called the "Hatikvah," or "The Hope." And hope proved to be the spark which was probably more encouraging

as such than the individual successes of landing and landing again. This persistent hope was proof that human pride and dignity are not easily killed and can be called to life even in the worst of times.[123]

A WEDDING STORY

Months before, I had already done the Aufruf—how do you call it? [banns]—at the temple. We had made up our minds already one way or another to get married. Now, my mother-in-law, if she should know about it she would have gotten a heart attack. It's the truth.

So, I went to my friend's house. Her father was a tailor making me a suit. I wanted to get married at least in a suit, because it was not the time of the gown anymore. And my friend says, "If you get married tomorrow it's between Passover and Shavuoth, so you cannot get married." But tomorrow was the last day of the month, so there was an exception. So, tomorrow we could get married. And once I got married I could get a Czechoslovakian passport. So I left the suit there, forgot about taking measurements, and I called Ernest. "If you want to come to the Seitenstetten temple"—the very famous Seitenstetten temple—"we can get married tomorrow." Well, no we couldn't, they had weddings from early morning til late at night. Everybody was getting married. But I tell them my fiance is German, which wasn't really true, but I had to get married. So, okay, they called a different district, the tenth Bezirk. "Okay, come tomorrow at 10 o'clock," the rabbi said.

I came home, and said, "Mama, I am getting married tomorrow."

"How about Ernst's mother?" she asks.

"He is afraid to tell her, she will get a heart attack."

So she said she doesn't want to go to the wedding, if she [Ernst's mother] is not. So my sister went, and I was very disappointed he [Ernst] couldn't get flowers, he couldn't find flowers. But, anyhow, we got married, and the rabbi said, "You will be just as happy even though you don't have all the nice things." From there I went straight to the Czechoslovakian consulate. It was jammed with people and nobody could see the consul, but I managed to see him anyway. And I walked out with a passport. And from there I went straight to Dr. Perl's office.

Irene Rischeles Wiesner. March 2003

PARTIAL PAYMENT

An Austrian patriot like his son, Wilhelm Weinberger returned to Vienna from his holiday in the south of France hoping to cast his vote in the March 1938 plebiscite. He did not stay long, merely a day or two before leaving again, never to return to Austria. The Gestapo went to Blaasstrasse looking for him—and, more importantly, for his money. Ludwig thinks Frau Neumann, a clerk at the firm and a Nazi party member—although no one knew it—was probably responsible for the speed with which the family came under scrutiny.

The Gestapo found Ludwig instead of Wilhelm, still in uniform although dismissed from the Army.

"'Where is the money? the gold?' they kept asking. 'You must know where it is.' But I didn't," Ludwig says. "I could say I didn't know, that I was with my regiment when my father left the country."

The Gestapo returned to the Weinberger offices periodically, demanding information on the whereabouts of firm assets and family members who might provide information. A longtime Weinberger employee, Franz Mertel, was the designated *Kommissarischer Verwalter,* Acting Manager, the required Gentile overseer. He had always been friendly to Ludwig—they often discussed books—and, in these grave circumstances, he did all he could to protect the family by vouching for their ignorance of Wilhelm's finances.

"We had many very loyal people, the employees, not all of them Jewish," says Ludwig. "My father's driver, Miksche, told me they'd have to kill him before he'd let them take me."

Within a year of the *Anschluss,* control of the Wilhelm Weinberger Firm was transferred to three outsiders: Franz Herkner, Franz Schmidt-Zabierow, and Max Wessely. Whether any of them were acquaintances of Wilhelm no one in the family knows. Their names appear on numerous documents Ludwig and his cousin Gretl gathered over the years relating to the disposition of Wilhelm's assets, the first of which is dated October 1938, just six months after the Nazis marched into Austria.

> Deputy Chief of the Trade Association and Its Divisions
>
> Vienna, 18 October, 1938
>
> URGENT
>
> To the Office of Transfer of Assets
> Attention Dr. Hummer
> Re: Wilhelm Weinberger Firm, Linoleum, Carpets, and Draperies Shop, Vienna 10, Favoritenstrasse 98 and 6 branches.
>
> I support the request for permission for the sale of the firm Wilh. Weinberger, with its business locations at
>
> X., Favoritenstrasse 130
> IX., Währingerstrasse 61
> V., Schönbrunnerstrasse 105

XX., Wallensteinstrasse 16
XXI., Floridsdorferstrasse 44
The business is in such condition as to be worthy of acquisition.

The locations at
X., Favoritenstrasse 98 and
IX., Währingerstrasse 64
are, however, because of general and local conditions to be liquidated.

I support the joint request of the applicants

Franz Herkner, XVIII., Schulgasse 13,
Franz Schmidt-Zabierow, III., Am Modenapark 3,
Max Wessely, VIII., Strozzigasse 15

for the takeover of the above mentioned firm, with the five business locations, in view of their professional suitability, as well as the availability of financial means. Under condition that the stock

There the letter breaks off and we have found no subsequent page. Assuming that the Trade Association is a professional organization rather than a governmental body, it could be that some of the very people who supported Wilhelm's application for *Kommerzialrat* or took his tax advice or attended with him meetings of the Rug Merchants Association blessed the handover of the company he had built "from nothing," as Ludwig says.

The following letter from the new owners turned up in a batch of documents, but with no indication of its addressee.

As is known, we have acquired the W. Weinberger Firm with the permission of the Office of Transfer of Assets.

We now intend to deposit into a blocked
account of the Länderbank Vienna a sum of
50,000RM [about $12,500][124] towards the
purchase price to the seller, the Jew Wilhelm
Weinberger, over which sum the Office of
Transfer of Assets has the right of disposal.
Although the purchase price is not yet due,
pending a decision on the part of the Office of
the Transfer of Assets, we request nevertheless
that you approve this partial payment.

Vienna, 13 January, 1939
Franz Herkner,
Franz Schmidt-Zabierow,
Max Wessely

On June 16, 1939, the Office of Transfer of Assets issued
an invoice to Herkner, Schmidt-Zabierow and Wessely that
lists the purchase price of the Weinberger firm as 295,089.12
reichsmark [about $73,780]. A bargain, to be sure.

Neither the extent of Wilhelm's "fortune" nor its whereabouts has ever been firmly established, although the Austrian government made its own estimation decades later, reported in a January 2000 letter to Ludwig from his cousin
Gretl Frisch:

For your information I can tell you that the
conversion value of the estimated fortune,
according to the rate at the time, is circa 45
million schillings [$3.6 million]; naturally
this does not mean that one—or we—will
get even a fraction of that. The banks have
agreed among themselves on a return of altogether 500,000 schillings [$40,000] which
is not even a fraction of the interest! When
this will be distributed is still written in the
stars.

At age 87, Ludwig received a share of the settlement. Gretl received hers too, just before she died.

FINAL NOTICE

All the legal jargon and numbered statutes cannot disguise the diabolically simple scheme the Nazis devised for seizing Jewish property. They imposed a *Reichsfluchtsteuerbescheid*— a "flight tax"—on Jews who left Austria. Of course, those who left would not receive the tax notice, so they could not comply with the law, and faced arrest if they returned, presumably even for the purpose of paying the tax. The seizure of their property, then, was "legal."

The following document from the *Vermögensverkehrstelle*, the Office of the Transfer of Property, was addressed to Wilhelm "Israel" Weinberger, in care of his attorneys at the firm of Zollinger Thun:

> 20 July 1939
>
> Declaration of Tax Owed by Persons Fleeing the Reich
> Final Notice
>
> According to my determination you have given up your residence in Austria or any other place in the Reich. According to Paragraph 13, 14 of the first decree for the establishment of the Tax Regulations in the land of Austria of 14 April 1938 (Reich Law Gazette I, page 389), you must pay a Flight Tax. Any dependents who have emigrated with you have the same obligation (wife, children) insofar as they have been or liable to be assessed with you for income tax or wealth tax.
>
> The total of assets belonging to you and your wife as well as to your children amounted, according to my information, as of 1 January 1938, to 990,906 reichsmark [about $248,000].

According to paragraph 15, the Flight Tax has been set as a fourth of that sum: 249,976 reichsmark [about $62,500]. This tax is levied in accordance to paragraph 5 of this law, and is due 15 May 1938.[125]

Penalties: According to paragraph 6 of the law, the tax increases by 1% of the total every month, but the minimum is 2%.

You may raise objections or protest this decision. You can submit it in writing or by proxy, but only within a month after the receipt of this tax declaration; that is to say, a month from the day it was mailed. Because you object does not mean a restriction on the tax or alter your obligation to pay.

Consequences of nonpayment: If payment, as well as any interest, has not been paid within a month of the due date: 1) there will be initiated against you criminal proceedings; and 2) an arrest warrant will be issued and your property seized. The warrant for arrest and confiscation will be advertised in the Reich notices at your expense. Should you be found in the country after the publication of your name in the notices, then every official of the police or security service, tax and custom offices, as well as any other official of the finance ministry who has been deputized, will be obligated to arrest you.

PAUPER

Whether he carried much more than his Czech passport, I don't know, but Wilhelm Weinberger left Vienna on March 11 or 12, 1938, and boarded a train to Pilzen, only to be turned back at the border. Austria was a country in the process of being invaded, willingly or otherwise, and for at least a short time its borders were secured while German troops marched in. It must have been a tense 24 hours for Wilhelm, fraught with anxiety not only over his own fate, but those of his wife, children, family, and business. He made it to Pilzen, where he had property and business interests, but it was just a way station to Destination Unknown. From all I have heard and read from survivors, it seems all plans were by necessity contingent, improvised. Of one thing, however, the Jews of Vienna—of Europe—could be sure, that no other nation could be relied upon to help them. Individuals, yes, but nations, no. They were on their own.

Again, too few details. I know only that Wilhelm's route took him from Czechoslovakia to Switzerland, where he stayed for some months, both in the spa town of Bad Ragaz and in Zurich. There, in the summer of 1938, he saw his son, Ludwig, for the last time. From Switzerland he traveled to England, but was turned away, not allowed to enter the country. His daughter Nora was there, as well as his niece, Gretl, both of whom had gotten permits to work as housemaids. His sister, Luise Wiesner, was also in England, and perhaps by that time, Alice, his wife. He was able to see none of them, retreating to Paris, and then booking passage on a boat bound for Palestine. On the boat, he met a lawyer, who recorded his new will, a document that divided his estate between his children and his sister, Rudi Fischer. He made no provision for Alice.

Ernst Wiesner saw his Onkel Willi in Tel Aviv in late 1939, where, he reports, Wilhelm lived frugally. One day he ran into him in a coffeehouse. Wilhelm told Ernst, "I come here to read the papers so I won't have to buy them." That made an impression on the young man, for although reading the papers in one's *Stammcafe* was a time-honored custom in Vienna, it was appalling to Ernst that the *Herr Kommerzialrat* was forced to practice such economies.

Soon after, hearing that his uncle was unwell, Ernst and Irene went to his apartment.

"It was a beautiful apartment in one of the nicest neighborhoods," Irene told me. "But it was empty. He had only a bed in the middle of a large room; I don't think he had even a table next to it."

"He died like a pauper," said Ernst.

MISFORTUNE

22 November 1939

Dear Aunt!
You will already have learned from Mother and Ernst about the most heavy misfortune that has befallen us. Our poor father died suddenly of a heart embolism on the 8th of November at 9:15 in the evening.

You can well believe that we are all totally stunned. Everything is quite horrible and our fate so gruesome and hard.

Poor mother is so despondent and the nights are so terrible for us.

God is testing us so severely.

Please stay healthy and don't lose heart regarding a better future.

Many kisses,
Your Nora

PERISHED

Regine Fürth, Ludwig Weinberger's maternal grandmother, was deported to Theresianstadt, where she was murdered. *Frieda Weinberger Mayer,* Ludwig's paternal aunt, and her husband, *Oskar,* were deported to Auschwitz, where they were murdered. *Nora Mayer,* Frieda and Oskar's daughter, was reportedly killed during an air raid in Berlin, where she had been working as a housemaid for the family of the Swiss ambassador. *Grete Wiesner Adler,* Ludwig's first cousin, and her daughter, *Natascha Adler,* were deported first to Theresianstadt, then to Auschwitz, where they were murdered.

Emil Adler, Grete's husband, was deported to Mauthausen and was murdered there. *Hermine Weinberger,* Ludwig's step-grandmother, was deported to and murdered at Auschwitz. In 1939, *Wilhelm Weinberger* died of a heart attack in Tel Aviv at age 55. His brother, *Julius,* about 50, died two years later, also in Palestine.

VIENNA, 1948

It was terrible. I saw this after the war—the misery. To find a hotel was not so easy. They didn't have glasses for the windows. I saw pictures of Stalin. Basically, they were lucky, they had not so much damage like the cities in Germany. And they had food. I bought so many books, sent them to Montevideo.

They offered me a credit from the bank, Creditanstalt, if I stayed in Vienna and helped to build up the company again. I didn't want this. It was all Russian now. I didn't want that Bobi [G. J.] goes to school there. And Jula didn't want to go there. I only wanted what belonged to me. I didn't want to steal anything, like they did. They stole everything. And if the bank gives me the money, everything is kosher. But I couldn't go back.

After they knew what we went through, they didn't like to see these people again [meaning the Jews]. They didn't like to see me either. We were Jewish foreigners now, who come back again. "He's still alive, he comes back." For the Jewish who went back there was an animosity. Let's face it. I went through all this, I know. "Die Jüdische sind wieder da."

Did I tell you when I went with a taxi to Wallensteinstrasse 16, to see the store? The first time? Wallensteinstrasse was a big—not a department—but a big store with one floor partly for my aunt to make the draperies, with steps up to it, a very big store. The building, partly it was owned by my father. They gave me a couple thousand dollar. It was in the Russian zone, you know. It used to be a Jewish neighborhood—twentieth Bezirk, Brigittenau. So, I came with the taxi only for curiosity, to see this. After all, I had been there every week, you know, once a week. And I stepped out and in front of our entrance was a newspaper kiosk. And he [the proprietor] recognized me after so many years. He says, "Why are you still alive?" [Sarcastically] It was nice to hear this. He didn't mean it—it was stupidity. Stupidity. I turned around. I said to him in German, "You didn't catch me."

Ludwig Weinberger, July 2002

10 City of the Dead

BEAUTIFUL CORPSE

It always comes back to language, doesn't it? To unravel the mysteries of Vienna, one must grapple with its idioms. Here's a good one: *schöne Leich'*—"beautiful corpse." It refers not to the aesthetics of the deceased but to the custom of putting on a good funeral, one with the second most essential ingredient, an appreciative audience for whom acquaintance with the departed is not actually required.

> When I die, die, die,
> The Fiakers will carry me
> And the zithers play along the way,
> How I'll love, love, love that,
> Play a dance loud and clear,
> Always merrily!

Many Viennese, I am told, belong to a burial society to which they pay dues, a kind of insurance that guarantees them not only the funeral of their dreams but a cadre of mourners, without whom there can be no *schöne Leich.'*

> Oh, dear folks, folks, folks,
> Tell the vagabonds
> Who are banging on the wooden tubs,
> To sing with joy, joy, joy,
> At my grave
> Always merrily! [126]

The Cemetery Run

The #71 trolley is best known for its stops at the Zentral-friedhof, Vienna's vast Central Cemetery, which lies to the south of the inner city in Simmering, the eleventh *Bezirk*. G. J. told me this story he found in the *Weanerisch* book:

Two old women are on board the #71, after having visited the graves of their husbands. Sitting across from one another, eyeing each other, they silently come to a mutual dislike.

Finally, one asks, "How old are you?"

"Seventy-seven," the other replies.

"And you still wear make-up?"

"How old are you?" the other queries in return.

"Eighty-seven."

"And you're still coming home from the cemetery?"[127]

A Street Called "Graves"

In the heart of the *innere Stadt,* at the intersection of the Stephansplatz and Kärntnerstrasse, begins a pedestrianized street of smart shops and outdoor cafes, a kind of open air parlor for the Viennese, called Graben. The word *Graben* can be translated both as "ditch" and as "graves." It is the former for which it is actually named; in Roman times there was located here a section of ditch, probably a moat, part of the defensive fortifications of the settlement. Yet I cannot help but think of graves when I stroll past the street's most striking monument, a fantastically baroque plague column, dedicated to the Holy Trinity.

Such monuments are common throughout central Europe, erected by pious rulers to mark the end of episodes of epidemic disease that periodically wreaked havoc on their cities. Vienna was no exception. It suffered outbreaks of plague or other disease over a span of nearly a thousand years, between the ninth and eighteenth centuries. The last occurred in 1713/14, claiming some 9,000 lives, and when it was over, Emperor

Karl VI ordered built one of Vienna's landmark churches, the beautiful high baroque Karlskirche.[128]

Tourists on the Graben lounge about the enormous base of the column, the *Pestsäule,* which was commissioned by Leopold I after the devastating plague of 1679 that killed 12,000 in Vienna.[129] One guidebook writer describes Leopold as having been "extremely ugly," his "Habsburg lip and protruding chin extremely prominent."[130] The figure of him kneeling before the Holy Trinity, a *putto* holding his gilt crown, certainly bears out this claim. He may have ordered his architects to depict him as humble before God, but there is nothing modest about his plague monument; indeed, like the emperor's chin, it is excessive. Several architects worked on the piece, including the great master of Austrian baroque, Fischer von Erlach. The vertical structure is covered with *putti* and archangels hovering about billowing stone clouds, leading the eye up to the dove of peace poised before a burst of gilded rays. But there is something to me more medieval than baroque about its movement, something that reminds me of a Breughel painting—a stomach-jarring, eye-blurring crowd of figures and symbols. As a monument it is meant to be laudatory, but the whole thing gives me a sinking feeling whenever I pass by. I don't think it is just Leopold's ugly face, which survived the plague year, but also the unsettling depiction of an old woman being tossed into Hell by one of that band of angels. Lucky blessed Leopold, unlucky damned old lady. One is delivered from plague through God's mercy, the other not. This always strikes me as an odd image with which to inspire loyalty to either crown or church.

PLAGUE SONG

Leopold's column is not the only legacy of the Plague of 1679. Another is one of the world's most famous folksongs, immortalizing an otherwise obscure Viennese musician, a player of the *Dudelsack*—bagpipes—named Augustin. *Lieber* Augustin, the story goes, got good and drunk one night and passed out in the street. He was tossed into a mass grave, mistaken for dead by the fellows whose lovely job it was to round up all the dead bodies. He awoke among the corpses, and managed to hoist himself out. As he suffered no apparent consequences—he must have had some hangover, though—his story gave rise to the theory that wine is a good prophylactic. The Viennese seem to think so still.

> Oh, dear Augustin
> Money's lost, man is lost,
> Oh, dear Augustin
> Everything's lost!
>
> Of money I will not talk,
> If I could grab life back,
> But oh, dear Augustin,
> Everything's lost!
>
> I'd be rid of life now,
> If I had no credit,
> But credit seems to follow me,
> One step by step!
>
> And even rich Vienna is
> Poor as Augustin
> And sighs along with him for
> Everything's lost!
>
> Everyday was feast day,
> But now we have plague,
> Just one great big corpse nest,
> That's all that is left!
>
> Oh, dear Augustin,
> Get in the grave now,
> And you, my dear Vienna,
> Now everything's lost![131]

INTO THE CELLAR

"There are tunnels and cellars and mass graves everywhere beneath the inner city," said Barbara Timmermann, leader of a walking tour called "Underground Vienna. "Basically, the whole of the *innere Stadt* is a cemetery!"

There was something incongruous about this attractive young woman in jeans and tee-shirt delivering so cheerfully on a sunny autumn afternoon a lecture full of grim details.

Barbara led us, an assortment of German- and English-speaking tourists, from our meeting point at the Roman-era ruins on the Michaelerplatz—"possibly a red-light district, but it could also have been a marketplace or the temple district"—to Am Hof, a wide cobblestoned square that retains a medieval cast, despite generous doses of baroque detail. The first royal residence, that of Archduke Jasomirgott (Henry II), was located here in the twelfth century. Today, though, one of the square's most striking features is the municipal firehouse, crowned with graceful figures holding up a golden globe. That is where Barbara took us, into the station courtyard, then down a narrow staircase and into a firefighters' lounge, a pretty awful looking place turned into a game room for rest periods, complete with a miniature motor speedway, the figure-8 race track lined with tiny cars ready to zoom off at the flick of a switch.

Distributing flashlights, she led us deeper underground, through a pitch black series of stairs and rooms and tunnels, damp from dripping water, where firemen once drilled, shut in below ground to practice putting out fires in the dark. Such cellars, Barbara told us, are typical of Vienna. Citizens often dug lower than the Roman-era level, so layer upon layer of rooms exist below ground throughout the city center. These served as effective air raid shelters during World War II. When the rubble was cleared after the bombing, some building owners discovered even deeper cellars they hadn't known existed.

After a short walk from Am Hof to Freyung, we entered the gift shop of the Schottenstift, the former monastery of the so-called Scottish Church founded by Irish (mainly) Benedictines in the twelfth century. Down into the nether regions we headed, into a vast, brick lined barrel shaped series of rooms, well lighted, some 2,000 square meters of what is now exhibition space. Tables from a recent wine seminar were still set up, and placards announced the forthcoming exhibit of—I blinked my eyes to be sure—Barbie dolls.

"It's all state of the art," Barbara pointed out, "And fully wired for Internet."

A block or two away, on the Schottengasse, we entered the Tostmann Trachten shop, housed in an old building and comprising inviting rooms featuring traditional Austrian dirndls and lederhosen and loden coats and bolts and bolts of tiny flower-strewn cotton prints. Down the stairs we trooped, through a little museum of antique costumes to have a look at the shop cellars, a series of them giving way to dark passageways, some of them now ending in brick walls.

"There is a true story," Barbara said, "of a shop girl who got lost in the dark down here. All night she kept following the tunnels, hoping to find her way back to the shop. Do you know where she ended up? Under the Stephansplatz!"

What a dark journey that must have been, with all those bones Vienna has buried beneath its streets cropping up at every turn. No doubt it was the longest mile that poor girl ever traveled.

By Royal Decree

Emperor Josef II was a practical man and, one might even say, a proto-environmentalist. In 1784, he decreed the use of a recyclable coffin in order to conserve both land and lumber. The dearly departed was to be placed first into a sack and then into a specially built box. Once all the rituals had been conducted, the coffin lowered into the grave and the mourners departed, the corpse could be dropped from the collapsible bottom and the coffin raised to the surface to be put into service again. But it was not, evidently, a concept whose time had come. The idea met with such resistance from the public that Josef was forced to rescind the decree a few months later.

An old model of Josef's coffin lies in state, so to speak, at Vienna's Funeral Museum (*Bestattungsmuseum*) in the fourth *Bezirk*. In keeping with the Emperor's vision of pure functionality, it is a plain wooden box adorned only with a cross. It pales in comparison with most of the rest of the collection of accessories and accoutrements the Viennese found indispensable when dispatching their dead: coffin banners, draperies and bunting (light blue for virgins, black for everyone else) to decorate the houses of the deceased, casket photographs, mourners' jewelry, funeral invitations, death masks and the like.

But all that is for, well, after the fact. Also on display is a coffin rigged with a bell, should the not-quite-dead awaken, a frightening notion that prompted in the eighteenth century a whole series of royal decrees governing funeral practices. In 1753, Maria Theresa issued a mandate for a 48-hour waiting period before burial, amended in 1755 to exclude those claimed by plague or other contagious disease. Those poor souls were interred immediately. In 1771, another decree established the construction by local parishes or communities of a *Totenkammer*, a chamber for the dead, where bodies would be stored until burial. In a city where two families often shared a single room, *not* having to live with the body for two days would have been a blessing, especially in the summer. And in 1797, the monarchy ordered that coffins be outfitted with an alarm system, as noted above, consisting of a rope attached to a bell that was placed in the hand of the corpse. Just in case.

Despite all the precautions and regulations, fear of live burial persisted—persists, I should say. But there was one reassurance Vienna's undertakers could offer, a stab to the heart with a stiletto, an antique example of which is on display in the museum.

People still request this service," the docent told G. J. and me. "They want to be sure they're dead."

DEATH OF AN EMPRESS

During his residence in Vienna, Mark Twain witnessed one
of the city's most august and rare events, the funeral of a
Habsburg. The Empress Elisabeth, the beautiful, restless, odd
and unhappy wife of Franz Joseph had been assassinated on
September 10, 1898, stabbed in the heart by an Italian anarchist as she was about to board a steamer on Lake Geneva.
Such a shocking end prompted a great outpouring of sympathy for the aging Emperor, if not overwhelming grief for the
loss of Elisabeth, for whom the Viennese developed little true
affection.

Twain was offered a prime spot from which to view the
funeral procession, a room in the new Krantz Hotel on the
Neuer Markt, directly across the square from the Church
of the Capuchin Brothers and its imperial burial vault, the
Kapuzinergruft, where the Empress would be laid to rest. In
his posthumously published essay, "The Memorable Assassination," Twain described the "Sunday-like" atmosphere of the
city; the black flags draping houses; the mourning dress of the
citizenry; the men who, he noted, refrained on this day from
smoking. From his vantage point overlooking the square, he
witnessed the magnificent spectacle of the gathering of dig-
nitaries and military, and marked off the stages in the slowly
unfolding drama that built to its climax at the church door:

> At four-twelve the head of the funeral pro-
> cession comes into view at last. First, a body
> of cavalry, four abreast, to widen the path.
> Next, a great body of lancers, in blue, with
> gilt helmets. Next, three six-horse mourning
> coaches; outriders and coachmen in black,
> with cocked hats and white wigs. Next,
> troops in splendid uniforms, red, gold, and
> white, exceedingly showy.
>
> Now the multitude uncover. The soldiers
> present arms; there is a low rumble of drums;
> the sumptuous great hearse approaches,

drawn at a walk by eight black horses plumed
with black bunches of nodding ostrich feathers; the coffin is borne into the church, the
doors are closed.[132]

What Twain was not able to hear, despite the hush of the
crowd, was the ritual exchange between the Habsburg sur-
rogate and the Capuchin friar, a petition for entry into the
crypt. Elisabeth's petition would have gone something like
this:

The courtier leading the procession knocks with his stan-
chion on the church door.

"Who is there?" the Capuchin gatekeeper asks.

"Her Majesty, Elisabeth, by God's grace Empress of Austria, Queen of Hungary, Queen of Bohemia," the courtier an-
nounces according to formula, adding Elisabeth's full array of
titles and honors.

"I do not know her," the Capuchin states, keeping the
door locked.

The courtier raps again, and to the same question, offers
an abbreviated list of Elisabeth's titles. Again, the Capuchin
remains unmoved and unmoving: "We know her not."

The courtier makes a third appeal for entrance.

"Who seeks entry?" asks the Capuchin.

"Our sister Elisabeth," states the courtier, "A mortal sin-
ner."

The door opens.

THE KAPUZINERGRUFT

The unadorned façade of the Capuchin Church and its adjoining entrance to the burial crypt seem at odds with the
lavish palaces where the Habsburgs lived, ruled, dallied, and
loved. But since 1633, the bodily remains of 145 Habsburg
monarchs, consorts, offspring, in-laws, and one close family friend of Maria Theresa's (the Countess Caroline Fuchs-
Mollard) have been placed here in dim underground vaults.

Most of the bodily remains, that is. The Habsburgs decided at some point to spread themselves around Vienna: their hearts are kept in urns in the Augustinerkirche and their entrails in a crypt in St. Stephen's.

Until my last visit to Vienna a couple of months ago, when I found the entrance to the crypt renovated—that is, modernized, complete with computer spitting out admission tickets—I had long enjoyed the quiet ritual of handing over a few schillings to an old brown-robed friar who sat at a table inside the entrance and silently pointed the way to the stairs down to the crypt. A sign over the lintel at the bottom admonished SILENTIUM. Visitors do not always comply, alas. It is down here an altogether strange dim world, often pierced by flash bulbs as well as echoing voices.

I like to pay particular homage to Maria Theresa (1717–1780), perhaps the most remarkable and energetic Habsburg of them all. No, she wasn't always wise, and she was no friend to the Jews, and although she might have been a fond mother, she nearly always put political expediency before her children's best interests. She made frequent use of the Habsburg principle of practical diplomacy: *Bella gerant alii, tu, felix Austria, nube*—"Others wage war, but you, happy Austria, marry." Her daughter, Marie Antoinette, was all but sold into marriage to Louis XVI. And she forced her son, Joseph II, still grieving over the death of his beloved wife, Isabella of Parma, into a second marriage with Maria Josepha of Bavaria, a woman he despised and did his best to ignore.

But for all Maria Theresa's flaws, she was sturdy, ambitious, musical, and highly intelligent. She outlawed torture, instituted public education, and gave birth to 16 children while ruling a vast empire. They just don't make empresses like her anymore.

Maria Theresa shares a huge and elaborately decorated double tomb with her husband, Franz Stefan of Lorraine, and it reminds me that not all Habsburg marriages were disasters. True, Franz had mistresses, but the marriage was reportedly happy. He dabbled in the sciences—he was keenly interested in alchemy—and collected coins, minerals, fossils. He also amassed a sizeable fortune with some astute investments, and more or less kept his nose out of politics. The couple is depicted reclining atop of their elaborate sarcophagus, facing one another as equals. Maria Theresa, however, holds in her left hand a mighty big sword.

In her guide to the Imperial Vaults, Gigi Beutler notes that Maria Theresa had planned ahead for her inevitable end, purchasing her wooden coffin, her modest black burial outfit and shoes years ahead of time. Not long before she died in 1780, the Empress paid a visit to the Kapuzinergruft to pray at Franz Stefan's tomb. She had by that time grown fat and had to use a specially devised lift in order to descend into the crypt. On her way out, one of the cables snapped and she was suspended, stuck, in midair. Although eventually rescued, she reportedly said, "That was a sign. The crypt doesn't want to let me go." And three weeks later, at age 63, she died.[133]

Schubert Died Here

Not long ago when I visited the small second-floor apartment on the Kettenbrückengasse where Franz Schubert died in 1828, I startled the poor ticket seller into stuffing her half-eaten sandwich into a drawer. Perhaps visiting the "death houses" (*Sterbehäuser*) of famous folk *is* scraping the bottom of the tourism barrel, even in Vienna, and thus my disruption of her quiet routine an anomaly.

The three tiny rooms were once the home of Schubert's older brother Ferdinand, and here the composer came to be looked after in his last illness. There is, at first glance, nothing remarkable to see, mainly displays of documents and musical manuscripts and portraits and prints that one expects to find in such memorial rooms, along with a writing desk and piano that may have belonged to Ferdinand. I need several minutes to focus, to find the *something* among the miscellany that will illuminate, reveal, speak to me in some small way of this Viennese genius's life, or of his death.

I find, in fact, many somethings: a lock of the composer's hair encased in a medallion, obtained during the first of two exhumations. Poor Schubert—he was most certainly not allowed to rest in peace. First, people clipped the hair off his corpse for souvenirs, then during the second exhumation, I read somewhere, measurements were taken of his skull, no doubt prompted by some nineteenth-century preoccupation with phrenology. God knows what else he might have endured.

I come across a municipal document, an inventory of his modest belongings at the time of his death: nine vests, one hat, five pairs of shoes, and so on. Nearby is an invitation to his funeral, the service to be held at the parish church in Margareten. A listening station offers a selection of recordings. One of Schubert's last *Lieder*, "Die Taubenpost"—"The Pigeon Post"—is gloriously sung by Bryn Terfel. I am satisfied.

Then, I spotted a book in a glass case, *Der Lotse* (*The Pilot*), by James Fenimore Cooper, and next to it a letter to his dear friend Franz Schober, the last Schubert wrote. I can make out only some of it, recognizing, however, Schubert's plea to his friend to send him some books:

> Be so kind as to come to my aid in this desperate situation with something to read. I have read Cooper's *The Last of the Mohicans*, *The Spy*, *The Pilot*, and *The Pioneers*. If you have anything else by him I beg you to leave it for me with Mrs. v. Bogner. My brother (who is the very epitome of conscientiousness), will bring it to me most conscientiously. Alternatively, another book. Your friend, Schubert.[134]

Oh, Mark Twain would have been sorely disappointed. He despised Cooper's tales. But nothing could please my patriotic heart more than the discovery that the boyish musical genius of Vienna loved these novels of the American frontier. And so do I. And I can think of no more poignant image to carry with me from Vienna than that of the young bespectacled composer, feverish and ill, escaping into the wilderness with Natty Bumppo.

HEAVENLY ORCHESTRA

I spotted on my map a patch of green in the eighteenth *Bezirk* called Schubertpark and set off to take a look, boarding the #5 *Bim* in my neighborhood and leisurely crisscrossing districts for a pleasant 20 minutes, a route that took me past the old Weinberger store on Wallensteinstrasse, now a Libro book shop. Walking up the Währingerstrasse the rest of the way, I passed two more of Wilhelm's shops, one now a Volksbank and the other a seedy-looking video store, before reaching my destination, a smallish patch of grass dotted with a few benches and a sandbox, a little untidy looking for a Vienna park, I thought, squeezed between apartment buildings and sitting atop an underground parking garage.

Nestled against a wall, blending into its shadow, I found the pair of lovely old monuments that once marked the graves of Schubert and Beethoven. These and an old gate facing Währingerstrasse are all that remain of the Biedermeier cemetery where the composers were originally buried. Ferdinand Schubert wrote to his father that Franz mumbled in his delirium what he understood to be a desire to be buried near Beethoven, who had died the year before. The two composers had met but once, and then only briefly, as Beethoven lay on his own deathbed in March 1827. Beethoven, however, had recently seen copies of some of Schubert's *Lieder,* including the *Schöne Müllerin* cycle and, according to one biographer, remarked, "Truly, there is in Schubert a divine spark!"[135]

Beethoven's funeral had been a huge affair, one of the city's greatest send-offs. Thousands, including Schubert, thronged the streets in a procession that began in the parish church of Alsergrund (now the ninth *Bezirk*) and ended in the Währing cemetery. Grillparzer wrote a graveside eulogy, delivered by Burgtheater actor Heinrich Anschütz:

He was an artist but also a human being, a human being in the highest sense. Because he secluded himself from the world, they called him hostile, and because he avoided emotion they called him unfeeling [. . .] He fled the world because in the entire realm of his loving nature, he found no weapon with which to defend himself. He withdrew from other people after he had given them everything and received nothing in return. He remained lonely because he found no soul mate, but up to his last moment he kept a human heart towards all people, a fatherly one to his relatives, and offered his goodness to the entire world. This is how he was, this is how he died, and this is how he will live for all times.[136]

The following year Schubert, too, was conducted to the same small cemetery, but in a more modest fashion. Vienna, it seems, had not yet taken full stock of the genius in its midst. Years later, Schubert's friend, the writer Eduard Bauernfeld, wrote a tribute tinged with bitterness:

A true Viennese and a genius!
The whole nation is amazed;
But the Viennese never realized it,
Except at third hand.[137]

In the 1880s, coffins were being dug up in Vienna's parish cemeteries and transferred to the new Central Cemetery— the *Zentralfriedhof*—in the suburb of Simmering. The main route out from the city center to the cemetery, the Simmeringerhauptstrasse, was frequently jammed with traffic from the processions for these reburials, which were well-attended by the public. As many have noted, the Viennese tend to appreciate their dead more than their living.

In 1888, Beethoven and Schubert, too, were moved from Währing to their new places among the "Graves of Honor," the *Ehrengraben*. They lie now in Section 32A, one of the most visited and touching sights in Vienna. Each time I stroll along the shady, lush green landscape of the cemetery to wander in and among the graves of so many illustrious dead, I am struck anew at how utterly different a place this is from the austere New England cemeteries where my own dead are buried, where plain slabs of granite reflect controlled passions and stoic temperaments. I marvel here at the architecture of grief, the monuments, lavish with sculpture and sentiment. Here is Brahms atop a pedestal, deep in thought, eyes downcast, hand to forehead, his handsome beard and flowing hair exquisitely rendered. Some admirer has placed a red votive before him, beside which lies a single red carnation, still fresh. There are flower tributes everywhere, tucked into cellophane cones and laid before favorites. There is Schubert's little Greek temple, where he is crowned with a laurel wreath by a comely goddess and attended by a cherub. Yellow roses, now wilting, have been placed into their marble hands. The base of Beethoven's obelisk is strewn with bouquets, and I discreetly stand back while two Japanese visitors set up a pretty camera pose, she placing her flowers just so.

All the Strausses are here, too, the father and his three musical sons. And Josef Lanner, and von Suppé, Gluck, Hugo Wolf, Karl Millöcker, Edmund Eysler, Eduard Kremser, Max Weinzierl, all keeping each other company, I would like to think, and arguing in true Viennese fashion about New School, polyphony, twelve-tone scales and such. Now, here's another fantasy: what if they joined up with their colleagues from 32C? That would bring Carl Michael Ziehrer, Alfred Grünfeld, Adolf Kirchl, Arnold Schönberg, Robert Stoltz, Ludwig Gruber, among others, to a most intriguing heavenly orchestra. But who, I wonder, will conduct this Parnassian array of musical egos? Perhaps Hans Swarowsky? Or, maybe they can persuade Willi Boskovsky to come over from 33G and lift his baton once more.

An Old Joke

There is an old joke about the Central Cemetery that I am sure originated with one of Vienna's coffeehouse wits. It goes something like this: "It's half the size of Zurich, but twice as lively." It may well be true that geographically speaking the cemetery may comprise a vastly smaller territory than Zurich, but it has, with over three million residents, nearly eight times the "population."

Beyond the First Gate

G. J.'s second cousin, Gaye Wiesner, Henry's daughter, once asked us to visit the gravesite of a Wiesner relative buried in the old Jewish section of the Zentralfriedhof. So we went to pay our respects and to bring back to Gaye some photographs of the stone, hopping off the #71 at the *erste Tor,* the first of the cemetery's five entrances along the Simmeringerhauptstrasse. Had we been visiting Beethoven or Schubert or Strauss, we would have gone to the *zweite Tor,* the second gate.

The Jewish cemetery that lies beyond the first gate is an altogether different realm than what one finds beyond the second, or third, or fourth, although the discrepancy may not be immediately apparent. The farther one wanders into the graveyard, the more visible the difference, the more it appears ravaged by time and neglect, the more plots one sees overgrown with weeds, dense with debris, the headstones toppled over or broken or just crumbling.

We followed Gaye's directions, but it was impossible to identify precisely the spot where her relative—very likely G. J.'s relative, too—is buried. The individual rows and plots were indistinguishable, and we got scratched and bruised trying to sort them out. We later related all this to Gretl, who knew very well the cemetery's condition. There was no money, she told us, "And who was there left in Vienna after the war to look after all those graves?" (Gretl herself is now buried next to her grandfather, Bernhard Weinberger, in the new Jewish section beyond gate four.)

When we last visited the old section, we looked for the grave of Leo Weinberger, Wilhelm's youngest brother, who was killed on the Russian front during World War I while serving in the Austrian Army. Gaye sent us a copy of a picture postcard she had found among her father's papers, a faded black-and-white photo of five young soldiers posing before a canvas backdrop painted with birch branches and foliage. Leo is seated on the left, a good looking and round shouldered fellow, his expression calm. A note is scribbled on the bottom—*Received card today and waiting longingly for the package*—and on the back, another message:

> Dearest Parents, I'm sending you an instant [schnell] photograph of me as a soldier. I'm looking good, no? Heartfelt greetings and kisses, Your son, Leo. Unfortunately, I couldn't come to Vienna.

G. J. remembered having found Leo's grave in the *Heldenfriedhof,* or Heroes Cemetery, some years ago, but now we couldn't find it and kept circling about. Two workmen greeted us as we passed. They stood before the open doors of their van, enjoying a smoke, tools scattered on the ground around a low white marble mound.

"Should the letters be black or gold," one of them asked. "Whaddya think?"

He had started to do the job in gold, so I said "Gold."

"I think so, too."

We chatted for awhile. They had been sent by the *Kultusgemeinde,* the Jewish community, to clean and reletter the twin marble stones dedicated in 1934 by the Association of Austrian Jewish Veterans of the Front to commemorate their fallen comrades whose remains still lie in foreign lands.

While we're talking we spot Leo Weinberger's stone—it is right in front of us. We had been looking for a low marker, not this handsome, shiny grey granite headstone. *Leo Weinberger,* it reads, *Unforgotten!* Eva later told us Gretl had ordered the new stone before she passed away. The old one, however, remains at the site, propped up against the new. It was proving difficult to read, so one of the workmen took a chisel from his van and scraped off the grime and lichens accumulated over nearly a century. It reads:

Here lies

The darling of his parents and siblings and of all people who knew him.

Leo Weinberger

The Headstones of St. Marx

There is one Vienna sight I dearly wish to see, the lilacs in bloom in the cemetery of St. Marx. Its grassy paths are lined with them, densely surrounding and often obscuring with their teardrop leaves the old Biedermeier gravestones abundant with angels and draped urns. I can imagine the fragrance, magnified a thousand-fold on a May afternoon. It is how heaven must smell.

Most people come to St. Marx to see where Mozart was tossed into a mass grave, and to take pictures of his simple monument, a broken column flanked by a single, boy-sized angel. But I come to read the old headstones of the widows and tradesmen and civil servants of nineteenth-century Vienna who are buried here. The inscriptions are as proud and sentimental as the stones themselves; in small ways, they offer glimpses into the city's social structure, reflect its respect for position and titles, and hint at family tragedies. Anna Kabelka, her headstone reveals, was a "head bookkeeper's widow"; Andreas Unger was a "guest house proprietor and homeowner" who lived at Landstrasse 339. Frau Elisabeth Mayer was the Leopoldstadt wife of a "citizen master chimney sweep," only 45 years old when she died and "deeply mourned by her husband and four children." Johann Franta died at age 46, a "citizen canal cleaner" buried next to his son, who died three years later at age 19. My "citizen" does not quite convey the meaning of *bürgerlich,* that ubiquitous modifier connoting tax-paying, middle-class citizenship. Herr Alois Ferstler, who died September 18, 1863, was not simply a coffeehouse proprietor, but a *bürgerlicher Kaffeehaus-Inhaber,* which suggests a man of at least modest estate.

There is poetry, too, inscribed on these stones. On the grave of a mother and son, Frau Anna Gerber (grocer's wife) and Josef Lorenz Gerber (shop clerk), who died three months apart in 1858, I read:

> Rest softly, the grief of life
> No longer presses on your noble heart;
> The slumber of the grave embraces you,
> With me alone remains the pain.

I come across another, the grave of Frau Theresia Arco, formerly Lauterbach, wife of a royal and imperial civil servant, citizen, and property owner, who was herself an assistant in the Noblewomen's Association and a property owner; in other words, a woman of substance.

> Full of melancholy I saw you sink,
> And always I will always think of you,
> Until the time of our resurrection
> When we will see one another again and
> forever.
> Still, what you lovingly accomplished here,
> Will never sink into dark night,
> For blessed will it beget blessing
> And raise itself up to God's throne.

Oh wanderer, stay here a moment and recite for her an Our Father.

That is a plea this wanderer cannot ignore, although she stumbles over the barely remembered words.

OUTLIVED

Ludwig and G. J. are not the only ones haunted by the dead in Vienna. Returning here I am always reminded of how in early 1990, the phone rang too loudly in our tiny room in a hotel on the Krugerstrasse. It was my mother, making an unprecedented overseas call. "It's Daddy," she said.

My father, Paul Knight, lay dying in Cape Cod Hospital, his poor damaged heart finally giving out, and I was in Vienna with a date that evening to meet Gretl for dinner and tickets to the Volksoper to see Strauss's *Eine Nacht in Venedig,* "A Night in Venice." G. J. escorted Gretl to the theater after a cheerless dinner while I stumbled off to the hotel to pack. I wanted desperately to see my father, to whisper to *him* my love and my thanks and my goodbye, and not to the drab walls of a rented room 5,000 miles away. By the time we landed in New York, however, he had passed. He couldn't wait, and it hurt for a long, long time that I hadn't been where I belonged, at his bedside with my mother and brothers and sisters, instead of in Vienna. Vienna. . . . I suddenly hated the place.

When we went back later that year, my resentment lingered. I refused to stay in our usual hotel, felt uneasy, jumpy. I kept waiting for the phone to ring. And it did, eight years later. This time the call was from my brother, John. Mother had had a heart attack, not a devastating one, but serious enough and wholly unexpected. Mother was, and remains, a sturdy woman who has brooked little illness throughout her now 81 years. We flew home and instead of taking leisurely strolls through the Volksgarten or *Jause* with Gretl and Eva at the Café Europa, I went to Cape Cod and rode my bicycle to the post office to fetch the mail and tried to persuade Mother to eat frozen yogurt instead of ice cream sundaes with extra whipped cream.

I was home in Connecticut when the most recent family catastrophe struck, home barely two weeks after my June trip to Vienna. My sister Marianne, our Mikey, did not survive the heart attack that struck her early one morning. True, she

had never had our mother's robust constitution, but her relative youth—she was 54—should have made up for that, as
well as her generous nature, her wicked sense of humor, and a
thousand other things that should, *should,* have kept her alive.
But they did not, and I am off soon again to Vienna, which
seems now my own private city of mourning.

11 Vienna Voices

A Gnädige Frau

In Vienna I have occasionally been addressed as *gnädige Frau:* merciful lady, gracious lady, dear lady. The very sound of the phrase pleases me and its old fashioned courtesy warms me on a cold evening, at least a little. I am grateful for each *gnädige Frau* I receive because, I suppose, it signifies the Vienna I wish to believe in, engages my illusions and makes the Vienna of my dreams a real place for a few seconds.

It strikes me more and more, however, that the honorific is evidence I am aging, an acknowledgment of my substance. I am beginning to look the part—a middle-aged, rather serious looking woman with horn rimmed glasses one might size up as likely to be responsive to compliments. Is there something the matter with me that I don't mind?

At the Griechenbeisl, which claims to be the oldest restaurant in Vienna and where Wilhelm, Ludwig tells me, dined occasionally, the city's vaunted charm is still embodied in the solicitous and, it must be noted, tidy waiters. They dress in handsome *Trachten* and speak English perfectly well, most of them, but I have listened—eavesdropped—and not once have I heard one address an English-speaking woman as "dear lady." One winter evening, when I dined there alone and to my immense satisfaction managed the comings and goings and the entire meal completely *auf deutsch,* I collected five *gnädige Fraus.* Every passing male, it seemed, wished me, "*Mahlzeit, gnädige Frau.*"

Needless to say, I required no dessert.

INVISIBLE

I am alone in Vienna and it is winter, so I take Peter Altenberg's advice and go *in's Caféhaus* to seek refuge and find peace, refreshment, a comforting warmth. Instead, I discover my invisibility. Is it because I come in from the icy cold in a big heavy coat that swallows me up? Or do I look too much the lost tourist and therefore inspire no concern as I wait at this table—and wait and wait—for a *heisse Schokolade,* hot chocolate, which I desperately need?

This café in the upscale Ringstrasse Gallerie is not one of my usual haunts and not even Viennese but Belgian, but here it is and the hot chocolate is sure to be divine, and I will order it with extra *Schlag,* whipped cream. I take up residence at a tiny table mall side, just outside the café door. The Fräulein looks out and sees me. I smile. She busies herself inside.

In ten minutes I tire of waiting and bundle up for the short walk around the corner to the café at the Hotel Bristol. Not one of my usual places, either, but it's that or the Starbucks across the street and I cannot bring myself to patronize Starbucks while I am in Vienna. That would be heresy, wouldn't it, in a city full of quirky, smoky, legendary coffeehouses? There is a free table at the Bristol, a little too conspicuous and noisy for my taste, but all the quiet corners are occupied. The counterman sees me but does not break off his conversation with the two waiters to tell them they have a customer. A few minutes later the two turn and walk past me. I gesture to one, who says, *Yes?* Not, *May I take your order?* or, heaven forbid, *Grüss Gott, gnädige Frau, what may I get for you?* Just, *Ja?* which sounds to me like *Whaddayawant?* My hot chocolate does not satisfy, but perhaps nothing tastes good when one is feeling invisible.

Three hours later it is lunch time and I am cold again from the unrelenting Arctic blasts beating the city and from being invisible. I am spiritually at low ebb, for I am in Vienna and it is winter and I am cold and I am without G. J. And now I am hungry. I go to the Café Griensteidl, which *is* one of my favorite cafés, not least for its nonsmoking section and its robust *Gulaschsuppe* that makes my tongue tingle from the paprika. I will listen to the hum of voices and the rattling of the newspaper pages, and the electronic songs of the *Handys* that no one in this city ever turns off except in the theatres and concert halls, and feel not quite so alone in Vienna. My glasses fog up as I enter, and I stumble a little trying to see, and I see that there are no free tables in the nonsmoking section. I find a spot on the smoking side, take off my coat, try to defog my glasses, and sit down. I wait. But I am again invisible, for the *Kellner* in his black suit and bow tie pays me no heed, while he delivers soup and coffee and cheese strudel to people all around me, even to the American who sits next to me reading *The Herald Tribune*. His German is worse than mine, I can hear that, but he gets his soup while I must wait for the *Kellner* to acknowledge my existence. He prefers, however, to banter with his colleagues, to avoid my glances and ignore my gestures, to settle the bill with the lady in the mink hat.

I think of Stephen Crane: "A Man Said to the Universe / 'Sir, I exist.'"

"*Herr Ober, die Menükarte. Bitte!*"

Herr Ober, who is not really the head waiter—but this is a useful little Viennese fiction—looks startled, as if he had heard a voice from the grave. The invisible woman speaks. The soup arrives quickly, hot and savory.

LISTENING FOR SILVIA

Patrick Wertheimer is not the only Viennese twenty-something second-cousin-once-removed of G. J.'s. Among his maternal relatives is Silvia Mieses, whom, oddly enough, we have not yet met, although we visit her parents, Louis and Marion, whenever we are in Vienna. As it happens—and I don't know why I still find this fact remarkable—our relatives on both sides, Weinberger and Mieses, are acquainted. Silvia attended the Lycée Française along with Patrick, although she was ahead of him by two or three years. And the tiny elderly lady I met at Eva's one Rosh Hashanah—"the little Lisl," Eva calls her—was Gretl's dearest friend and Silvia's great-aunt. Vienna's small Jewish community is intertwined in such ways.

When I was in Vienna last fall, it seemed everyone I met knew Silvia or, rather, had heard her read the news on ORF, Österreichischer Rundfunk, the Austrian equivalent of the BBC. I kept the radio in our apartment tuned to her station, 99.9 FM, Hitradio Ö3, but never seemed to catch her hourly news updates. Sometimes, though, I got the feeling that I had just missed her. One of Eva's friend's said one evening when the subject came up, "Oh, Silvia Mieses. I heard her just this afternoon when I had the radio on in my kitchen." Her voice seems tantalizingly and frustratingly just out of hearing.

People have asked Louis and Marion how she got such a plum job. They don't believe she was hired on merit alone and the very question, naturally, rankles.

"She applied and was accepted," Louis says. "She is a smart girl. But here they think you can only have such a job if you know somebody." *Protektion.*

Since I discovered I can get Ö3 here in Connecticut over the Internet, I continue to listen for Silvia. A couple of clicks and live from Vienna come the latest *Schlager*—hits—the same ones, more or less, as here in the States. Whenever I remember, or feel that strange sort of longing for Vienna, I tune in, but on Ö3 am treated not to Strauss, Schubert, Schrammel, or even the Stoakogler Trio, but to Dido, Outkast, and Nelly Furtado. I try to make out the traffic and weather reports, feel a little thrill at hearing the Viennese accents of the DJs, and on the hour strain to catch the newsreader's name.

So, I'm listening, Silvia. What news from Vienna?

THE PUMMERIN

It is 6 p.m. in Connecticut on December 31—midnight in Vienna. A new year begins in the City of Dreams, and I attend its birth via the Internet. The ORF announcer counts down the seconds: *zehn, neun, acht, sieben.* . . . There is a second of silence, then commences the ringing of the Pummerin, the great bell of St. Stephen's cathedral. Twelve times it is struck, sounds that one imagines can be heard around the world even without the benefit of radio broadcast, sounds to mark the beginning of time or its end, solemn and sonorous.

The Pummerin is one of several legacies of the 1683 Turkish siege of Vienna. Coffee, I might add, is another, for the Turks left behind sacks and sacks of beans which, legend has it, came into the possession of an enterprising citizen who opened the city's first coffeehouse. But that is another story. The Turks also left behind a sizeable number of cannon, and the original Pummerin was cast from these in 1711. It weighed some 10.2 tons, and was dragged from a foundry in Leopoldstadt through the streets of the *innere Stadt,* a task that required some 200 men (although one source puts the number at 400) and the reinforcement of cellars and vaults beneath the streets of the procession route. The bell was eventually hoisted into the cathedral's south tower, where it rested on two mighty oak beams. It was not rung, however, until several weeks later, at the coronation of Karl VI.

For nearly all of its 234 years, until 1945, the Pummerin marked only Vienna's holiest days, while the Dom's smaller bells rang daily to mark devotional—and sometimes public—duties. The nineteenth-century bell called the "Feuering" was used as a fire alarm; an older and smaller one announced closing time of the local pubs. That one was known as the "Bieringerin," the beer bell.

In the last weeks of the Second World War, a fire in the cathedral brought down the south tower and the Pummerin. Although many assume the cathedral was bombed, it did not take a direct hit; its roof, however, was pierced by the bullets of the departing Reich soldiers as the Russian troops approached the inner city. Shops surrounding the Dom fell prey to looters, who are believed to have set fires to cover their crime. Sparks and flames from nearby buildings were probably sucked into the cathedral's cool interior through the holes in the roof, and so the fire began inside and spread to the south tower, whose old wooden trusses collapsed. The Pummerin was smashed to pieces.

Out of its shards a new bell was cast in 1952, which in 1957 was installed in the north tower. It bears the inscription:

> Cast was I from the booty of the Turks when the city, after almost total exhaustion, overcame the foreign power and rejoiced. 1711.
>
> Burst apart did I in the white heat of the conflagration. I fell from the devastated tower as the city moaned under the burdens of war and fear. 1945.[138]

On New Year's Eve, as the final strike of the Pummerin fades, the hauntingly familiar opening bars of "The Blue Danube Waltz" begin. I am 5,000 miles away, but these sounds of Vienna are transporting. I wish I were there, shouting *Prosit Neujahr* with the crowd gathered on the Stephansplatz, the old stones of the cathedral all lit up and golden. How nice it would be to take G. J.'s arm and head to some warm *Beisl* for a glass of champagne with which to toast the new year.

Happy Is She . . .

Before the Pummerin tolls on New Year's Eve, another venerable tradition plays out in Vienna. The city's two opera houses, the Staatsoper and Volksoper, stage Johann Strauss, Jr.'s *Die Fledermaus*. What could be more appropriate on the one evening of the year, when the entire world is tipsy anyway, than journeying back through this extravagantly melodic and narratively convoluted operetta to a late nineteenth-century Europe of elegant surfaces and naughty hypocrisies? The story has everything: revenge, infidelity, mistaken identity, tax evasion, a couple of dishy housemaids, a masked mystery woman, and a drunken jailor named Frosch ("Frog"). It hardly matters, though, whether or not one can follow the plot. Just listen.

Strauss's score is better than a bottle of champagne for raising the spirits and putting a happy sheen on the world, no matter what miserable state it is in. Its most famous lyric, *"Glücklich ist, wer vergisst, was nicht mehr zu ändern ist"*—"Happy is he who forgets what can no longer be changed"—has become a motto of the Strauss era, and of the city's mythological hedonism.

An odd sort of collision, or perhaps the correct word is collusion, of source material resulted in Strauss's operetta masterpiece and the lyric that put a gloss on a time and a place. Strauss's collaborators, Richard Genée and Karl Haffner, borrowed the book from the Meilhac and Halévy 1872 comedy *Le Réveillon* or *Christmas Eve*. Meilhac and Halévy had based their story on Roderich Benedix's *Das Gefängnis* or *The Prison,* which means that a German play was transformed into a French farce and then back into a German-language comedy set to Viennese music, which debuted on an Easter Sunday but is now performed mainly on New Year's Eve.[139]

But Genée and Haffner probably borrowed the *carpe diem* sentiment ("*Glücklich ist, wer vergisst . . .*") from Schopenhauer's recently published and popular translation into German of *Oracolo Manual* (*The Practical Art of Wisdom*), written by a seventeenth-century Spanish monk, Baltasar Gracián.[140] Gracián, in turn, probably borrowed it from Seneca. So much for a purely "Viennese" philosophy.

However it ended up in a Strauss operetta, the Viennese and much of the rest of the world continue to think that forgetting what cannot be changed is not an entirely unworthy way to begin a new year.

L'Shana Tovah

Eva Wertheimer's oldest friend, Ivi Adler, stands at the head of her table and begins the New Year's blessing: *Baruhk atah Adonai, Elohaynu, melekh ha-olam* (*Blessed are You, Lord, our G-d, king of the universe*). Rich, reverent, unwavering, his voice earns a place among so many others in my memories of Vienna, the voice of ancient ritual, the voice of a still vital Jewish life in this city. Ivi takes a slice of apple from a bowl and dips it in honey: *Blessed are you, Lord, our G-d, king of the universe who creates the fruit of the tree.* The apples are handed around and those gathered at Eva's table share a common hope for a sweet new year.

This is Eva's big night, a celebration she hosts every autumn for a dozen or more close friends and family. She offers up a feast, one that has been in the making for days, if not weeks. It is impossible not to feel loved, and just as impossible to believe that she managed it all from her tiny disaster of a kitchen. With her usual aplomb, she waves away all expressions of awe.

"I am very organized, you know," she says. "But, really, it is not at all difficult. I had time even to meet my girlfriend for coffee this afternoon."

She cannot, however, entirely hide the tiredness in her eyes.

Eva's modest living room is dominated this evening by a long table covered in white cloth and dotted with pomegranates, whose copious seeds are a reminder of the good deeds of which we are all capable. She has brought out her best Rosenthal china and gaudy, gem-colored Bohemian crystal goblets. She ladles the soup from a large tureen: full flavored beef broth—*Rindsuppe*—thick with tiny strands of noodles, a meal unto itself. Next, we pass around the starters: glistening gefilte fish, a mound of chopped liver, chunky egg salad, taboule fragrant with parsley, fresh spinach salad, beet salad enlivened with horseradish. I sample a bit of everything, resisting Pauli's orders to take more and Eva's exhortations to fill my plate.

The German language swirls around me, a little island onto myself as a Gentile and as an English speaker. For the thousandth time I feel the isolation, the frustration, of the language barrier. I am certainly not ignored. Ivi's daughter, Tanya, tells me about her studies at the university. Eva's friend Evelyn chats about her visits to Chicago and California. But I long to join the conversations I cannot take part in, the ones I catch in fragments, talk of politics, the war in Iraq, Israel. I want to find out things, but cannot summon up either the language or the courage. How does it feel to be a Jew, today, Rosh Hashanah, in *this* city, *this* Vienna?

Are there ghosts at this feast?

But, no, even if I could manage it, this is not the occasion. It may be the season of reflection, but tonight's celebration is about a new beginning. Better, I realize, to enjoy the company, the festive mood, and *more* food. Eva brings forth the beef roulade, veal schnitzel, spiced chicken legs, and big serving dishes overflowing with noodles and rice.

"Eva, so little to eat?" asks Ivi.

And still more. It is close to midnight and we have been at the table for three hours, and now it is time for spice cake, and a compote laced with cinnamon, and the best fruitcake I have ever tasted. The room is smoky and the windows are open. Patrick and his friends have already left the table to look up the soccer results on the Internet and to watch Ali G. on MTV. Tomorrow is a work day and reluctantly old friends rise and prepare to leave.

"*L'shana Tovah,*" someone says, and the rest join in. Happy, sweet, new year.

Nusskipferln

My mother recently came across "Choice Recipes," an old stained booklet published in 1932 by the Ladies' Aid Society of the North Granby Congregational Church. It contains my grandmother Maisie's gingerbread recipe. Reading it is like hearing her voice, which I recall only faintly, for it is the kind of recipe women exchange over coffee, approximate, rather than exact: "Take a good cup of this, and then mix in a handful of that, and bake in a hot oven til it's done."

Such legacies are precious, though, and I treasure not only Maisie's recipe but also the one left to me by my mother-in-law, Jula. She was not a great cook, which she unabashedly admitted. Her creative talents lay elsewhere. She sewed beautifully and made most of her own clothes; she could knit, crochet, embroider, and in her younger days even made hats. If most of her cooking was, shall we say, uninspired, she did from time to time serve up a very good *Gulasch* and a tasty "meatloaf surprise" (the surprise was a hot dog stuffed in the center).

She passed along to me her recipe for *Nusskipferln,* nut crescents, a lovely buttery Viennese cookie. She scribbled it on a piece of notepaper, not elegantly, but in that characteristically European cursive, round fat letters lavish with curlicues. Every December I bake a batch and thus again hear her soft Viennese accents:

> Jeel: you take the Butter and the Sugar and cream them. Then you mix in the Wanilla and the Flower and the Nüsse. Take a little bit of the Dough and make into lit-tle Balls and then make them into Kipferln, little horns. Bake them for about 15 minutes, nicht? And when you take them from the Offen, sprinkle the powered Sugar on them. While they are hot. Fairy eesee, Jeel.

"I Hope to End my Life in Freedom"

When Sigmund Freud was finally persuaded to flee Vienna in June 1938, he was 82 and frail. He was, he thought, too old for exile, but a visit from the Gestapo to Berggasse 19 and the daylong detention of his daughter, Anna, convinced him of its necessity. With the help of influential friends, he and his family made the journey to England.

Freud's voice in exile can still be heard, thanks to an audio clip posted to the Freud Museum's website. In the month following his arrival in London, he recorded a statement for the BBC, sounding every bit the cliché of an old Viennese professor accustomed to lecturing. He reads not haltingly but deliberately, and slurs some words, which I don't doubt is the result of the many treatments he underwent for oral cancer, rather than a lack of English proficiency. Indeed, there is something musical about his English, its cadence lifting syllables out of their usual rhythm. He hits the minor notes, a true Vienna voice, and something like a waltz.

Yet, I hear assertiveness, defiance, even, as he summarizes in the broadest of outlines the substance of his career and achievements. And then, in an unexpected shift into German, he makes the most plaintive of statements:

> I started my professional activity as a neurologist trying to bring the relief to my neurotic patients. Under the influence of an older friend and by my own efforts I discovered some important new facts about the unconscious excitements of life and the role of the sexual urges and so on. Out of these findings there grew a new science, psychoanalysis, a part of psychology and a new method of treatment of the neurosis. I had to pay heavily for this bit of good luck. People did not believe in my facts and thought my theories unsavory. Resistance was strong and unrelenting. In the end, I succeeded in acquiring pupils and building up an international psychoanalytic association. But the struggle is not yet over.
>
> *Im Alter von 82 Jahren verliess ich infolge der deutschen Invasion mein Heim in Wien und kam nach England wo ich mein Leben in Freiheit zu enden hoffe.*
>
> [At the age of 82 I left my home in Vienna as a result of the German invasion and came to England where I hope to end my life in freedom.]
>
> *My name? Is Sigmund Freud.*[141]

"A Trauma of My Generation"

I do not think that I belong to Austria. I live here, and I cannot change this anymore, but that's all! I would not regard Vienna as "my home." I do not feel uncomfortable to live here; nobody does or says anything to me, but the Austrian population—in my opinion—is not "honest." If they say Austria is not an antisemitic country, it's not true (on the other hand, can you show me a country where there is not antisemitism?). Only, Austria is different; the Austrians were guilty of what happened during the Nazi era, only they don't admit it, they think that they have done nothing wrong and that they were victims themselves and this is not true. They were welcoming Hitler like a Messias, if I may use this word in connection with Hitler at all, and I cannot forget it. I have seen the masses shouting and—it may sound unrealistic—but the older I get the more I can hear them shouting and welcoming this man. I believe it must be a trauma of my generation (the last one which survived the Holocaust) that with increasing age we visualize things of the past more vividly. It is a fact that I think *now* more about all the terrible things which happened, than I did when I was young.

Gretl Fischer Frisch, Letter, September 1992

A Poem in a Window

On a Sunday morning stroll last autumn, G. J. and I spotted a poem, signed only "mf," pasted to a ground floor window in the ninth Bezirk:

Ich bin nicht schuld.
Ich kann mich nicht erinnern
Ich bin zu spät geboren.

[I am not guilty.
I cannot remember
I was born too late.]

Gerade deshalb will ich nie vergessen,
was ich—Gnade des Schicksales—
nicht miterleben musste!

[For this very reason I will not forget
What I—by the grace of destiny—
Did not myself witness.]

THE CITY OF SONG

My friend Jane Hikel and I stopped at the Café Schwarzenberg for a bite to eat before our concert at the Musikverein. I had been boycotting the place since G. J. injured himself there the year before. He tripped on a piece of loose carpet, tore his pant leg and scraped his knee. He wasn't seriously hurt, but his poor knee looked a bloody mess and he was a little shaken. To our amazement, no Herr Ober, no waiter, no bus boy, no patron offered him a hand up off the floor. I threw some money on the table and led him limping out of the place to the trolley, and have harbored unkind thoughts about the establishment ever since.

Jane and I were in a bit of a hurry, though, and the Schwarzenberg lies only a short distance from the concert hall. Expedience overruled resentment. I wanted, perhaps, to kiss and make up anyway, because this is a fine old coffeehouse, the oldest remaining on the Ringstrasse, and had been frequented by all the Weinbergers and Wiesners before the *Anschluss*.

This evening a performance was under way in the back of the room. Standing before the piano an old lady sang in a thin and wavery soprano. Jane and I were transfixed for a time by the picture she formed in the uneven light. While mostly obscured by shadow, her face was lighted, rendered an ethereal white. A brown hat sat primly on her wispy grey hair. She sang slowly some sweetly sad *Wiener Lied,* a song of the city.

Later, Jane said, "I think she was singing for her supper. Remember? The waiter brought her a plate of food."

That could be. Maybe she was once a star of the Volksoper who had fallen into a pathetic old age. Or maybe she was just a slightly dotty old lady who liked to sing and came into the café once a week for a meal and a song. She didn't look entirely tragic. She might have had a million euros' worth of gold bullion stashed under her mattress, or an original Schiele hanging in her dining room. Whatever the case, she was accorded her dignity, and I don't doubt even a *gnädige Frau,* at the Schwarzenberg and that redeemed the place in my eyes. I don't know that G. J. will be so forgiving, however.

Half an hour later, Jane and I took our seats at the Golden Hall of the Musikverein, one of the most illustrious concert halls in the world. We were surrounded by other foreign tourists, awaiting the music of classical Vienna, an all-Mozart sampler performed by the Wiener Mozart Orchester, and in fine fashion, by musicians in periwigs and jewel-toned frock coats and gowns. But those gorgeous arias from *Le Nozze di Figaro, Don Giovanni, Die Zauberflöte,* and *Die Entführung aus dem Serail,* those movements from *Eine kleine Nachtmusik* and the Symphony no. 40 did not entirely drown out that old, quivery voice from the café. Surely, she was still singing, and surely she was singing this: "*Wien, Wien nur du allein, sollst stets die Stadt meiner Träume sein.*" "Vienna, only you alone will always be the city of my dreams."

Madam Conductor, Virtually

Tuning in to the Viennese temperament: the eternal tuning of an unequal-tempered orchestra.

Karl Kraus, *Dicta and Contradicta*[142] (1923)

One afternoon at Vienna's Haus der Musik, a truly extraordinary museum devoted both to the science of sound and to the city's culture of music, I realized a girlhood fantasy. Standing before a large screen projection of the august Vienna Philharmonic orchestra, its members in black tie, poised and ready to play, I (in my black and white Keds) picked up the baton and signaled my selection of music. For my conducting debut, there was but one choice. Another signal from me—I had merely to raise my baton—and the orchestra began to play "The Blue Danube Waltz."

Almost immediately I felt the full weight of responsibility for keeping the tempo, for raising and lowering that suddenly heavy baton in some semblance of regular motion. Why was it so difficult? True, I hadn't "conducted" much after the age of 15 (having switched to air guitar) and so was sadly out of practice, but this was nearly impossible to manage. I heard the music speed up, and then slow down, until it finally came to a crashing halt. An irate concertmaster faced me from the screen, and delivered a blistering critique:

> Warum sagt niemand was? Das is ja entsetzlich, man kann nicht so spielen! Sagen Sie, haben Sie das Stück denn nie gehört?
>
> (Why does no one say anything? This is dreadful, one cannot play like this! Say, have you never heard this piece before?)

Utterly humiliated, I stepped away, out of the path of a ten-year-old awaiting his turn, perhaps to play out his own fantasy. Energetically but erratically he slashed the air with the baton to the opening bars of *Radetzky March,* urging the orchestra to play at breakneck speed. The concertmaster implored, *"Aber bitte, so nicht! Entscheiden Sie sich für irgendein Tempo und dabei bleiben Sie!"* ("Please, not like that! Decide on a tempo and stay with it!") At least I had that satisfaction, not to be shown up by a child.

I wandered away from the Virtual Conductor installation, but was sorely tempted to go back, to have another go, this time to take firm command of the orchestra. I would close my eyes and lose myself in the music, my arms rising and falling with it in perfect accord, just as they did all those years ago. I would remember what it was to be 13 again and unafraid to be myself—at least in private. And should I fail, should I displease that exacting, grumpy old Viennese concertmaster—"Have you even heard this piece before?!"—I would have my own ready reply:

> Aber, ja, mein Herr. I have indeed heard your waltz, moved to its infectious, spinning rhythms, and taken to my heart its joyful, wistful sounds. Yes. For how exquisite is the music of your Vienna. And how unsettling its voices.

Notes

[1] These statistics come from various sources: William Perl, *Operation Action* (New York: Ungar, 1983) 19; "Time Line of the History of the Jews of Vienna," 2 July 2003 <http://www. virtualvienna.net>; and "The Database of Jewish Communities: Vienna," 2 July 2003 <http://www.bh.org.il>.

[2] Alfred Granger, *The Spirit of Vienna* (New York: McBride & Co., 1935) 214–15.

[3] Georg Kreisler, "Wien ohne Wiener," *Wien im Gedicht*, ed. Hertha Kratzer (Vienna: öbv&hpt Verlag, 2001) 70–1. Trans. G. J. Weinberger.

[4] Karl Kraus, *Half-Truths and One-and-a-Half Truths*, ed. and trans. Harry Zohn (Manchester, UK: Carcanet Press, 1986) 32.

[5] Dr. J. Alexander Mahan, *Famous Women of Vienna* (Vienna: Halm and Goldmann, 1930) 284.

[6] "Waluliso." *aeiou Encyclopedia*, 11 Nov. 2003 <http://www. aeiou.at>.

[7] Joseph Roth, *The Radetzky March*, trans. Joachim Neugroschel (Woodstock, NY: The Overlook Press, 1995) 69–70.

[8] Lady Mary Wortley Montagu, *Letters from the Levant during the Embassy to Constantinople: 1716–18*. (1838; New York: Arno Press, 1971) 37–38.

[9] Francis Russell, *The World of Dürer: 1471–1528* (New York: Time, Inc., 1967) 119.

[10] Eva Hoffman, "The New Nomads," *Yale Review* 86.4 (1998): 48.

[11] Ernst Waldinger, "Ich bin ein Sohn der deutschen Sprache," *Austria in Poetry and History*, ed. Frederick Ungar (New York: Ungar, 1984) 318. Trans. G. J. Weinberger.

[12] Wolfgang A. Mozart, "To his sister, in Salzburg (postscript)," *Mozart's Letters, Mozart's Life*, ed. and trans. Robert Spaethling (New York: Norton, 2000) 45.

[13] Ruth Kluger, *Still Alive: A Holocaust Girlhood Remembered* (New York: The Feminist Press, 2001) 200.

[14] Mark Twain, "The Awful German Language," *Essays and Sketches of Mark Twain*, ed. Stuart Miller (New York: Barnes & Noble, 1995) 280.

[15] Twain, "The Awful German Language," 277.

[16] Carl Dolmetsch, *Our Famous Guest: Mark Twain in Vienna* (Athens: U Georgia P, 1992) 316–17.

[17] Dolmetsch, 47–48.

[18] Karl Kraus, *Half-Truths and One-and-a-Half Truths* 69.

[19] Jonathan McVity, "The Twist: *Dicta and Contradicta* in Context," Karl Kraus, *Dicta and Contradicta,* ed. and trans. Jonathan McVity (Urbana: U Chicago P, 2001) 130.

[20] William M. Johnston, *The Austrian Mind: An Intellectual and Social History, 1848–1938* (Berkeley: U California Press) 1972.

[21] Kraus, *Dicta and Contradicta* 82.

[22] Edward Timms, *Karl Kraus: Apocalyptic Satirist* (New Haven: Yale UP, 1986) 88.

[23] Kraus, *Half-Truths and One-and-a-Half Truths* 65–8.

[24] Mark Twain, "Stirring Times in Austria," *The Man That Corrupted Hadleyburg and Other Stories and Essays* (New York: Oxford UP, 1996).

[25] Hermann Hakel, ed. *Wien von A—Z* (Vienna: Wiener Verlag, 1953) 265. This and subsequent citations from *Wien von A-Z* are reprinted with the kind permission of the IG Autorinnen Autoren/Wien.

[26] "One Hundred Years of Vienna Public Transport," *Enjoy: Wilkommen in Wien* September, 2003: 6.

[27] Verhehrsverbund Ost-Region, Verkehrslinienplan *Wien 2003.*

[28] Patrick Leigh Fermor, *A Time for Gifts* (London and New York: Penguin, 1977) 212.

[29] Kaiser Franz Joseph I, "Es werde die Ringstrasse," *Trau, Schau, Wien,* ed. Paul W. Stix and Erik G. Wickenburg (Vienna: Zsolnay, 1973) 62–3.

[30] William M. Johnston, *Vienna, Vienna: The Golden Age, 1815–1914* (Milan: Mondadori Editore, 1980) 6.

[31] Gottfried Heindl, ed. *Leg' mich zu Füssen Majestät* (Vienna: Neff, 1985) 142.

[32] Ferdinand von Saar, "Zweite wiener Elegie," *Austria in Poetry and History,* ed. Frederick Ungar (New York: Ungar, 1984) 188. Trans. G. J. Weinberger.

[33] Astrid Weigelt, "Schaffnerlos: Sieben Jahre ist sie jetzt her, die Fahrt des letzten Schaffners in Wien," *Vor Magazin.* 17 (2003): 28–29.

[34] Oskar Jan Tauschinski, *Wien von A–Z* 269.

[35] "Horror tram accident leaves man dead," English edition, 7 Aug. 2002 <http://diepresse.com>.

[36] "The Shore Line Trolley Museum," 27 Oct. 2003 <http://www.bera.org>.

[37] Arthur Schnitzler, *Aphorismen und Betrachtungen* (Frankfurt a/M: S. Fischer, 1983) Trans. G. J. Weinberger.

[38] Stefan Zweig, *The World of Yesterday* (Lincoln, NE: U of Nebraska P, 1964) 6. Used by permission of Viking Penguin, a division of Penguin Group (USA) Inc.

[39] Favoritenstrasse 98, Ludwig insists, was the first retail store Wilhelm established and remained the flagship store until 1938. However, records suggest there may have been modest predecessors, including one at Favoritenstrasse 78.

[40] Franz Kafka, "Letter to His Father," *Dearest Father: Stories and Other Writings,* ed. Max Brod, trans. Ernst Kaiser and Eithne Wilkins (New York: Schocken, 1954) 150–51. Used by permission of Schocken Books, a division of Random House, Inc.

[41] Ernst Wiesner, however, left the family firm in 1937 to seek employment elsewhere, judging there was no real future for him in it, not with Ludwig as heir apparent.

[42] The President of the Austrian Republic at that time was Dr. Michael Hainisch.

[43] Paul Hofmann, *The Viennese: Splendor, Twilight, and Exile* (New York: Anchor, 1988) 26–27.

[44] Göding is the German name for Hodonin, the small Moravian city to which Mikulschitz, Wilhelm's birthplace, was administratively attached.

[45] Ludwig can provide no other information. Research has yielded a possibility, an artist who specialized in bronzes by the name of Felix Weiss, born 1908 in Vienna. There is, however, no way to confirm his acquaintance with Wilhelm Weinberger.

[46] Ernst Lothar, *The Door Opens* (New York: Doubleday, 1945) 16.

47 In the hierarchy of Viennese schools, the *Realschule* was a step below the *Gymnasium*. According to Arthur J. May's *Vienna in the Age of Franz Josef* (Norman: U Oklahoma P, 1966), "Newer secondary schools, *Realschulen,* preparing youths for technological and commercial colleges, never attained the prestige of the *Gymnasia,* but both were attended largely by children of well-to-do homes." 47.

48 Zweig, *The World of Yesterday* 36–37.

49 "Spunda, Franz," *aeiou Encyclopedia,* 11 Nov. 2003 <http://www.aeiou.at>.

50 "Hohlbaum, Robert," *aeiou Encyclopedia,* 11 Nov. 2003 <http://www.aeiou.at>.

51 "Hans Holzer—Psychic Investigator." 29 Mar. 2004 <http://groups-beta.google.com/group/ alt.religion.clue>.

52 "Hans Holzer—Psychic Investigator."

53 "Franz Spunda: Der magische Dichter," 7 July 2002 <http://home.t-online.de/home/ turbund/spnd.htm>.

54 "Franz Spunda: Der magische Dichter."

55 "NS-Literatur," 5 Apr. 2004 <http://www.dhm.de/lemo/html/nazi/kunst/nsliteratur>.

56 Robert Hohlbaum, "*Wie ich zu Grillparzer kam . . .* ," *Völkischer Beobachter* 22 Mar. 1938: 11.

57 Carl von Lützow, "Über die Universität," *StadtChronik Wien,* ed. Christian Brandstätter et al. (Vienna: Christian Brandstätter Verlag, 1986) 335.

58 Helga H. Harriman, "Introduction," *Seven Stories by Marie Ebner-Eschenbach* (Columbia, SC: Camden House, 1986) xvi.

59 C. E. Gates, "Introduction," Marie Ebner-Eschenbach, *Die Kapitalistinnen und zwei andere Novellen,* Crofts' German Series (New York: Crofts, 1930) xii-xiii.

60 The University has placed a commemorative plaque in the courtyard in memory of faculty who were expelled and victimized during the Nazi years.

61 Gottfried Heindl, *Und die Grösse ist gefährlich: Wahrhaftige Geschichten zur Geschichte eines schwierigen Volkes* (Vienna: Neff, 1969) 130.

62 Heindl, *Und die Grösse ist gefährlich* 131.

63 Arthur Schnitzler, *Paracelsus and Other One-Act Plays,* trans. G. J. Weinberger (Riverside, CA: Ariadne, 1995) 36.

64 Hofmann, *The Viennese* 50.

[65] Inge Lehne and Lonnie Johnson, *Vienna: The Past in the Present* (Riverside, CA: Ariadne Press, 1995) 97.

[66] Andrew Barker, *Telegrams from the Soul: Peter Altenberg and the Culture of fin-de-siècle Vienna* (Columbia, SC: Camden House, 1996) xviii.

[67] Peter Altenberg, "To the Coffeehouse," *Trau, Schau Wien*, ed. Paul W. Stix and Erik G. Wickenburg (Vienna: Zsolnay, 1973) 229.

[68] Cited in Dolmetsch, *Our Famous Guest* 152.

[69] Karl Kraus, "The Demolished Literature," *The Vienna Coffeehouse Wits: 1890–1938*, ed. and trans. Harold B. Segel (W. Lafayette, IN: Purdue UP, 1993) 65. This and the following citations from this work are reprinted by permission of the Purdue University Press.

[70] Kraus, "The Demolished Literature" 69.

[71] Kraus, "The Demolished Literature" 72.

[72] Kraus, "The Demolished Literature" 74.

[73] Karl Gutzkow, "Reiseeindrücke aus Deutschland, der Schweiz, Holland und Italien."

[74] Kraus, "The Demolished Literature" 72.

[75] Egon Schwarz, Introduction, *Arthur Schnitzler: Plays and Stories*, The German Library 55 (New York: Continuum, 1998) xvii.

[76] Schnitzler, *My Youth in Vienna* 303.

[77] Arthur Schnitzler, *Tagebuch 1917–1919* (Vienna: Verlag der Österreichischen Akademie der Wissenschaften, 1985) 211. This and subsequent citation from Schnitzler's diaries are used with permission of the Österreichische Akademie der Wissenschaften.

[78] Dolmetsch, *Our Famous Guest* 113.

[79] Dolmetsch 117.

[80] "Hugo Thimig über das neue Burgeheater," *StadtChronik Wien* 342.

[81] Heindl, *Und die Grösse ist gefährlich* 151.

[82] Zweig, *The World of Yesterday* 170.

[83] Arthur Schnitzler, *Tagebuch 1879–1892* (Vienna: Verlag der Österreichischen Akademie der Wissenschaften, 1987) 302–303.

[84] Heindl, *Und die Grösse ist gefährlich* 42.

[85] Felix Salten, *Wurstelprater* (Vienna: Wilhelm Goldmann Verlag, 1973) 116–123.

86 Arthur Schnitzler, *The Great Puppet Play,* trans. G. J. Weinberger, *Paracelsus and Other One-Act Plays* 161.

87 "Freud as Archeologist," 17 May 2004 <http://www.freudmuseum.at>.

88 Jeffrey B. Berlin, Afterword, *Arthur Schnitzler: Professor Bernhardi and Other Plays,* trans. G. J. Weinberger (Riverside, CA: Ariadne, 1993) 370. Used by permission of Ariadne Press.

89 Arthur Schnitzler, *Tagebuch 1920–1922* (Vienna: Verlag der Österreichischen Akademie der Wissenschaften, 1993) 318–19.

90 Sigmund Freud, "On Dreams," *The Freud Reader,* ed. Peter Gay (New York: Norton, 1989) 165.

91 Arthur Schnitzler, *Der Schleier der Beatrice, Die dramatischen Werke* vol 1 (Frankfurt: S. Fischer, 1962) 576.

92 Joachim Ringelnatz, "Der Briefmark," *German Verse,* ed. G. Schultz, 2nd ed. (Melbourne: Macmillan of Australia, 1970) 217.

93 *Die Presse.* English Edition. 15 July 2002 <http://www.diepresse.at>.

94 Christian Schönfelt, *Wiener Walzer* (Vienna: Belvedere Verlag Wilhelm Meissel, 1970) 18–19.

95 "Der Wiener Opernball—der Ball der Bälle," *Enjoy Vienna Magazine,* Feb. 2004: 5.

96 Christiane Tauzher and Sandra Schönthal, "Alles Walzer," *Kurier,* 20 Feb. 2004: 14.

97 Michael Kelly, *Reminiscences* (New York: J. & J. Harper, 1826) 130–31.

98 John Whitten, "The Origin of Johann Strauss' opus 314, 'On the Beautiful Blue Danube,'" *Johann Strauss* (Vienna: Historical Museum of the City of Vienna, n.d.) 27–30.

99 Whitten 28–29.

100 Joseph Wechsberg, *The Waltz Emperors: The Life and Times and Music of the Strauss Family* (New York: Putnam, 1973) 167.

101 Wechsberg 170.

102 Wechsberg 167.

103 Franz von Gernerth, "An der schönen blauen Donau," 4 Aug. 2004 <http://ingeb.org/Lieder/ donausob.html>. Translated by G. J. Weinberger.

104 Josef Weyl, "An der schönen blauen Donau," 4 Aug. 2004 <http://ingeb.org/Lieder/ donausob.html>. Translated by G. J. Weinberger.

[105] Werner Hanak, "Quasi una fantasia: Zur Dramaturgie einer Ausstellung," *Quasi una fantasia: Juden und die Musikstadt Wien,* ed. Leon Botstein and Werner Hanak (Vienna: Wolke Verlag, 2003) 23.

[106] Wechsberg 24.

[107] Cited in Wechsberg 24.

[108] Sara Trampuz and Wolfgang Dosch, "Charles Kalman im Gespräch mit Wolfgang Dosch und Sara Trampuz über sich, seinen Vater und die Stadt der Lieder: Grüss mir mein Wien," *Quasi una fantasia* 120.

[109] Frederic Morton, Foreword, *My Youth in Vienna,* by Arthur Schnitzler xi.

[110] Otto Brusatti, *Johann Strauss* (Graz: Verlag Styria, 1999) 15.

[111] Wechsberg 178–79.

[112] Wechsberg 180.

[113] Eduard Hanslick, "Lohengrin," *Vienna's Golden Years of Music: 1850–1900,* ed. and trans. Henry Pleasants III (New York: Simon and Schuster, 1950) 59.

[114] Hanslick, "Der Meistersinger," *Vienna's Golden Years of Music: 1850–1900* 125.

[115] Henry Pleasants III, Preface, Vienna's *Golden Years of Music: 1850–1900.* xxiii.

[116] Hanslick, "Bruckner's Eighth Symphony," *Vienna's Golden Years of Music: 1850–1900* 304.

[117] Hanslick, "Strauss, *Don Juan,*" *Vienna's Golden Years of Music: 1850–1900* 309.

[118] Hanslick, "Strauss, *Don Juan*" 325.

[119] Gordon Brook-Shepherd, *The Austrians: A Thousand-Year Odyssey* (London: HarperCollins, 1996) 333.

[120] Brook-Shepherd 332.

[121] Brook-Shepherd 327–8.

[122] William R. Perl, *Operation Action: Rescue from the Holocaust* 69.

[123] Perl 9.

[124] Conversion of reichmarks to dollars is figured at 4 RM per dollar. See Perl, *Operation Action* 27.

[125] Wilhelm Weinberger had left Austria in March, 1938.

[126] Karl Rieder, "Wann I amal stirb!" *Wienerlieder: Von Raimund bis Georg Kreisler,* ed. Jürgen Hein (Stuttgart: Reclam, 2002) 14–15.

[127] Josef Köber, *Weanerisch: Geschichten und Wörterverzeichnis für Freunde des Wiener Dialekts* (Vienna: Wiener Verlag, 1993) 19.

[128] "Pest," *aeiou Encyclopedia of Austria*, 30 Nov. 2004 <http://www.aeiou.at>.

[129] "Pest," *aeiou Encyclopedia of Austria*.

[130] Gigi Beutler, *The Imperial Vaults*, trans. John Kennedy. (Vienna: Beutler-Heldenstern, 1999) 30.

[131] "Ei, du lieber Augustin," *Wienerlieder: Von Raimund bis Georg Kreisler* 9.

[132] Mark Twain, The Memorable Assassination," 23 Nov. 2004 <http://www.underthesun.cc/ Classica/Twain/whatisman/whatisman23.html>.

[133] Beutler 44.

[134] Peter Ian Waugh, trans. *Franz Schubert: Birthplace, Memorial Apartment* (Vienna: Historical Museum of the City of Vienna, n.d.) 57.

[135] Charles Osborne, *Schubert and His Vienna* (London: Weidenfeld and Nicholson, 1985) 150.

[136] Franz Grillparzer, *"Am Grab Beethovens: Heinrich Anschütz Deklamiert Grillparzer." StadtChronik Wien* 243.

[137] Eduard Bauernfeld, "Franz Schubert" (1851), *Wien im Gedicht* 99.

[138] Reinhard H. Gruber, *St. Stephan's Cathedral in Vienna*, trans. Jeffrey and Effie McCabe, 2nd ed. (Vienna: Domkirche St. Stephan, 2001) 80.

[139] Wechsberg, *The Waltz Emperors* 195.

[140] Moritz Csáky, "More than 'Nonsense on Stage Taken Seriously': Cultural Historical Remarks on Viennese Operetta at the Turn of the Century," *Österreichische Musikzeitschrift.* Special English Edition (1999): 22–23.

[141] "Sigmund Freud on-line," sound recording, 17 May 2004 <www.freud-museum.at>.

[142] Karl Kraus, *Dicta and Contradicta* 98.

Works Cited

Barker, Andrew. *Telegrams from the Soul: Peter Altenberg and the Culture of fin-de-siècle Vienna*. Columbia, SC: Camden House, 1996.

Berlin, Jeffrey B. Afterword. *Professor Bernhardi and Other Plays*. By Arthur Schnitzler. Trans. G. J. Weinberger. Riverside, CA: Ariadne, 1993. 363-77.

Beutler, Gigi. *The Imperial Vaults*. Trans. John Kennedy. Vienna: Beutler-Heldenstern, 1999.

Botstein, Leon, and Werner Hanak. Eds. *Quasi una fantasia: Juden und die Musikstadt Wien*. Vienna: Wolke, 2003.

Brandstätter, Christian et al. Ed. *StadtChronik Wien*. Vienna: Christian Brandstätter Verlag, 1986.

Brook-Shepherd, Gordon. *The Austrians: A Thousand-Year Odyssey*. London: HarperCollins, 1996.

Brusatti, Otto. *Johann Strauss*. Graz: Verlag Styria, 1999.

Csáky, Moritz. "More than 'Nonsense on Stage Taken Seriously': Cultural Historical Remarks on Viennese Operetta at the Turn of the Century." *Österreichische Musikzeitschrift*. Special English Edition (1999): 19-30.

"The Database of Jewish Communities: Vienna." 2 July 2003 <http://www.bh.org.il>.

Dolmetsch, Carl. *Our Famous Guest: Mark Twain in Vienna*. Athens: U Georgia P, 1992.

Fermor, Patrick Leigh. *A Time for Gifts*. London and New York: Penguin, 1977.

"Franz Spunda: Der magische Dichter." 7 July 2002 <http://home.t-online.de/home/ turbund/ spnd.htm>.

"Freud as Archeologist." 17 May 2004 <http://www.freud-museum.at>.

Freud, Sigmund. "On Dreams." *The Freud Reader*. Ed. Peter Gay. New York: Norton, 1989. 142-72.

Gates, C. E. Introduction. *Die Kapitalistinnen und zwei andere Novellen.* By Marie Ebner-Eschenbach. Crofts' German Series. New York: Crofts, 1930. i-xv.

von Gernerth, Franz. "An der schönen blauen Donau." 4 Aug. 2004 <http://ingeb.org/ Lieder/ donausob.html>.

Granger, Alfred. *The Spirit of Vienna.* New York: McBride & Co., 1935.

Gruber, Reinhard H. *St. Stephan's Cathedral in Vienna.* Trans. Jeffrey and Effie McCabe. 2nd ed. Vienna: Domkirche St. Stephan, 2001.

Gutzkow, Karl. "Reiseeindrücke aus Deutschland, der Schweiz, Holland und Italien." *Trau, Schau, Wien.* Eds. Stix, Paul W., and Erik G. Wickenburg. Vienna: Zsolnay, 1973: 199-201.

Hakel, Hermann. Ed. *Wien von A – Z.* Vienna: Wiener Verlag, 1953.

Hamann, Brigitte. *Hitler's Vienna. A Dictator's Apprenticeship.* Trans. Thomas Thornton. NY: Oxford UP, 2000.

"Hans Holzer—Psychic Investigator." 29 Mar. 2004 <http:// groups-beta.google. com/group/ alt.religion.clue>.

Harriman, Helga H. Introduction. *Seven Stories by Marie Ebner-Eschenbach.* Columbia, SC: Camden House, 1986. i-xxxvi.

Hein, Jürgen. Ed. *Wienerlieder: Von Raimund bis Georg Kreisler.* Stuttgart: Reclam, 2002.

Heindl, Gottfried. Ed. *Leg' mich zu Füssen Majestät.* Vienna: Neff, 1985.

—. *Und die Grösse ist gefährlich: Wahrhaftige Geschichten zur Geschichte eines schwierigen Volkes.* Vienna: Neff, 1969.

Hoffman, Eva. "The New Nomads." *Yale Review* 86.4 (1998): 39-50.

Hofmann, Paul. *The Viennese: Splendor, Twilight, and Exile.* New York: Anchor, 1988.

"Hohlbaum, Robert." *aeiou Encyclopedia.* 11 Nov. 2003 <http:// www.aeiou.at>.

Hohlbaum, Robert. "Wie ich zu Grillparzer kam. . . ." *Völkischer Beobachter* 22 Mar. 1938: 11.

"Horror tram accident leaves man dead." http://diepresse.com. English Edition 7 Aug. 2002.

Johnston, William M. *The Austrian Mind: An Intellectual and Social History, 1848-1938.* Berkeley: U California Press, 1972.

—. *Vienna, Vienna: The Golden Age, 1815-1914*. Milan: Mondadori Editore, 1980.

Kafka, Franz. *Dearest Father: Stories and Other Writings*. Trans. Ernst Kaiser and Eithne Wilkins. New York: Schocken, 1954.

Kelly, Michael. *Reminiscences*. New York: J. & J. Harper, 1826.

Kluger, Ruth. *Still Alive: A Holocaust Girlhood Remembered*. New York: The Feminist Press, 2001.

Köber, Josef. *Weanerisch: Geschichten und Wörterverzeichnis für Freunde des Wiener Dialekts*. Vienna: Wiener Verlag, 1993.

Kraus, Karl. "The Demolished Literature." *The Vienna Coffeehouse Wits: 1890-1938*. Ed. and trans. Harold B. Segel. W. Lafayette, IN: Purdue UP, 1993. 65-86.

—. *Dicta and Contradicta*. Ed. and trans. Jonathan McVity. Urbana: U Chicago P, 2001.

—. *Half-Truths and One-and-a-Half Truths*. Ed. and trans. Harry Zohn. Manchester, UK: Carcanet Press, 1986.

Kreisler, Georg. "Wien ohne Wiener." *Wien im Gedicht*. Ed. Hertha Kratzer. Vienna: öbv&hpt Verlag, 2001. 70-1.

Lehne, Inge, and Lonnie Johnson. *Vienna: The Past in the Present*. Riverside, CA: Ariadne, 1995.

Lothar, Ernst. *The Door Opens*. New York: Doubleday, 1945.

Mahan, Dr. J. Alexander. *Famous Women of Vienna*. Vienna: Halm and Goldmann, 1930.

May, Arthur J. *Vienna in the Age of Franz Josef*. Norman: U Oklahoma P, 1966.

Montagu, Lady Mary Wortley. *Letters from the Levant during the Embassy to Constantinople: 1716-18*. 1838. New York: Arno Press, 1971.

Morton, Frederic. Foreword. *My Youth in Vienna* by Arthur Schnitzler. Trans. Catherine Hutter. New York: Holt, 1970. ix-xiv.

Mozart, Wolfgang A. "To his sister, in Salzburg (postscript)." *Mozart's Letters, Mozart's Life*. Ed. and trans. Robert Spaethling. New York: Norton, 2000. 45.

"NS-Literatur." 5 Apr. 2004 <http://www.dhm.de/lemo/html/nazi/kunst/nsliteratur>.

"One Hundred Years of Vienna Public Transport." *Enjoy: Wilkommen in Wien* Sept. 2003: 6.

Osborne, Charles. *Schubert and His Vienna*. London: Weidenfeld and Nicholson, 1985.

"Over 20,000 hoarded letters. . . ." 15 July 2002 <http://diepresse. com. English Edition>.

Perl, William R. *Operation Action: Rescue from the Holocaust.* New York: Ungar, 1983.

"Pest." *aeiou Encyclopedia of Austria.* 30 Nov. 2004 <http://www. aeiou.at>.

Pleasants, Henry, III. Ed. and Trans. *Vienna's Golden Years of Music: 1850-1900.* New York: Simon and Schuster, 1950.

Roth, Joseph. *The Radetzky March.* Trans. Joachim Neugroschel. Woodstock, NY: The Overlook Press, 1995.

Russell, Francis. *The World of Dürer: 1471-1528.* New York: Time, 1967.

Salten, Felix. *Wurstelprater.* Vienna: Wilhelm Goldmann, 1973.

Schnitzler, Arthur. *Aphorismen und Betrachtungen.* Frankfurt a/M: S. Fischer, 1983.

—. *Dream Story.* Trans. Otto P. Schinnerer. 1927. Los Angeles: Green Integer, 2003.

—. *My Youth in Vienna.* Trans. Catherine Hutter. New York: Holt, 1970.

—. *Paracelsus and Other One-Act Plays.* Trans. G. J. Weinberger. Riverside, CA: Ariadne, 1995

—. *Der Schleier der Beatrice. Die dramatischen Werke* vol. 1. Frankfurt a/M: S. Fischer, 1962.

—. *Tagebuch 1879-1892.* Vienna: Verlag der Österreichischen Akademie der Wissenschaften, 1987.

—. *Tagebuch 1917-1919.* Vienna: Verlag der Österreichischen Akademie der Wissenschaften, 1985.

—. *Tagebuch 1920-1922.* Vienna: Verlag der Österreichischen Akademie der Wissenschaften, 1993.

Schönfelt, Christian. *Wiener Walzer.* Vienna: Belvedere Verlag Wilhelm Meissel, 1970.

Schultz, G., ed. *German Verse.* 2nd ed. Melbourne: Macmillan of Australia, 1970.

Schwarz, Egon. Introduction. *Arthur Schnitzler: Plays and Stories.* The German Library 55. New York: Continuum, 1998. xvi-xviii.

"The Shore Line Trolley Museum." 27 Oct. 2003 <http://www. bera.org>.

"Sigmund Freud on-line." Sound recording. 17 May 2004 <http:// www.freud-museum.at>.

"Spunda, Franz." *aeiou Encyclopedia*. 11 Nov. 2003<http://www. aeiou.at>.

Stix, Paul W., and Erik G. Wickenburg, eds. *Trau, Schau, Wien*. Vienna: Zsolnay, 1973.

Tauzher, Christiane, and Sandra Schönthal. "Alles Walzer." *Kurier* 20 Feb. 2004: 14.

"Time Line of the History of the Jews of Vienna." 2 July 2003 <http://www. virtualvienna.net>.

Timms, Edward. *Karl Kraus: Apocalyptic Satirist*. New Haven: Yale UP, 1986.

Twain, Mark. *Essays and Sketches of Mark Twain*. Ed. Stuart Miller. New York: Barnes & Noble, 1995.

—. *The Man That Corrupted Hadleyburg and Other Stories and Essays*. New York: Oxford UP, 1996.

—. The Memorable Assassination." 23 Nov. 2004 <http://www.underthesun.cc/Classica/Twain/whatisman/whatisman23.html>.

Ungar, Frederick. Ed. *Austria in Poetry and History*. New York: Ungar, 1984.

Verhehrsverbund Ost-Region. *Verkehrslinienplan Wien 2003*.

Waldinger, Ernst. "Ich bin ein Sohn der deutschen Sprache." *Austria in Poetry and History*. Ed. Frederick Ungar. New York: Ungar, 1984. 318.

"Waluliso." *aeiou Encyclopedia*. 11 Nov. 2003 <http://www.aeiou. at>.

Waugh, Peter Ian. Trans. *Franz Schubert: Birthplace, Memorial Apartment*. Vienna: Historical Museum of the City of Vienna, n.d.

Wechsberg, Joseph. *The Waltz Emperors: The Life and Times and Music of the Strauss Family*. New York: Putnam, 1973.

Weigelt, Astrid. "Schaffnerlos: Sieben Jahre ist sie jetzt her, die Fahrt des letzten Schaffners in Wien." *Vor Magazin* 17 (2003): 28-29.

Weyl, Josef. "An der schönen blauen Donau." 4 Aug. 2004 <http:// ingeb.org/Lieder/ donausob.html>.

Whitten, John. "The Origin of Johann Strauss' opus 314, 'On the Beautiful Blue Danube.'" *Johann Strauss*. Vienna: Historical Museum of the City of Vienna, n.d. 27-30.

"Der Wiener Opernball—der Ball der Bälle." *Enjoy Vienna Magazine* Feb. 2004: 5.

Zweig, Stefan. *The World of Yesterday*. Lincoln, NE: U of Nebraska P, 1964.

About the Author

Jill Knight Weinberger (PhD, University of Connecticut) is an Associate Professor of English at Central Connecticut State University, where she teaches courses in creative writing and American literature. Her travel writing has appeared frequently in the *New York Times*, *Boston Sunday Globe*, and *Los Angeles Times*. In 2000, the Society of American Travel Writers Foundation recognized her writing with a Lowell Thomas Award for Travel Journalism.

Photograph of the author by Jake Koteen.
Used by permission.

Printed in the United States
61141LVS00002B/112